Missing Knowledge

What If?

By Nathan L. Jarrett

The information in this book is for educational purposes only.

ISBN-13: 978-0-578-13209-9
ISBN-10: 0578132095

First Edition
Published; October 2013
Revised March, 2014
Jarrett Publications
Printed in the United States of America

Table of Contents

Introduction

We have always searched for knowledge, and wanting to know more and more. That concept, that desire to obtain this information dates all the way back to the Garden of Eden. Adam and Eve's quest for wanting to learn more cost them the place we all want to be at all the time. Where we work part of the time, but don't have to worry about money, going to the grocery store to buy food, to have to take the car to have it fixed when need to be, etc.

The Garden of Eden was a place where they basically lived one big long vacation. It's believed the animals spoke to them. Their needs were taken care of for them. They were almost treated royally. They never got sick. The temperature was always constant. They could get a suntan when they wanted. Later they allowed themselves to be talked into doing something they were told not to do. Afterwards, death entered into their lives, and we have been judged by these actions ever since.

Adam and Eve sought after knowledge and paid the price. Now that we have crossed that threshold, we still seek knowledge. However, there are times when people don't care or wish to expend the energy to continue to learn.

Hosea 4:6; *my people are destroyed from lack oj knowledge. "Because you have rejected knowledge, 'l also reject you as my priests; because you have ignored the law oj your God, l also will ignore your children.* (New International Version)

Why are some books the Bible refers to are not in it?

Why do most pastors and churches avoid the topic of Nephilim that roamed the earth thousands of years ago? These Nephilim are a part of every ancient civilization in one form or another. The Bible states some of them were heroes, men of renown. They would be politicians and people in leadership positions or celebrities.

What height did these Nephilim reach? Were they actually giants? What happened to them? Is there evidence of their existence today? Are they among us now?

Who had the technical knowledge to build the pyramids? Are the pyramids just in Egypt?

How were these superstructures built that have been around for thousands of years? They didn't have the use of bulldozers, cranes, and heavy equipment machinery. If we were to try to construct them today, it would challenge our engineering knowledge.

What really happened at the Tower of Babel? What was the final height of that tower? What happened to it? Does this tower and Nimrod affect our culture today?

Is there going to be another nuclear war? If so, when and where? Do we know how many people will die? Will we destroy ourselves?

Do Greek and Roman gods still influence our society today?

Did the Abraham of the Bible have other tests of faith other than the situation with his son Isaac?

Did people in the past actually travel in time?

Is there a difference between fallen angels and demons?

Why are all these massacres happening today and with greater frequency?

Are you wondering what is going on in our society? Something just doesn't feel right. Something is changing, and it just doesn't seem it is for our greater good.

Could our Heavenly Father, the God of Abraham, Isaac, and Jacob really be misunderstood as to why there were all the battles that raged which He commanded to His people Israel to perform? He gave commands to wipe out every man, woman, child. They were told to kill all their animals and livestock. He seemed to be instructing the Israelites at times to commit what we nowadays call genocide. It just doesn't make sense does it? Or does it make sense? Could we have misunderstood God the Father as we read the Old Testament all this time?

As you can tell, the above questions and topics are somewhat wide ranging. What this book will do is connect them all together so you can see things in a different light. Many of the concepts and ideas in this book will be, for some of you, something completely different.

As you start reading this book, you will start to see, to understand, and to ask questions you have thought about before, but maybe didn't know how to ask or properly phrase the question. At times, I will use some ancient text to shed some more light on the subjects contained in this book.

The Book of Revelation in the Bible is starting to be unlocked for us, more and more in these days. As we are in the days of Noah right now, so shall it be with the coming of Jesus.

Simply beware of those who will challenge these ideas.

2 Peter 3:1-7;
1 Dear friends, this is now my second letter to you. I have written both of them as reminders to stimulate you to wholesome thinking.
2 I want you to recall the words spoken in the past by the holy prophets and the command given by our Lord and Savior through your apostles.
3 Above all, you must understand that in the last days scoffers will come, scoffing and following their own evil desires.
4 They will say, "Where is this 'coming' he promised? Ever since our ancestors died, everything goes on as it has since the beginning of creation."
5 But they deliberately forget that long ago by God's word the heavens came into being and the earth was formed out of water and by water.
6 By these waters also the world of that time was deluged and destroyed.
7 By the same word the present heavens and earth are reserved for fire, being kept for the day of judgment and destruction of the ungodly. (New International Version)

Focus on the word 'deliberately' forgot. They didn't think it was that significant or possibly didn't think it was necessary at all. They didn't want to believe that LORD God would do this sort of thing.

Those that laughed at Noah when he was building the ark changed their attitude, stopped their laughing and their scoffing when the LORD sealed up the ark and the rains started to come down, and the earth opened up allowing the water from inside of it to spring forth. The ones left behind tried to get into the Ark, but were pushed aside in a unique way, turned away, to their own demise and death.

Keep in mind what is coming up during the great tribulation period, as it is called, will be worse than anyone can EVER imagine. Such pain and suffering will be brought onto mankind like has never been done before or will be again.

Again, this book will help you get some answers to your questions in these days we live in now. Yes, there are answers, the answers you need to hear.

Acknowledgments

I would like to, graciously thank, Herbert Eisengruber for allowing me to use some of the pictures he took in this book. I would suggest you go to his website and check out the other pictures and information he has listed there. He has done some extensive traveling to some exciting places and some of the pictures he has taken I haven't seen before. One of them is America has its own version of Stonehenge.

http://paleoseti.com/index2.htm

I would also like to graciously thank Wolfgang Kaehler for allowing me use of one of his photos in this book. Check out his website for some stunning pictures. He is a professional photographer!

http://www.wkaehlerphoto.com

Our World Today

With all that is going on around us today, we are genuinely seeking some heartfelt answers to what is happening around us. Something that we can grab a hold of. Something that will help us to understand what is going on around us. Whether we realize it or not, it affects us. It should bother us greatly for many reasons.

Sometimes we Christians have a tendency to glaze over Scripture and sometimes we don't dig deeper into it. We hear stories of different Bible characters. We heard sermons on different topics from the Bible. Yet we don't dig deeper so we can understand it. We read these precious Scriptures but sometimes fail to realize that the answers we are seeking are in it or will point us in the right direction to get the answers.

We all are trying to find the answers as to what is going on in our society. We seek for the answers and yet are not following up in the correct way. Sometimes the tangible escapes us. We need to change our mindset so we can see the truth of what is happening and why. Then, and only then, can we push forward and change the things which need to be corrected.

Remaining in a teachable state includes us listening to information which might be contrary to what we think we know. Otherwise, all the answers you are seeking, all the questions you have, which are nestled within the depths of your heart, can go unanswered. The opportunity you want, the mate you are seeking, the calling you want to bring about and make manifest in your life could be delayed or could bypass you because you are not heeding the information put before you.

The very word 'research' is really looking at something someone else has looked at and seeing if we see or find something different. Have you have heard the saying, 'I need to have another set of eyes look at this just to make sure I'm not missing anything here'.

We see all the violence, hatred, wars, rumors of wars, and betraying one another. But sometimes we need to look back in time to see what could happen in the future. So let's start there.

Matthew 24:1; *Then many will lose faith. They will betray and hate each other.* (GOD'S WORD® Translation)

Mark 13:22; *For false messiahs and false prophets will rise up and perform signs and wonders so as to deceive, if possible, even God's chosen ones.* (New Living Translation)

Matthew 24:12; *And because there will be more and more lawlessness, most people's love will grow cold.* (GOD'S WORD® Translation)

The verse that states people's love will grow cold is something that I'd never thought I would see in my lifetime. Yet it is here now and growing. It troubles me greatly for many reasons seeing this unfold right before my very eyes. Why is it people care less and less about each other? Why do they hold grudges? Why all the retaliation when they perceive they have been wronged? What happened to being patient with one another and forgiving others like it used to be when I was growing up?

Luke 17:26; *"And just as it happened in the days of Noah, so it will be also in the days of the Son of Man:* (New American Standard Bible)

Matthew 24:37; *"When the Son of Man returns, it will be like it was in Noah's day.* (New Living Translation)

Some Christians have heard these verses quoted from time to time. Yet sometimes we don't put two and two together. As Christians, we look forward to the second coming of Jesus the Messiah. If we are indeed waiting for His return, we must also realize that the times when He does return will be like the days when Noah lived before the great flood occurred. So the same things that happened when Noah lived will be present here during the time when our Messiah will return.

We will learn what the conditions were like before and right up to the time of the flood. It affected Israel, the rest of the world and has tremendous impact on our lives even today. It has more far-reaching consequences than most of us can ever imagine.

We are going to start by looking at some super structures that dot the world's landscape. They would be engineering marvels by today's standards. We will not be looking at these structures which were built up to one hundred years ago years ago but at some of them built thousands of years ago.

Ancient Superstructures of the World

The Pyramids

Pyramids are usually four-sided structures. Some of them rise to a point while others do not. They come in different sizes and heights.

The biggest collection of pyramids is in Egypt, from 97 up to 138.

(Source; History Channel, 2010)
(Source; http://en.wikipedia.org/wiki/Egyptian_pyramids)

One of the largest pyramids in the world is Giza in Egypt. It is also known as the Great Pyramid of Khufu. Today it's called the Great Pyramid at Giza. According to the "Inventory Stela", it is thought that Khufu did not actually build it. Ancient texts tell us he did some maintenance to it.

What is the "Inventory Stela"? It is a document that gives information about the Sphinx and the Great Pyramid at Giza. Some dismiss it as being revisionists' writings while others feel the truth is within the document. Those who saw it wrote Khufu just repaired the great pyramid. These records are supposed to be sealed off so no one can view them again. Why?

You are probably wondering why I'm discussing this pyramid rather than talking about the "Days of Noah". Believe it or not, there is a link. A connection you see as you continue reading.

Here are some interesting details and observations about the Great Pyramid at Giza.

1. It is eight sided, not four which most people think.
2. It was built to withstand earthquakes that leveled most everything else in the area but this pyramid. There are a few other pyramids in the area along with the Sphinx.
3. There are an estimated 2.3 million limestone blocks in it. Some of these blocks weigh between twenty five to eighty tonnes each. The eighty tonne blocks are at the base. A tonne equals about two thousand, two hundred four pounds. That is more than an American ton. (Source; http://en.wikipedia.org/wiki/Great_Pyramid_of_Giza)
4. There are writings that supposedly say this was built in about twenty years. If you do the math, here is how many stones they would have to do every hour to get this done in twenty years.
    a. 2,300,000 ÷ 20 years = 115,000 pieces of multi ton stones that would they were squared, cut them to size, lifted out of the limestone bedrock, transported, put them in place, every year.
    b. 115,000 ÷ 275 days = 418 pieces per day were put into place. 275 days allow for ninety days per year of no work because the Nile flooding.
    c. 418 ÷ 12 hours = 35 per hour. That's thirty five pieces of multiton stone per sixty minutes.
    d. If you were to add back in the ninety days of the Nile flooding, the amount of the blocks that would need to be laid would go down to 26 per hour.
5. How did they cut them out of the quarry, lift them up and get them ready for transport?
6. How did they create ninety degree angles and corners?
7. The quarry where these stones were located are miles away. How did they transport them to the site?
8. Interestingly enough, there is no capstone on this pyramid. Why? All the rest of the pyramids has them. So why doesn't it have one? Or did it have one, and it was removed?

9. It appears this pyramid on the outside was beautiful when it was finished. It had a highly polished stone that reflected the light of the sun, which lasted into the night. As you can tell by looking at them now, most of that stone or possibly granite that had reflected that light has been removed. Some believe it was used to build mosques in Egypt. There was gold in some of those pyramids while some had other precious metals in them also.
10. There is an interesting entry made in Flavius Josephus Complete Works. Chapter 2:3;
    All these proved to be of good dispositions. They also inhabited the same country without dissensions, and in a happy condition, without any misfortunes falling upon them, till they died. They also were the inventors of that peculiar sort of wisdom which is concerned with the heavenly bodies, and their order. And that their inventions might not be lost before they were sufficiently known, upon Adam's prediction that the world was to be destroyed at one time by the force of fire, and at another time by the violence and quantity of water, they made two pillars, the one of brick, the other of stone: they inscribed their discoveries on them both, that in case the pillar of brick should be destroyed by the flood, the pillar of stone might remain, and exhibit those discoveries to mankind; and also inform them that there was another pillar of brick erected by them. Now this remains in the land of Siriad to this day.
    Flavius, Josephus (2013-01-21). Josephus Flavius: Complete Works and Historical Background (Annotated and Illustrated) (Annotated Classics) (Kindle Locations 9011-9015). Annotated Classics. Kindle Edition.
    It appears Adam knew there was going to be a massive flood that will destroy the earth. Then at another time, the world was going to be destroyed by fire. As a result, they decided to engrave in brick and in stone all their discoveries, so they would not be lost in the destruction. Could the carvings in the pyramids be the ancient

discoveries Josephus was talking about in the above passage?

With all the theories about how they were built and why, when the question is asked how they lifted these huge limestone blocks up and put them in place, they just do not know. Egyptologist do not have a good answer as to how they were moved into place.

Levitation from time to time rears its head up, but to be practical, I don't see this as a possible solution at all. Why? If we would be able to levitate, it would be widely used today. Now granted, we can levitate things today. That is a fact. However, the devices that are used to produce the levitation state needs electricity to help create the effect. There was a manufacturing process to create the device that electricity uses to create the effect. In other words, some factory used machinery to create and mold the parts that are used to create the effect. At this point, there is no evidence that we have discovered so far that leads us to believe the ancients had any such production facilities.

The largest granite stones in the King's chamber weighs between twenty five to seventy tonnes. Some of the stones are thought to weigh more than one hundred tonnes. How did they move these huge stones into place in those days? There is no evidence of having bulldozers, cranes or the like back in those days. Moving stones of that size would be considered an engineering marvel by today's standards.

Here are some questions for you to ponder. Why didn't they just use smaller blocks of stones? How did they get those stones quarried, cut to perfection, and sanded down to get a smooth surface? Again, how did they transport them from many miles away from the quarry to the building site? Was it over land or by water or both? There is no evidence they had ships back then that could move anything close to that amount of weight. There is reason to believe they had sail boats, like the one that was found at the foot of the Great Pyramid at Giza in 1954. It was 143 feet in length. Yet to carry any weight that could be remotely close to carrying that many tons is not even possible. Allow me to give you some quick facts about shipping tonnage by a cargo vessel in our time period.

Ships today come in many different sizes. Some freighters can handle up to four hundred thousand metric MT (400,000) DWT. A metric ton is slightly more than an American ton. Now some of these supertankers of today can handle more DWT. DWT stands for "dead weight tonnage". What that means is all of the weight this ship is designed to hold has to include the weight of all of the following; sum of the weights of cargo, fuel, fresh water, ballast water, provisions, passengers, and crew. Almost all of the cargo that is aboard these ships today is placed into containers which are the size of a trailer on a semi truck. They can have thousands of these trailers on these ships. Then you can get close to the maximum tonnage this ship can carry because it is evenly distributed on the ship. So does it make sense that this ship can handle up to 400,000 total tonnage, but would struggle handling these huge rocks weighing up to and over 100 tons? The challenge is getting them centered properly, so the weight is evenly divided on the ship so it can be safely transported. Then there is the challenge of lifting and removing the rocks when it gets to its destination. Keep reading and you will understand why I'm asking these questions. More than likely, other people may have thought about these same things, but never asked or spoke about them.

So how were these blocks moved from miles and miles, upwards to fifty miles in distance?

Some scholars believe ancient man could NOT have built these pyramids when the wheel and all it can do had not yet been invented yet. Stop and think for a minute. They have yet to understand the full impact of the wheel, and yet the Egyptians are using and building a technical marvel? One of the seven marvels of the world? There are many geometric dimensions that were included in the design of these structures. The pyramid of Giza faces almost exactly true north, east, west, and south. It's been said it is just a three sixtieth of a degree off of true north. Today we can get within something like nine sixtieth of a degree. To add to that, some of these pyramids exactly match up with the different constellations in the sky.

There are some that believe it was only off by a 3/60th of a degree of true north. That is absolutely incredible.

Known Pyramids From Around the World

Mexico, Mayan pyramid of Inscriptions at Palenque and Mayan pyramid of the Magician at Uxma, This site presents a five-terraced Tlahuizcalpantecuhtli Pyramid, Cholula, and Tzintzuntzan.

Illinois, USA. It's called Monk Mound. It is similar to the ones found in China.

Grand Canyon, it appears to be a natural, though it is not perfect in shape as those constructed elsewhere.

Alaska, buried near Mount McKinley.

Bermuda Triangle, There appears to be at least one located there. There may be two. It could be located almost right in the middle of the triangle. Some triangle researchers are observing vortexes appearing on the ocean surface. Maybe that could be caused by the underwater pyramid(s). That certainly would explain why so many phenomena take place when aircraft or ships are lost in that area. What is interesting is this pyramid appears to be partially translucent. Some believe it is larger than the Great Pyramid of Giza. If that is the case, it certainly would change the story we are told about the Great Pyramid of Giza wouldn't it? The Giza pyramid is a technical marvel. Yes, it is and more advanced than we ever realize. But what this does imply is there might be bigger ones located in other parts of the world. Now the question I'm asking is how did that pyramid get under the water? Or was it built before the flood of Genesis 7? It appears the water levels in the world were lower before the flood than they are now. I would like to know why there is no expedition planned to check it out. It was discovered sometime around the mid-1960's. Or did they check it out and no one is talking about it? If you would think about it, that pyramid has been underwater and has withstood the test of time. It has many tons of water weight on top of it all of these thousands of years.

Guatemala has the Pyramid of Tikal.

Europe has them in Bosnian (old Yugoslavia), Montevecchia and Florence/Tuscany Italy, In Maribor Slovenia, near the Austrian border.

Are you surprised these pyramids are all over the world?

In England, there is the Silbury Hill pyramid. In Glastonbury, there is a tall monument that sits on top of what some believe is a natural pyramid. A natural pyramid is a huge mound or hill that uses dirt, grass, and weeds and is shaped to look like a pyramid. There are myths that include this is the area where the Holy Grail is located. The Holy Grail is supposed to be the cup that Jesus used during the Last Supper with his disciples.

Ireland, some call the mound in Boyne Valley (Newgrange) a pyramid.

In Nice France, there is one that is partially erect. The Barnenez mount actually looks like a pyramid in its overall design.

Turkey. They are mostly natural mounds and look almost perfect in shape.

Sudan has thirty five of them. Some of them are smaller. Others have some unique designs.

Greece, there are sixteen pyramids.

Off the western coast of Morocco in Africa, is a complex of pyramids in one location on Tenerife Island in the Canary Islands group.

Australia had several pyramids. All but one were bulldozed in the 1950's. The remaining one is privately owned and off limits to visitors. It is actually the largest free standing natural pyramid in the world at nine hundred and twenty two feet in height. Do a search on the Internet for Australia Pyramid.

Japan, most of the pyramids are under water.

Russia has two of them in Nakhodka. It is a port city off the Sea of Japan. It is west of Japan and north of North Korea.

Indonesia, one is located in Java.

Tahiti. But today it's mostly just a mound of stones.

As you realize now, these pyramids are located throughout the world in completely different cultures and in different languages. And I'm sure we will probably find more of them. So how many of them are in the world? No one is sure. Some sources state that China had one hundred of them. If I were to guess, I would think there are possibly five hundred (500) or more in the world.

While you look at these structures, you may think, "wow, why were these huge structures erected in the first place?" It's simpler than you think!

I'm going to discuss some theories about why these pyramids were built the way they were.

1. Some believe they were worship centers. Some of the pyramids in other parts of the world actually had evidence of human sacrifices in them. In some, the smoke of the human burnt offering rose up from the inside of it and out through its top.
2. There are some of these pyramids which were actually centers of healing. There seems to be information that backs up this claim. There are testimonies of people who went into one of these pyramids and came out being healed of cancers, etc. Some websites actually sell a size of a pyramid that fits inside your home. Another size you can hang over your bed. Custom sizes can be purchased too. If a person had enough property or room in their backyard, one could build a bigger model of one. However, I'm not suggesting you do this. There seems to be a lot of science involved in their design and especially their placement on the earth. It appears there can be no metal in it unless it is metals like gold or platinum, or the like. Hence, they are made of either all stone, brick (which doesn't hold up to the test of time), or dirt. There is some interesting reading on this topic.
3. The designs of some of these pyramids have channels like return ducts in a house. Might these 'ducts' be used to collect energy and distribute it or to generate and distribute it? How did they cut out these channels through solid rock?
4. It is thought the pyramid is a cheap copy of what the Holy City of Jerusalem will be like in the Book of Revelation.

Revelation 21:15-22;
15 The angel who was talking to me had a gold measuring stick to measure the city, its gates, and its wall.
16 The city was square. It was as wide as it was long. He measured the city with the stick. It was 12,000 stadia long. Its length, width, and height were the same.
17 He measured its wall. According to human measurement, which the angel was using, it was 144 cubits.
18 Its wall was made of gray quartz. The city was made of pure gold, as clear as glass.
19 The foundations of the city wall were beautifully decorated with all kinds of gems: The first foundation was gray quartz, the second sapphire, the third agate, the fourth emerald,
20 the fifth onyx, the sixth red quartz, the seventh yellow quartz, the eighth beryl, the ninth topaz, the tenth green quartz, the eleventh jacinth, and the twelfth amethyst.
21 The 12 gates were 12 pearls. Each gate was made of one pearl. The street of the city was made of pure gold, as clear as glass.
22 I did not see any temple in it, because the Lord God Almighty and the lamb are its temple. (GOD'S WORD® Translation)

5. While some would have you believe these pyramids were simply a huge burial site for the pharaohs, they really were not. Of the few pharaohs who were found inside these pyramids, there is a possibly these places were healing centers, which could be the reason why they were buried in it so that whatever be the cause of their death, they would be healed and come back to life.
6. There is another theory that states these were simply power centers that took the energy from the earth itself and generated all this enormous power so it can be harnessed and used to provide the energy they need to do the experiments they wanted to do back then. So the question is what experiments am I talking about? There's a possibility that they wanted to control the

weather, change the planet size, to disrupt what the LORD had created; and destroy it. Some call it terraforming. The idea might have been to have all these pyramids built all over the world so they could change different things in the world whenever they wanted. I remember seeing an episode about terraforming in one of the most popular outer space series ever. I didn't pay much attention to it at the time, but now I understand what is going on here.
What is interesting about another theory is their location on the planet. There seems to be a formula to the placements of these pyramids. With that said, I want to present to you a possibility that is probably not widely known. Among those that have studied the earth's magnetic energy fields they notice there is possibly that an enormous amount of energy is released from under the earth and is enhanced when it is funneled through these pyramids. That way, they could tap into it. (Source, http://en.wikipedia.org/wiki/Plate_tectonics),
What is also interesting in this energy discharge is its strongest in the morning and is the weakest when the sun goes down. Could it be for most people, why our best and most refreshed part of the day is the dawn? Could this energy spring forth from the earth and regenerate us? It could mean the earth is also recharging itself over the night. Then this can add a slightly different perspective on these following verses.

Genesis 1:3-5;
3 Then God said, "Let there be light!" So there was light.
4 God saw the light was good. So God separated the light from the darkness.
5 God named the light [day], and the darkness he named [night]. There was evening, then morning-the first day. (New International Version)
Genesis 1:16; *God made two great lights--the greater light to govern the day and the lesser light to govern the night. He also made the stars.* (New International Version)
Proverbs 4:18; *The path oj the righteous is like the*

morning sun, shining ever brighter till the full light of day. (New International Version)
We are supposed to sleep and recharge our bodies at night. Could it be the same thing for the earth? Could the LORD have designed the earth so that the disappearance of the sunlight onto the earth in the evening be a type of signal for it to recharge itself? As the earth rotates, could the approaching sunlight be a signal… so to speak? Does this mean with all of the lights and the activity at night that happens on this planet, could we be tapping into or draining the power from within the earth itself? It could mean the earth doesn't fully recharge itself. These questions are something to ponder.

If you have seen the inside of a pyramid either in person, in a photo, or on a TV program, you will see that in some areas, there is a lot of engraving, chiseling, and coloring of the artwork done deep inside of their walls. So the question I have is, how did they perform all that work? By hand of course. So after the pyramid is in place and completed, how did they illuminate the areas where they worked? They needed to see the wall or column so they can work on it. The sunlight didn't reach that far down into it.

Let's take a look at the Baghdad Battery. I watched someone build one using just some cork, copper sheathing rolled up, an iron rod, some pottery that was about four inches tall, and some electrolyte solution. Another person built a salt water battery with using just a container, salt water, a piece of copper, and a piece galvanize in each container. They attached an ampere meter to the battery, and it showed electrical current. Could this have been a potential source for electricity?

All of these huge stones have texts on them. What are these ancient texts saying and who are they addressing them to? The meaning is still unclear. In order for us to determine that, it's best to understand Genesis 6 and what really happened. It's best to understand the truth of what Jesus told us, 'As in the days of Noah…' Could all this be part of the end times? Are those writings just guidance from the powers of darkness as to how to operate the pyramids and what to expect when their energy is unleashed? Could those that built them before the flood of Genesis 7 left us instructions as to what they are and how to operate them? Or have these instructions have already been decoded?

There are many pictures of Egyptian life during the thousands of years during the Pharaoh's reign. There doesn't seem to be carvings of people building the pyramids. Maybe there are. If that is the case, how come they haven't shown them to us in video or picture form? But if there are no paintings or carvings describing these building events, why are we being deceived from the "world scholars" that state the Egyptians built them? We need to start questioning these things. If they are telling us something that is less than truthful, then what else are they lying to us about?

There are a few who believe that some of these pyramids have healing powers that are performed by dark or black magic. Don't believe there is dark or black magic that has healing powers? Let's look at these passages.

Revelation 13:3; *One of the heads of the beast seemed to have had a fatal wound, but the fatal wound had been healed. The whole world was astonished and followed the beast.* (New International Version)

Zechariah 11:16-17;
16 I'm about to place a shepherd in the land. He will not take care of those that are dying. He will not search for the young. He will not heal those that have broken their legs or support those that can still stand. But he will eat the meat of the fat animals and tear off their hoofs.
17 "How horrible it will be for the foolish shepherd who abandoned the sheep. A sword will strike his arm and his right eye. His arm will be completely withered. His right eye will be completely blind." (New International Version)

Now let's take a look at just a few of some ancient super structures!

Other Super Structures

The design of these enormous structures is absolutely incredible. The questions still remains, how were these huge stones quarried, transported, and put into place with such perfection. We would be extremely challenged to do that today. As you read through the following pages, you will begin to understand why I asked the question.

Let's look at other ancient superstructures that are located all over the world.

The Ancient Ruins of Malta

Malta is an island located 93 miles south of Sicily, Italy. Its under 200 square miles in size. It is part of the British Commonwealth.

It's been said by Maltese 'tall tales' that the megalithic pagan temples built throughout the region were built by giants. One of the temples, Ggantija, is ironically meaning 'giants tower'. Some of these eleven temples were built approximately between 3600 to 3000 B.C. Some say these pagan temples may have been built before the pyramids. This means it was built before the Genesis 7 flood.

One of these massive stones weighs around twenty tons. To put that into perspective, a mid size car can weigh around 1.75 tons. So that one stone is equivalent to almost eleven and a half cars. How were these massive stones lifted and put into place? Some are ten or twenty feet high off the ground. (Source; History Channel)

Afamia in Syria

How did the roofing trim pieces (that's what I call them) get placed some one hundred feet in the air? The stones weigh between 80 to 120 tons.

Stonehenge, England

This site is probably one of the most widely known stone structures of this kind.

Stonehenge, United States

The U.S. has its own version of Stonehenge similar to the one which is in England. It's located here at this site in Salem, New Hampshire. Photo is courtesy of Herbert from his website.

Hampi, India

Carnac Stones, France

There are supposed to be over three thousand stones lined up for two miles at this location. They are the largest collection of these types of Megaliths stones in the world. Some weigh from fifty, seventy-five, and upwards to three hundred and fifty tons.

Who and how did they line up these massive stones?

Source; History Channel, Ancient Aliens Season 2

Mycenae, Greece

This fortress city in southern Greece has local folklore stating that a giant had built some of the buildings here. This giant is known as the Cyclops. There are huge carved stones at this site. One piece that is high above the entrance shown slightly to the right is estimated to weigh two hundred tons. This is called the Lions Gate. That massive piece above the entrance supports the surrounding wall. Who put it up there and how?

Gobekli Tepe, near Sanliurfa, Turkey

It has taken archeologist thirteen years to excavate only five percent of this site. Some columns weigh more than fifteen tons. So far they haven't found any stone cutting tools like they usually do at other sites. They haven't found any agricultural tools either.

Source, History Channel Ancient Aliens second season.

Hissarlik, Turkey

This one is interesting. This is from the ancient city of Troy. Does Troy sound familiar? Homers book, the Iliad? Doesn't it look like an amphitheater?

Nemrud Dagi, Turkey

Puma Punku, western Bolivia.

Located in the Andes mountains, this location is twelve thousand feet above sea level. Some of these megalithic stones are twenty-seven feet long and weigh over one hundred tons each. The stones are polished to such smoothness that the method used thousands of years ago is not supposedly in existence today.

Source, History Channel Puma Punku

This monolith of a stone is estimated to weigh over 300 tonnes. That well over 600,000 lbs or converted to lbs would be about 661,386 lbs. That is getting near to being almost ¾ of a million lbs.

Sacsayhuaman, near Cuzco Peru.
Look at the size of these stones. They are interlocked to where you cannot get a razor blade between them. This site is located on a side of a mountain.

Hayu Marca, Peru

Located about 800 miles southeast of Lima Peru is what appears to be a rectangle cut out of a wall of solid stone. It is one of the strangest things that you might ever see. As you can tell, it looks like some type of doorway. Though you can't see it in the picture, there appears to be some type of indentation on the right side. And that indentation is located about where a door knob is placed.

Tiahuanaco, southern Peru.

Located near Puma Punku. Notice the massive pieces of stone?

Lake Titicaca, Peru

Located near Puma Punku.

Baalbek, Lebanon

Look at the size of these stones right up front in one part of the temple of Jupiter. They are estimated to be around 500 to 750 tons. They were carved out and moved into place.

Ollantaytambo, Peru

Notice the size of these stones. Engineers have said these were built and placed in such a way that they will move up and down during an earthquake. Who designed that and placed these onto the side of a steep mountain? There is evidence that they were put into place (with such great precision) to where you couldn't put a thin piece of paper between the two stones.

(Source, History Channel Ancient Aliens third season)

Teotihuacan, Mexico

This site is massive. This picture only shows part of it.

Tabasco, Mexico

They just carved out an image of a head out of this one stone. On this site, there are many of these types of carving of stone. Does this look familiar to you? Like you have seen this before? How about from the site mentioned before (page 18) at Nemrud Dagi, Turkey?

Copan, Honduras

This alter would probably belong to the Mayan. Notice the craving on that huge rock, which weighs tons. Look at that sign to the right too.

Easter Island, Off of South America

Some of these weigh as many as 75 tons. What is interesting is why are they facing in the direction they as looking in? Was there something there in the direction they were facing at one time, which is no longer there?

Where they simply lookouts, so to speak? Maybe they were carved to be guardians of the land they sat on. Did the thing they were looking at fall into the ocean? Or could it be what they were looking at is no longer there because it's no longer attached to that land mass? In the beginning, it is believed that God made the earth with one primary huge land mass. But today, it's divided up. If so, when did the earth become divided up? More on that later.

Baalbek, Eastern Lebanon

This location has some of the largest stones in the world. The stone shown here in this picture is estimated to weigh over one thousand tonnes. That

is over two million lbs. Remember, the weight in tonne is more than the American ton.

Throughout the world, these types of stone blocks were cut and placed so perfectly together that you can't put a razor blade between them. This was done thousands of years ago. Others like this one were used for the temples and weigh an estimated five hundred and fifty to one thousand tonne. Five hundred tons is over 1,000,000 lbs. It's thought these stones were quarried and moved to this site from five miles away. There are several ones at this site. Like the others, this one is just laying there like wood at a construction site. Today there are no cranes that can begin to lift that amount of weight.

In the Jupiter temple, there are fifty-four columns with each one weighing sixty tons while one corner block weighed over one hundred tons.

(Source: https://sites.google.com/site/theywatchus/evidence-of-nephilim-giants)

Let's put this into another perspective. The maximum weight limit for the newest bridges in the United States is 80,000 lbs. That is forty tons. Some of these carved stones could not be transported across our bridges. Keep in mind there are bridges that are rated far less than that weight too.

Some Arabs believe that Baalbek is the place where Nimrod's famous Tower of Babel was built. During Nimrod's reign over Lebanon, an Arabic manuscript (the name of it is unknown) stated he (Nimrod) sent giants over to the fortress of Baalbek to rebuild it. It's unknown whether it was an earthquake which damaged the fortress or the flood of Genesis 7 which was responsible. The name "Baalbek" was named in honor of "Baal". Baal is the god of the Moabites and worshipers of the sun. It is also believed that Zakaria El-Qazwini (an Arabian historian) claims King Solomon built an enormous castle there. It is also believed this is the place where Elijah confronted the priests of Baal (1 Kings 18:19-40); in their own temple. He brought down fire from heaven consuming the sacrifice. Right afterwards, 450 of the priests of Baal were killed by the Israelites. (Source; History of Baalbek; by Michael M Alouf. Published 1999.)

Messini, Greece

Did you think the above stone from Baalbek, Eastern Lebanon was the only one of its kind laying around? Well here is another one from Greece. This place is called the Arcadian Gate. I think they dropped this one because it appears to have had a few cracks in it. Maybe they were going to try to repair it or at least look at it more closely. They must have thought they can check it out better if it's laying on the edge... Now that is wild...

Roman Temple in Lebanon

They placed the above stone right here in this temple shown in the photo on the left. I've seen other structures that used this size of stone at its base also. Notice the long upright pieces. Now how did they move the millions of lbs of stone from the quarry to this location? Those same size stones are also used in Cahuachi, Nazca in Peru. Those ruins are on a side of a mountain. That's completely on the other size of the world.

Baalbek, Lebanon

Here is another one from Baalbek. How would you like to move this column? My guess is the builders were going to use it to support some structure. Then it might have cracked or it fell over, and then part of the top broke off so they leaned it against the wall. I would think they were going to do something with it. But whatever happened, they never came back to move it.

Luxor temple, Egypt

I've seen photos where they had an area where they carved out the image and then placed these huge multiton pieces into their present location. How did they get those stones up there?

Sphinx and Pyramid underwater during Genesis 7 Flood

I thought it would be a bit entertaining and interesting if you saw this underwater so you could get a perspective of what it looked like during the flood. Some sources have stated there were salt on the walls inside the pyramid. I think you can guess how it got in there…

Aswan Egypt

Here is an obelisk. It is still in the quarry. Notice the crack on top of it. I believe it is over 100 feet tall and weighs over 1,000 tons. This quarry is something like five hundred thirty five (535) miles away from the great pyramid at Giza. It's over two million (2,000,000) lbs in weight. How were they going to lift that up out of that hole? No wooden ship can carry that massive weight and size.

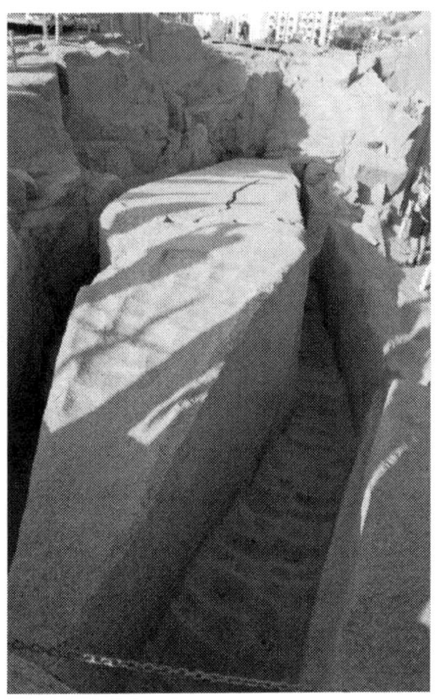

I would like to thank Wolfgang Kaehler for allowing me to use this photo. Check out his website for some stunning pictures. He is a professional photographer!

I was told this obelisk is also from Aswan. I'm not going to try to figure out how many tons it weighs. Could this one be at least one and half times the size as the one is above?

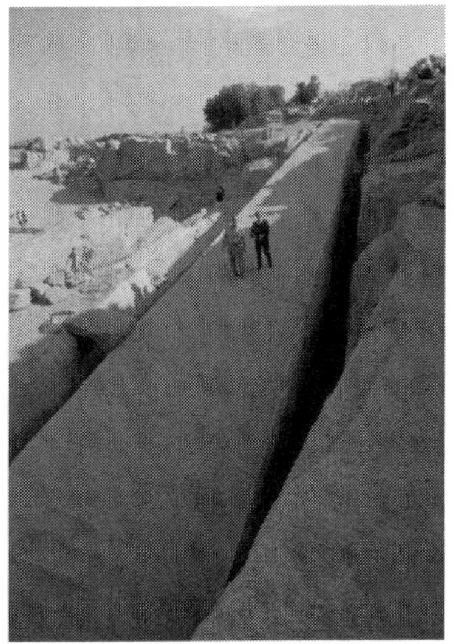

The question is, why is it still in the quarry? The sides of it are carved out. So most of the work was completed. Notice the top part of it is cracked in a few places. So they left it in place. If it were not cracked, it would have been obviously missing from this quarry. Then we would have had a bigger mystery to figure out. They wanted it to be a particular length… for some reason.

Are you thinking who engineered these designs? How were these stones shaped so concisely? Who put them in place, and with exacting precision?

Who built these structures? Why did they build them to look the way they did? What was the reason to place them where they are located now? Do you realize how long it would take to build these structures today? How did they know how deep to go in the ground so it will support the structure for thousands of years? To withstand the earthquakes which occur from time to time? If we built these today, we'd have done engineering studies, the plans would be laid out for these super structures in some engineering or drafting program on a computer. Then you have the environmental impact studies done in the area. Then quarrying the rock and transporting it to the site. Lifting it up and putting it into place, making sure it is aligned squarely with the other stones. After all of this, I doubt they would last as long as these have over thousands of years.

From the information I've provided you so far, what are your observations? Do you see a pattern emerging? Do you notice any commonality between these sites? Do you see anything that is similar? Of these sites, do you notice anything in common among them?

Let me give you my observations.

1. All the work is done in stone. The Tower of Babel was built with brick as I will discuss this later.
2. Notice the ninety degree angles on the stone work on many of the structures. These are stones that were carved thousands of years ago.
3. The structures have endured and survived countless earthquakes.
4. Notice the smoothness of the pieces that had carvings on them. On some of them; you will notice very specific attention to detail. For example, the one in Tabasco Mexico. Look at the detail in both the lips, in the eyes, and in the iris.
5. I noticed the grand style of these structures. It is as if they were building a city in some cases.

Notice inside these pyramids the elaborate paintings and etchings of the time. Some believe it was the Egyptians who were leaving behind what life was like during that time period. Others think there are some instructions, ancient secrets of the earth, which were used during the Genesis 6 time line.

This picture of the wall actually had color in it. But this photo being in black and white, you don't see it.

As many of the scholars would have you believe, they didn't have electricity back in those days. If that is the case, then how did they paint time-consuming pictures on the interior walls of some of the pyramids?

How did they see to paint them? There is no natural light that can make its way down into where these areas are located. Did they stop construction to paint these walls and ceilings within the pyramid?

Some will most certainly speak up and 'Ah, that is an easy one. They used candles!' Hmmm… Seeing how many of them were made in the time of Genesis 6 and up to maybe a thousand years later or so, candle making wasn't discovered until around 200 B.C. by the Chinese.
(Source; http://en.wikipedia.org/wiki/History_of_candle_making)

So the use of candles is out. What about mirrors?

Mirrors where made by polishing some types of stone so one could see their own reflection. But to reflect sunlight is clearly another matter. Those types of mirrors where invented well into 16th century. (Source; http://en.wikipedia.org/wiki/Mirror)

So mirrors are out too. Now how did they paint those pictures on the walls?

Transitions

There are passages in the LORD's Precious Word (the Bible) that don't completely reveal all that happened in some events or circumstances. There are many of them actually.

1. Did Enoch know ahead of time he was going to be taken up by the LORD?
2. What about Enoch's wife? Did she also know ahead of time? If not, did the LORD send her an angel down to inform her as to what happened to her husband?
3. Did the information come in a dream or vision or maybe not at all? Why wasn't more information given as to why the flood came?

I recollect thinking about what I just mentioned in the above paragraph and other things that have happened in the Bible. But it doesn't state how it happened or what happened to get them into that state. I was looking for a deeper meaning. More of an understanding of these events that happened in the Bible. Then a day or two later it came to me. The answers came to me along with some Scriptures.

How much of history does the LORD want to reveal to us in the Bible? Let's look at what Jesus said to His disciples after He rose from the dead.

John 21:20-25;
20 Peter turned around and saw the disciple whom Jesus loved. That disciple was following them. He was the one who leaned against Jesus' chest at the supper and asked, "Lord, who is going to betray you?"
21 When Peter saw him, he asked Jesus, "Lord, what about him?"
22 Jesus said to Peter, "If I want him to live until I come again, how does that concern you? Follow me!"
23 So a rumor that that disciple wouldn't die spread among Jesus' followers. But Jesus didn't say that he wouldn't die. What Jesus said was, "If I want him to live until I come again, how does that concern you?"
24 This disciple was an eyewitness of these things and wrote them down. We know that what he says is true.
25 Jesus also did many other things. If every one of them were written down, I suppose the world wouldn't have enough room for the books that would be written. (GOD'S WORD ® Translation)

If all of the works that Jesus had done were written down, let alone all the rest of the information which wasn't included in the Bible, all the books in the world would not contain them all. It makes us wonder how much more work we need to do to help and serve others while we walk with Him. Jesus was here for around thirty years. In his seventy-week ministry, all the works He had done could not be contained in all the books in the world.

The second revelation was when I was really seeking out some information for the concepts in this book. He had given me verse 25 above. Then the next one came.

Proverbs 25:2; *It is the glory of God to conceal a matter; to search out a matter is the glory of kings.* (New International Version)

The moment these verses were revealed to me. I just smiled and thanked Him. Hallelujah! That's why a lot of history is not included in the Bible. It would get too big for us to use. It's those things, if we seek them out, He will show them to us!

Proverbs 8:17; *I love those who love me, and those who seek me find me.* (New International Version)

Jeremiah 29:13; *You will seek me and find me, when you seek me with all your heart.* (English Standard Version)

Jeremiah 33:3; *Call unto me, and I will answer you, and show you great and mighty things, which you know not.* (King James Version)

Let's start with the human side of life. The human struggle we are sometimes faced with in our daily lives. They happen to all of us whether we notice it or not. When things don't turn out the way we expected or go as planned, we need to come up with another solution. So let's look at Adam and Eve. We'll briefly look at their lives and the decisions they made and what possibly happened or could have happened.

Adam and Eve Outside the Garden of Eden

Here is one of the moments of that interpersonal relationship Adam and Eve found themselves in after being banished from the Garden. Few people ever talk about what happened right after their expulsion from paradise, as some have come to call it.

In a sense, Adam and Eve were treated like royalty while they were in the Garden of Eden. Everything was provided. They didn't need clothes, food was everywhere. They worked to make sure the garden was well tended and so everything grew properly. There were no timelines to meet. The temperature was just right. They didn't need air conditioning or a furnace. At times, they could bask in the warm sunlight and enjoy the warmth of the sun's rays on their skin. The moonlit nights were wonderful and very enjoyable to experience. They talked to each other and sometimes a lion or tiger want to be petted or needed some attention from the both of them. Maybe Adam would wrestle a little bit with them in a playful way. He might have explained to Eve why he named this animal a tiger and that one a lion.

"Eve, you see that little creature to your side, that is a chipmunk. Isn't he a cute little guy? Well I think he is a guy. Let me check…" He gets up as if to pick it up, but she starts to giggle a little bit.

"Adam, instead of that, just kiss me. I like the way that feels."

Adam kisses her. Then something catches his eye. An eagle flies by and lands within a cubit of Adam.

"Hi, Adam and Eve. Thought I'd drop by and say hello", the eagle said.

"Hi. So what are you doing today? Find anything exciting?"

"I'm just flying around and enjoying all of the LORD's creation. I love seeing everything I can see. Praise His Name" the eagle answered. "I'll talk with you later Adam. I think my mate is calling me…" With that, the eagle takes off.

Revelation 5:13-14;

13 Then I heard every creature in heaven and on earth and under the earth and on the sea, and all that is in them, saying: "To him who sits on the throne and to the Lamb be praise and honor and glory and power, for ever and ever!"
14 The four living creatures said, "Amen," and the elders fell down and worshiped. (New Living Translation)

Psalm 148:5-12

5 Let them praise the name of the LORD, for at his command they were created,
6 and he established them for ever and ever— he issued a decree that will never pass away.
7 Praise the LORD from the earth, you great sea creatures and all ocean depths,
8 lightning and hail, snow and clouds, stormy winds that do his bidding,
9 you mountains and all hills, fruit trees and all cedars,
10 wild animals and all cattle, small creatures and flying birds,

11 kings of the earth and all nations, you princes and all rulers on earth,
12 young men and women, old men and children. (New Living Translation)

"Isn't this the life Eve?" He sprawls on his back on the ground. The warmth of the sun is shining on his skin. Adam proceeds.

"All this harmony. I think it is time for the LORD to stop by so we can talk with Him. I wonder what He is going to teach us today. You know, sometimes I wish He can talk with us more…"

Now whether or not that conversation or something similar took place won't be known until we get to heaven. But everything was great there. They did some work, there was plenty of good food, there was plenty of family time to enjoy, great conversations, and they had the Ultimate Teacher, the LORD.

Today, we long for that type of life. We know we need to work. But in our hearts, we long for that life style. I call it "The Garden of Eden" syndrome. We know we need to work, but don't want the stresses of it to accompany it.

Then the Bible says they ate of the fruit of the tree they were not supposed to eat from. And then they were banished from paradise.

I can picture them sitting on a rock, looking down at the clothes the LORD God made for them. The great feeling of paradise was gone. What they needed was all around them. They looked at the cherubim with its flaming sword flashing it back and forth so they couldn't go back inside. The cherubim was guarding the tree of life.

Then the Bible quickly goes to the birth of Cain after they left paradise. Nothing else is mentioned about the adjustments they needed to make to continue their lives together.

I wonder how Adam and Eve felt when an eagle flew by and looked at them. He called out to it. The eagle talked to Adam, but for the first time, Adam didn't understand what it said. Imagine the puzzlement and dismay that might have gone through his mind as the eagle flew in a different direction. Did the thoughts of "is that eagle mad at me?" cross his mind? A deer came nearby. Adam called out to it, but it said something and ran off. Adam couldn't understand what the deer just said to them either.

I often wondered at that moment when they sat there and maybe didn't say anything, watching that cherubim at the entrance with its flaming sword. Now they had to get their own food, grow crops, eventually find shelter and water. They will come to understand sickness and pain; both physical and emotional. Someday they will experience death.

Nowadays, when married couples (or even those in other relationships) face rocky times, there are thoughts about splitting up and going their separate ways. Sometimes they choose not to invest any more into each other to save the relationship. Adam and Eve basically went from royalty to homeless people. I wonder if they argued and had strong words for each other at that time. Consider the following scenario.

"Well Eve, that serpent was pretty convincing to you. I wish you wouldn't have listened to it and eaten of that tree." Adam said while still looking at the cherubim. They are both sitting on a rock looking at that cherub.

1 Timothy 2:14; *And Adam was not the one deceived; it was the woman who was deceived and became a sinner.* (New International Version)

"Yes he was. But wait, didn't you eat of that tree too?" Eve inquired of Adam.

"Well yes, but you gave it to me." Adam said sharply back.

"What was I supposed to do Adam? Not share it with you? I love you Adam and wanted to share with you the same things I had."

She jumps off the rock and turns her back to Adam, then tightly folds her arms while looking away.

"You know He told us not to eat of that tree." Adam continues.

"And why didn't you speak up mister I named all the animals? You could have spoken up and said something like, 'Eve, I don't think we should be eating that. Our God said so…' I would have listened to you Adam like I always did when we had our conversations together. But did you? Nope. I'm feeling bad enough now and on top of that, you are saying these things to me..." Eve says as she sharpens her tone to Adam.

Then she turns to Adam and unfolds her arms and places them on her hips and continues.

"I'm just wondering what is going to happen. How is this going to affect our children? What about our children's children? That serpent just... just… I can't think of the word I want to use…"

Roman 5:12; *Therefore, just as sin entered the world through one man, and death through sin, and in this way death came to all people, because all sinned.* (New International Version)

"You mean 'lied'?" Adam answered back in a softer tone.

"Yes thank you. That creature you named just lied to us. Now look at the mess we are in." Eve pauses.

John 8:44; *You belong to your father, the devil, and you want to carry out your father's desires. He was a murderer from the beginning, not holding to the truth, for there is no truth in him. When he lies, he speaks his native language, for he is a liar and the father of lies.* (New International Version)

"Now the LORD is mad at us. Now what do we do? Now He says we are going to die… And I'm not sure what exactly that means…" She looks down at the ground for a bit, then looks up at him and continues.

1 Corinthians 15:56; *The sting of death is sin, and the power of sin is the law.* (New International Version)

"Adam, could what we had done affect many of our great, great grandchildren? What did our Father say? Hold on, oh yes, what if this affects many generations to come?"

She sits down on the rock again and tears flow down her cheeks. They both notice them. They both look at each other.

"What is that running down your cheeks? It looks like water." Adam asks.

"I don't know" she responds.

Did they ponder going their separate ways? They were the only ones on the planet then unless Jesus came down to visit them. Their conversation continues.

Adam wrapped his arms around Eve and held her. Then she started crying.

"I feel so bad Adam. Look what I did!" Tears are really streaming down her face now.

"Don't blame yourself. It's my fault. I should have said something like you said. The LORD told me too not to eat of that tree.

"So why DID you eat of that fruit I gave you, Adam?"

Adam paused, looked away, then looked into her eyes and started to speak;

"I thought we would figure it out together Eve."

"Wait… Why would you do this to yourself Adam? Now you are going to die?"

"I know. But I need you, and I didn't want to be without you because I love you."

"Yes I know, Adam. But you gave up your life for me. And our God punished you for listening to me too."

Genesis 3:17; *To Adam he said, "Because you listened to your wife and ate from the tree about which I commanded you, 'You must not eat of it,' "Cursed is the ground because of you; through painful toil you will eat of it all the days of your life.* (New International Version)

"Maybe I had the greater sin Eve. I should have spoken up and said something about it… Let's figure this out together…"

Whether or not it went down like that, I don't know. Maybe it didn't enter into their thinking. But there was a time when they could have split up and gone their separate ways.

To stay alive, they struggled to find food, water, and shelter. Thankfully, it's believed the LORD did speak to Adam and Eve even though they were no longer in the Garden of Eden.

They eventually would have children named Cain, Abel and Seth. After the LORD's judgment on Cain for killing his brother

Abel, he moved to the land of Nod, which was east of Eden. Adam and Eve had other children too, both sons and daughters.

Genesis 5:4-5;
4 After Seth was born, Adam lived 800 years and had other sons and daughters.
5 Altogether, Adam lived a total of 930 years, and then he died.. (New International Version)

Too often we forget to have compassion, to be patient with other people. The world has tried to engrain into us what love is, but that is usually the exact opposite of how He wants us to act.

Someday we will return to the Garden of Eden. However, it will be more enhanced and more beautiful than ever.

Before we leave the Garden of Eden, I would like to bring to your attention the following information.

When we were in the Garden of Eden, we were vegetarians.

Genesis 1:29-30;
29 Then God said, "I give you every seed-bearing plant on the face of the whole earth and every tree that has fruit with seed in it. They will be yours for food.
30 And to all the beasts of the earth and all the birds in the sky and all the creatures that move along the ground—everything that has the breath of life in it—I give every green plant for food." And it was so. (New International Version)

As a side note, if all of us were vegetarians, both animals and us, then where did the teachings of the meat eating dinosaurs come from? Did someone make it up?

But, because of Eve's first sin and then Adam's sin following right after, the curse on the ground was revealed and that curse included death to the animals too.

Genesis 3:14; *Then the LORD God said to the serpent, "Because you have done this, you are cursed more than all animals, domestic and wild. You will crawl on your belly, groveling in the dust as long as you live.* (New Living Translation)

Did you catch that phrase? All the livestock and wild animals are cursed. But the serpent was indeed more cursed, by having to crawl on its belly for the rest of its life.

What isn't widely known is we were not supposed to eat meat until after the flood. That's when the animals, birds, creatures on earth and in the sea began to began to fear and dread us.

Genesis 9:1-4;
1 Then God blessed Noah and his sons, saying to them, "Be fruitful and increase in number and fill the earth.
2 The fear and dread of you will fall on all the beasts of the earth, and on all the birds in the sky, on every creature that moves along the ground, and on all the fish in the sea; they are given into your hands.
3 Everything that lives and moves about will be food for you. Just as I gave you the green plants, I now give you everything.
4 "But you must not eat meat that has its lifeblood still in it. (New International Version)

Pre-Flood

enesis 6:1-4;
1 When human beings began to increase in number on the earth and daughters were born to them,
2 the sons of God saw that the daughters of humans were beautiful, and they married any of them they chose.
3 Then the LORD said, "My Spirit will not contend with humans forever, for they are mortal ; their days will be a hundred and twenty years."
4 The Nephilim were on the earth in those days—and also afterward—when the sons of God went to the daughters of humans and had children by them. They were the heroes of old, men of renown.
5 The LORD saw how great the wickedness of the human race had become on the earth, and that every inclination of the thoughts of the human heart was only evil all the time.
6 The LORD regretted that he had made human beings on the earth, and his heart was deeply troubled... (New International Version)

There is a phrase and a word mentioned above which are different from most others in the Bible. The first one is “sons of God” and the other is “Nephilim.”

I am amazed how most people don’t know much about this passage of Scripture. And of those who do, avoid talking about it. Yet the beginning part of Genesis 6 is one of three events that have negatively impacted our lives up to and including today. Yet no one wants to discuss it at length.

The first event was the sin in the Garden of Eden.

Without a doubt, the second event was the actions of Genesis 6. In my mind, there is no doubt we are still plagued with what happened during that period of history. What was unleashed back then is still trying to torment us today in our daily lives.

The third event is Nimrod and the Tower of Babel. I will be discussing this also.

There are four theories as to whom the “sons of God” are. They are;

1. **Sons of Seth**. This is usually called the Sethite theory. This theory states the male descendant’s of Seth’s bloodline married the daughters of Cain’s bloodline. As the result of this union, the Nephilim were born. Before we go any further, I’m going to give you a quick overview of who the Nephilim are.
   I talk more of whom the Nephilim are, later in the book. The short overview of it is they were giants, of differing heights, possessed incredible strength and were widely known during that time period before and after the flood of Genesis 7. In some cases, they were heroes who live in legends of yesterday. They are actually talked about today by other names. I will cover that later on.
   If we look at the Sethite theory, we can see there is a problem with it. It says in Genesis 1 that all the plants and animals reproduce after their own kind. That means a bird produces another bird when it reproduces. A giraffe produces another giraffe. A tiger another tiger. The same thing happens with plants. They don’t cross the barriers of what the LORD has set up in the

beginning. You need to inject new DNA before this barrier is crossed. And that is the same thing with us. We can reproduce other human beings when a male and female reproduce. If that is the case, then how can two human beings create a Nephilim, a giant? They can't unless some new DNA enters into the picture. If you believe Adam and Eve were in their ancestry, then it can't be done. Kissing relatives don't produce Nephilim.

2. **Sons of Cain**. This is usually called the Cainite theory. This is not to be confused with the Canaanites mentioned after the flood of Genesis 7.
   This theory states the exact opposite happened. The male descendant's of Cain married the daughters of the Seth. This doesn't hold up either because they both are descendants of Adam and Eve. Again this is a kissing relative's situation.
   There is one possible variant of this theory. There are some who believe that something more happened in the Garden of Eden… other than eating of that forbidden fruit. There are some that believe Adam is not Cain's father. They believe satan is the father for many reasons. If you have heard the term "satan's seed," you might understand there might be a connection… however slight that it might be. One reason some believe in this theory is Cain is not mentioned in Adam's genealogically. The second is Eve bore Cain's brother Abel without saying Adam again knew his wife and bore Cain. That could mean Cain and Abel are twins. I have read it is medically possible. The third is where it says in the following verse;
   1 John 3:12; *We must not be like Cain, who belonged to the evil one and killed his brother. And why did he kill him? Because Cain had been doing what was evil, and his brother had been doing what was righteous.* (New Living Translation)
3. **Nobility or Aristocratic Leaders**. In this theory, it is supposed to have its origins somewhere during the fifth, sixth, or eighteenth centuries A.D. while others claim it has its root in 1800 B.C. The reasons for this theory is many were uncomfortable with the interpretation they

were fallen angels. They just couldn't comprehend this possibility. Yet this "leaders" theory is really no different than the Sethite or Cainite ones. Again, kissing relatives don't produce Nephilim.

4. **Fallen angels.** One translation that could help us with finding whom they were is the Jewish Study Bible. It translates the 'sons of God' into "divine beings;" I bolded it for you.

Genesis 6:1-4;

1 When men began to increase on earth and daughters were born to them,

2 the ***divine beings*** *saw how beautiful the daughters of men were and took wives from among those that pleased them.—*

3 The LORD said, "My breath shall not abide in man forever, since he too is flesh; let the days allowed him be one hundred and twenty years."—

4 It was then, and later too, that the Nephilim appeared on earth—when the divine beings cohabited with the daughters of men, who bore them offspring. They were the heroes of old, the men of renown.

(Jewish Publication Society of America (2000-12-01). Tanakh: The Holy Scriptures--The New JPS Translation According to the Traditional Hebrew Text)

"Divine beings" appears to eliminate the human factor. Nowhere in the Bible does it say man is a divine being. So in order to try and understand if they are indeed fallen angels, we need to seek out other methods to determine what this wording means. To do this, let's see what the original language states for the phrase "sons of God." This should debunk all the other theories.

I looked up the phrase "sons of God" in the Hebrew and searched to see if it is mentioned in other places of the Bible. And sure enough, it is. It is stated in the following verses.

Job 1:6; *One day when the sons of God came to stand in front of the LORD, Satan the Accuser came along with them.* (GOD'S WORD® Translation)

Job 2:1; *Again there was a day when the sons of God came to present themselves before the LORD, and Satan*

> *also came among them to present himself before the LORD.* (English Standard Version)
> **Job 38:7;** *when the morning stars sang together and all the sons of God shouted for joy?* (English Standard Version)
> In Job chapters 1 & 2 you see the "sons of God" are called to present themselves to the LORD. This is significant. Nowhere in the Bible does it state we, as human beings, are called to present ourselves to Him. You and I are called the sons of Adam. Jesus was called the Son of man.

In the writing below are some ancient texts from a well respected first century historian called Flavius Josephus.

Let me give you a little background on Flavius. He was a Jewish historian who was born just after the crucifixion of Jesus. He is well respected for his writings. To this very day, some modern day, spirit filled preachers, still reference his writings in one form or another. Some of his well known writings include 'War of the Jews' and 'Antiquities of the Jews.' You will notice he calls them 'angels of God.' I highlighted the text for you.

Antiquities of the Jews;
Chapter 3:1; NOW this posterity of Seth continued to esteem God as the Lord of the universe, and to have an entire regard to virtue, for seven generations; but in process of time they were perverted, and forsook the practices of their forefathers; and did neither pay those honors to God which were appointed them, nor had they any concern to do justice towards men. But for what degree of zeal they had formerly shown for virtue, they now showed by their actions a double degree of wickedness, whereby they made God to be their enemy. For many **angels of God** accompanied with women, and begat sons that proved unjust, and despisers of all that was good, on account of the confidence they had in their own strength; for the tradition is, that these men did what resembled the acts of those whom the Grecians call giants. But Noah was very uneasy at what they did; and being displeased at their conduct, persuaded them to change their dispositions and their acts for the better: but seeing they did not yield to him, but were slaves to their wicked pleasures, he was

afraid they would kill him, together with his wife and children, and those they had married; so he departed out of that land.

As you can tell, the "sons of God" are the fallen angels. I'm sure you may remember the following verse. How do I explain what Jesus said then? Let's look at it.

Matthew 22:30; *At the resurrection people will neither marry nor be given in marriage; they will be like the angels in heaven.* (New International Version)

Let's look at that verse again. Jesus is teaching us something here. The first thing is the time period. It states "At the resurrection". Was the time of Genesis 6 the resurrection? No, it wasn't. Was the time Jesus taught this the resurrection? No. He is talking about a time into the future. The second thing is the phrase "angels in heaven." Where are these fallen angels? In heaven? They are NOT in heaven.

Now let's look at that word Nephilim. Most of the translations use the word 'Nephilim' in Genesis 6:4. A few versions use the word 'giants.' Another one that I am aware of use the words 'fallen ones'.

I found it very interesting how many scholars struggled with how to translate that word "Nephilim". I think it is interesting the Israelites didn't have a problem with using that word for what they described. They knew who they were. The word "Nephilim" only appears twice in the Bible. Once in Genesis 6:4 and the other times in the following verse.

Numbers 13:33; *We saw the Nephilim there (the descendants of Anak come from the Nephilim). We seemed like grasshoppers in our own eyes, and we looked the same to them."* (New International Version)

Some believe Nephilim is the plural form of Nephat meaning, to fall, be cast down, to fall away, to desert. Yet there is another translation that defined it as 'the mighty ones'. When the Old Testament was translated into Greek, they used the word 'giants'.

Now Chuck Missler, a noted Biblical scholar, felt that the Greek word really should be 'earth-born' instead of 'giants'. The Greek Septuagint, an ancient translation of the Hebrew Bible, translates the work Nephilim as gigantes, which actually means "giant".

Here are some of the many translations of the word 'Nephilim'.

1. Giants
2. Fall
3. Fall away
4. Fallen ones
5. Be cast down
6. Mighty ones
7. To desert
8. Earth-born

As you can see, the writer of Genesis didn't really define what a Nephilim was back in those days. He knew what they were because he saw them. As to us, the friendly debate goes on. However, it doesn't change the outcome of that union. The discussion is merely based on what do we call the children of that union.

Michael Heiser, a scholar in the fields of biblical studies and the ancient Near East, believes that the word Nephilim does not mean "fallen ones" in Hebrew. The reason why is because of the spelling or the shape of the word. The following is from his website.

The word "Nephilim" is formed / spelled TWO ways in the Old Testament Hebrew text:

נְפִלִים (Genesis 6:4 and once in Numbers 13:33)

נְפִילִים (also in Numbers 13:33)

The difference between them, of course, is the extra letter in the second spelling:

This difference in spelling this "extra letter is critical to understanding where the word does and does not come from, which in turn informs us as to how it's to be or not to be

The extra letter is the letter *yod* (י), which has two functions: (1) the "y" sound; (2) to MARK the long "i" sound (as in "ee", like in English "machine"). In the case of *nephilim* (notice the English spelling with two "i" vowels), the *yod* serves to give us the long "i" vowel sound. Hence *nephilim* is technically (correctly) pronounced "nepheeleem."

translated.

The bottom line is the word Nephilim cannot mean "fallen ones", it means giants.

Here is his website. Check it out for more of a detailed account of the above.

(Source; http://www.michaelsheiser.com/nephilim.pdf)

It is this author's opinion that the Nephilim is the name of the offspring of the union between a woman and the fallen angels.

The Bible does clearly mention all living flesh that walked, crawled, on the earth, or flew in the air died in that flood, unless they were in the ark. So how did the Nephilim come back?

What did all the animals do that caused them to be destroyed too? These questions will be addressed in this book.

Man has always been wicked in his heart.

Genesis 8:21-22;

21 The LORD smelled the pleasing aroma and said in his heart: "Never again will I curse the ground because of humans, even though every inclination of the human heart is evil from

childhood. And never again will I destroy all living creatures, as I have done.
22 "As long as the earth endures, seedtime and harvest, cold and heat, summer and winter, day and night will never cease." (New International Version)

After the flood, the Nephilim returned. Here are some of their names.

1. Ammonities
2. Canaanites
3. Emim
4. Moabites
5. Philistines
6. Rapha
7. Raphah
8. Rephaim. That word alone is mentioned about 34 times in the Old Testament. You might enjoy doing a word study of this word. It opens up an entire world of information.

There are others not mentioned above. I just didn't include them all in this book. So the question I have is why isn't this studied and talked about in Christian circles? How about our churches? There is plenty of evidence these Nephilim and their descendant were around thousands of years ago. The LORD devoted many verses to them and their descendants. It's in the Word of God, the Bible…

What usually is the case is they are not sure how to preach on it or teach these events with them in it. As you continue to read this book, you will begin to see a pattern. Usually somewhere during this book, the light bulb comes on and they begin to view the Old Testament in a different light. Then the events and human interactions will be understood in a different light. That is when you start to see things differently.

In the Bible, the word "giant" is referred to about nineteen times. "Giants" are referred to about 30 times. There are other historical texts which give an account of these beings. You'll see that evidence/information in this book. Now we have these Nephilim inhabiting the earth again.

Timeline of Events in Early Genesis

In order to understand where I'm going with all this information, we should look at the past and what led up to the time period of Genesis 6. This is VERY important because when the time period of Genesis 6 is understood, then you will truly understand why the LORD brought about the flood. When that is understood, the events of today and what we are seeing now for only the second time in history will start to make sense. Then you will be prepared for the unique event we are in right now.... The days of Noah.

Here is an estimated timeline for the following events which occurred at the beginning of time on this earth. Some other Bible scholars believe in a slightly different timeline. Some date the first week of creation at around 4002, some 4004, and yet others 4111 B.C. The difference between the longest one and the one I will use below is about 136 years. Within the scope of about six thousand years, I don't think 136 years matter that much. This time line came from the Chronological Bible by Edward Reese. He was one of my professors in college. It's available to purchase on Amazon. I would recommend you get a copy of it. It places the entire Bible in a chronological order.

I prefer to follow the timeline listed below.

1. Around 3975 B.C. is the week of creation.
2. Cain is born in 3972 B.C.
3. Abel is born in 3971 B.C.
4. Around 3847 B.C. Cain kills his brother Abel. That means about 128 years had passed between the week of creation and Cain killing Abel.
5. Around 2439 B.C. is when Genesis 6:2 took place. (Source for of the above verses; Reese Chronological Bible).
   Genesis 6:2; *that the sons of God saw that the daughters of men were beautiful; and they took wives for themselves, whomever they chose.* (New American Standard Bible)
6. About 120 years later in 2319 B.C. (source; Reese Chronological Bible), Noah, his family, and the animals entered into the Ark.

Genesis 7:6-10;
6 Noah was six hundred years old when the floodwaters came on the earth.
7 And Noah and his sons and his wife and his sons' wives entered the ark to escape the waters of the flood.
8 Pairs of clean and unclean animals, of birds and of all creatures that move along the ground,
9 male and female, came to Noah and entered the ark, as God had commanded Noah.
10 And after the seven days the floodwaters came on the earth. (New International Version)

If we do the math, about 1,536 years had passed between the week of creation and Genesis 6:2.

So the time between the above murder of Abel by his brother Cain and the LORD deciding to start preparing to bring the flood to the earth is about 1,408 years. Now here is something to think about. All that time had passed. The Bible talks about some genealogies, Enoch walked with God, then God took Enoch, Noah was born, the great grandson of Enoch and other things (we will be discussing Enoch some more a little later on in this book). During this time, nothing violent was recorded in the Bible. Life just moved forward without much fanfare or significant events, apart from Enoch being taken. Now keep in mind, there was still wickedness on the earth by man. Man was still sinning. So I would call this in Biblical events, very quiet… or was it?

Then Genesis 6 happened. All of a sudden, Genesis 6:5 happens.

Genesis 6:5-7;
5 The LORD saw how great the wickedness of the human race had become on the earth, and that every inclination of the thoughts of the human heart was only evil all the time.
6 The LORD regretted that he had made human beings on the earth, and his heart was deeply troubled.
7 So the LORD said, "I will wipe from the face of the earth the human race I have created—and with them the animals, the

birds and the creatures that move along the ground—for I regret that I have made them." (New International Version)

Huh.... Did I miss something here? I must have missed something here. I checked different versions of the Bible to see if I missed something here. Man has always been sinful and wicked. So what happened? What changed?

By my estimates, there were at least 1 billion (1,000,000,000) people on the planet when the flood of Genesis 7 happened. Other Bible scholars estimate there were between 5 to 17 billion people on the planet (http://ldolphin.org/pickett.html). With all these people here, life just seemingly went right along.

A side note here. We have 7 billion people on the planet today. Why are governments and special interest groups complaining, stating there are too many people on the planet?

What happened in Genesis 6 that was so terrible that the LORD decided to destroy life that was on the earth, except for those on the ark? Think for a few moments. What happened or what changed?

Was the LORD just 'fed up' with man? I have yet to hear someone preach about this topic, but look at the passage; "...and his heart was deeply troubled." Dwell on that verse for a while. The LORD's heart was filled with pain. Have you had a loved one you were close to die? Maybe it was a parent, a child, a friend, a spouse maybe or a fiancé? Maybe you had a breakup with someone you thought you might marry some day or a lifelong friend passed away. Remember the intense feelings you went through when any of these things happened?

Well it seems because we are made in His image, in His likeness, He apparently goes through those same types of feelings we do. But with Him, multiply that by billions. Each and every one of us here on earth, every individual is just as important to the LORD as the other.

So what transpired that was so, so very hideous that He, our God, decided to wipe all life He created? What changed? What were the circumstances that surrounded this event? And will we experience it today?

A Major Rebellion

In review, we had the fall of mankind in the Garden of Eden. Then Cain killed his brother Abel around one hundred and twenty eight years after the week of creation. Then about 1,408 years later Genesis 6:2 happened. These angels married the daughters of men because they were beautiful. Then these women gave birth to the Nephilim.

Now we go from what seems like everything was just moving along just fine for the most part to suddenly our God going to destroy everything that breathes on the earth by way of a flood. This is serious stuff.

The greatest destruction upon the whole earth was about to take place with the flood, and hardly anything was written about it in the Bible. At the time of this writing, there hasn't been such a destructive power unleashed upon the earth since the time of that flood. That includes the atomic bomb detonations that have occurred since World War II. There have been over two thousand of those detonations since then too.

In Genesis 6, absolute anarchy broke out upon the earth by what these angels and the Nephilim did by marrying the women on earth. These angels taught men things they should not know. Here are some reasons why the LORD decided to destroy everything on the earth, except for those creatures in the water and those in the ark.

1. There are those people who believe the goal of satan and his fallen angels was to corrupt the lineage (blood line) of our LORD Jesus. They obviously didn't succeed. There are those who believe that they wanted to destroy the earth and everything that was on the earth.
   Between Genesis 6:2 and Genesis 7:16, about one hundred and twenty years will pass between those two above verses. Then He sealed all the animals in the ark along with Noah's family. Those one hundred and twenty years gives Noah time to grow the trees to the

right height, build the ark, and load the animals He sent to him. It took about five years for Noah and his sons to build it.

Book of Jasher, 5:34 - In his five hundred and ninety-fifth year Noah commenced to make the ark, and he made the ark in five years, as the LORD had commanded.

The Book of Jasher is actually referenced twice in the Bible. The word Jasher means righteous or upright.

Joshua 10:13; *And the sun stood still, and the moon stopped, until the nation took vengeance on their enemies. Is this not written in the Book of Jashar? The sun stopped in the midst of heaven and did not hurry to set for about a whole day.* (English Standard Version)

2 Samuel 1:18; *and he told them to teach the sons of Judah the song of the bow; behold, it is written in the book of Jashar.* (New American Standard Bible)

The verses above seem to say; 'Hey, this information is also in this book.' Some translations spell it as either Jashar or Jasher. Paul actually refers to this book in the following verse. How is that? Jannes and Jambres are only mentioned in the New Testament in 2nd Timothy 3:8-9. They are not mentioned in the Old Testament. But they are in the Book of Jasher.

2 Timothy 3:8; *Just as Jannes and Jambres opposed Moses, so also these teachers oppose the truth. They are men of depraved minds, who, as far as the faith is concerned, are rejected.* (New International Version)

Book of Jasher 79:27 And when they had gone Pharaoh sent for Balaam the magician and to Jannes and Jambres his sons, and to all the magicians and conjurors and counsellors which belonged to the king, and they all came and sat before the king.

2. The second possible reason was so they could corrupt man and alter God's creation. Why did man's great wickedness appear or manifest itself so quickly on the earth all of a sudden? What changed, what happened? What happened in Genesis 6 that caused the LORD to be grieved that He made man? You will learn that the

events that happened in the time period of chapter 6 of Genesis were so 'epic' in proportions that it will change the course of man forever. You will understand how man has been under heavy assault in so many areas. What is interesting is, because we are in the days of Noah time period now, I believe it will get worse than it did back then. These fallen angels decided to violate God's law and marry these daughters of men. They knew they were not supposed to do what they did.

In the 1st Book of Enoch, these angels were called 'watcher angels' because they were assigned to the earth. The word 'watcher' is mentioned three times in the Bible.

Daniel 4:13; *"I saw in the visions of my head as I lay in bed, and behold, a watcher, a holy one, came down from heaven.* (English Standard Version)

Daniel 4:17; *The sentence is by the decree of the watchers, the decision by the word of the holy ones, to the end that the living may know that the Most High rules the kingdom of men and gives it to whom he will and sets over it the lowliest of men.'* (English Standard Version)

Daniel 4:23; *In that the king saw an angelic watcher, a holy one, descending from heaven and saying, "Chop down the tree and destroy it; yet leave the stump with its roots in the ground, but with a band of iron and bronze around it in the new grass of the field, and let him be drenched with the dew of heaven, and let him share with the beasts of the field until seven periods of time pass over him,"* (New American Standard Bible)

Keep in mind, through my research there are many instances when the angels are mentioned as a holy one. This next passage is one of the key events that increased the seriousness of the war the powers of darkness will rage against God and all of His creation.

1st Book of Enoch,

10:9; And to Gabriel YAHWEH said, "Proceed against the bastards and the reprobates and against the children of adultery; and destroy the children of adultery and expel the children of the Watchers from among the people. And send them against one another so that they may be destroyed in the fight, for length of days have they not."

1st Book of Enoch, 6:1-8;

1 In those days, when the children of man had multiplied, it happened that there were born unto them handsome and beautiful daughters.

2 And the angels, the children of heaven, saw them and desired them; and they said to one another, "Come, let us choose wives for ourselves from among the daughters of man and beget us children."

3 And Semyaz, being their leader, said unto them, "I fear that perhaps you will not consent that this deed should be done, and I alone will become responsible for this great sin."

4 But they all responded to him, "Let us all swear an oath and bind everyone among us by a curse not to abandon this suggestion but to do the deed." Then they all swore together and bound one another by the curse.

5 And they were altogether two hundred; and they descended into 'Ardos, which is the summit of Hermon.

6 And they called the mount Armon, for they swore and bound one another by a curse.

7 And their names are as follows: Semyaz, the leader of Arakeb, Rame'el, Tam'el, Ram'el, Dan'el, Ezeqel, Baraqyal, As'el, Armaros, Batar'el, Anan'el, Zaqe'el, Sasomaspwe'el, Kestar'el, Tur'el, Yamayol, and Arazyal.

8 These are their chiefs of tens and of all the others with them.

These watcher angels knew what they were doing was wrong. But they decided to do it anyway. It gave the names of the leaders of the two hundred watcher angels above. So now these angels had done a deed that will plague man for thousands of years to come. The results of these deeds will bring wars and rumors of wars. It will bring increased death and destruction to the people on this planet. Misery and torment to those of us who live here. The results of their actions are still present today. But Jesus came, lived, and died so we can be freed from the captor. Just like in the Garden of Eden when the encounter with the serpent occurred, so now man is going to be corrupted again. This time, in ways most people would never have thought was possible. Do you think you have not been deceived?

Genesis 6:4; *The Nephilim were on the earth in those days, and also afterward, when the sons of God came in to the daughters of man and they bore children to them. These were the mighty men who were of old, the men of renown.* (English Standard Version)

The phrase 'and also afterward' means they would be here after the flood too. The Bible said every man, woman, and child died who were on the earth in those days, apart from Noah and those in the ark.

Genesis 7:20-23;

20 The waters rose and covered the mountains to a depth of more than fifteen cubits.

21 Every living thing that moved on land perished—birds, livestock, wild animals, all the creatures that swarm over the earth, and all mankind.

22 Everything on dry land that had the breath of life in its nostrils died.

23 Every living thing on the face of the earth was wiped out; people and animals and the creatures that move along the ground and the birds were wiped from the earth. Only Noah was left, and those with him in the ark. (New International Version)

Keep in mind there are a few ways of determining how long a cubit is. One cubit is seventeen plus inches tall. Others are eighteen inches long. Then there is one Hebrew cubit is around twenty five (25) inches long. Keep this in mind because we will use the measurement in a way that will allow you to look at the Scriptures differently.

So if the water rose 15 cubits above the mountains, that means it was between twenty two (22) to thirty (30) feet above the top of the mountains.

As I present more and more information for you to ponder, it will begin to make sense as to how these descendants of these fallen angels came back.

3. The third possibility is that satan, the fallen angels and the Nephilim were trying to figure out a way to get past the cherubim and the flaming sword so they could get to the Tree of Life, eat from it, and live forever.
   Genesis 3:22; *And the LORD God said, "The man has now become like one of us, knowing good and evil. He must not be allowed to reach out his hand and take also from the tree of life and eat, and live forever."* (New International Version)
   If they could have gotten to that Tree of Life, they could have taken and eaten of it. Then they would be able to negotiate with the LORD about their salvation.
4. A fourth possibility is satan was trying to create a race just like himself.

I mentioned "Book of Enoch". This book has some fascinating historical information in it. There is reason to believe the early Christians believed some of its writings. While it didn't make it into the Cannon of Scripture, it should be looked at as having historical information of what could have happened during that time period.

Let's look at the phrase 'mighty men who were of old, men of renown.' The reason why I brought this up is to explain some things that schools, colleges, universities and seminaries are teaching, which is plain wrong. It is a deception full of half-truths, spin, and simply ignoring the truth about the LORD God. Yet in other cases, they are outright lying and they know it.

The following provides an account of what they supposedly did that started the enhanced wickedness and violence that spread throughout the earth.

1st Book of Enoch, 7:1-6:
1 And they took wives unto themselves, and everyone respectively chose one woman for himself, and they began to go unto them. And they taught them magical medicine, incantations, the cutting of roots, and taught them about plants.
2 And the women became pregnant and gave birth to great giants whose heights were three hundred cubits.
3 These giants consumed the produce of all the people until the people detested feeding them.

4 So the giants turned against the people in order to eat them.
5 And they began to sin against birds, wild beasts, reptiles, and fish. And their flesh was devoured the one by the other, and they drank blood.
6 And then the earth brought an accusation against the oppressors.

How tall do you think these Nephilim reached? Ten, fifteen, twenty feet maybe? Think bigger.

1st Book of Enoch 7:2; And the women became pregnant and gave birth to great giants whose heights were three hundred cubits.

As we talked about earlier, there are various measures of length in how long a cubit is. A Hebrew cubit is twenty five inches. If we use that measurement and multiply that by 300, you get over six hundred feet (600).

Let's get a perspective of this size.

1. Some of the Nephilim were as long as the Ark. The Ark was 300 cubits in length.
2. They could look into the windows of the fifty-fifth floor of a skyscraper and wave hi! Their eyes were big enough to take up the entire floor. The old Sears tower is one hundred and eight floors in height. The Empire State Building is one hundred and two stories.
3. If they were to lay down on the ground, they would take up almost five complete football fields, from end-zone to end-zone.
4. A Nimitz class aircraft carrier averages about 1,092 feet in length. So they are longer than half of the length of this type of carrier.
   (Source, http://www.navy.mil/navydata/fact_display.asp?cid=4200&tid=200&ct=4)

However, Patrick Heron in his book, Nephilim and the Pyramid of the Apocalypse, also believes the Hebrew cubit to be just over twenty five (25) inches too. Yet others have reason to believe the cubit is just over eighteen inches. So whether you are over six hundred feet or over four hundred and fifty feet tall, that is still huge in stature.

Many of these Nephilim skeletons which have been uncovered over the years usually were between nine and a half up to forty to fifty feet in height. Some claim they have seen the remains of those between sixty to eighty feet tall. You will see some pictures of these giants' skeletons later in the book.

Here is what Azaz'el, the head "supervisor" of these fallen angels, taught the men of the earth.

1st Book of Enoch, 8:1-4:
1 And Azaz'el was the head of all the watcher angels. He taught the people the art of making swords and knives, and shields, and breastplates; and he showed to their chosen ones bracelets, decorations, shadowing of the eye with antimony, ornamentation, the beautifying of the eyelids, all kinds of precious stones, and all coloring tinctures and alchemy.
2 And there were many wicked ones and they committed adultery and erred, and all their conduct became corrupt.
3 Amasras taught incantation and the cutting of roots; and Armaros the resolving of incantations; and Baraqiyal astrology, and Kokarer'el the knowledge of the signs, and Tam'el taught the seeing of the stars, and Asder'el taught the course of the moon as well as the deception of man.
4 And the people cried and their voice reached unto heaven.

These watcher angels taught man and woman many secrets of the earth and within the earth. Metallurgy is one that actually advanced man so they can make better weapons of war. Notice they taught how to kill others or the art of killing their fellow man. They showed them dances involving Voodoo. The other teachings would turn into cult religions and martial arts. They showed them how to perform magic healing rituals, makeup, and astrology. I believe they taught them far more things than those listed here.

Why is this significant? Let's look at the progress of man in today's time. We are building things like trains, airplanes, automobiles, etc. Trains were started to be used sometime in the 1850's. Then it expanded from there. Later in the 1880's and beyond, a man by the name of Nikola Tesla actually designed and built the first wireless electricity that actually worked. He proved it out and was able to show people that he could light up a light bulb from miles away without wiring. You might find it interesting where he got the idea for this too.

Then around the turn of the century, Henry Ford started rolling automobiles off the assembly lines in 1903. As the years went on, his company increased manufacture of cars. We were still in the horse and buggy era, but it eventually came to an end. World War I happened, chemical weapons were used, and Germany lost. No major discoveries took place for the most part. Then prohibition happened in 1920 and the powers that be crashed the stock market in October 1929. Then the Great Depression took a firm grip and lasted till we were drawn into World War II. Again there were no great discoveries apart from wireless electricity. But it never made it to the market place. And it is an interesting story as to why it wasn't marketed too.

Up to this time, there were not many places that had air conditioning as we know it now. The television didn't take hold until the 1950's. The rifles used in World War II were not very advanced. They started building the world's largest aircraft during World War II. But it wasn't completed until 1947. It took its first flight on November 2, 1947. Some people might remember it was called the 'Spruce Goose' because of the material that was used to construct it. Howard Hughes had actually constructed and flown it. There weren't any computers back then, so design work was long and costly. Mankind really didn't leap forward much yet. Correct?

Then something happened that got everyone's attention. Something that shook the entire world. Something that would create an intense calm that would engulf the entire planet. And that is the atomic bomb.

Here, we are splitting atoms to create one of the most deadly destructive forces that man had ever created when we just got out of the horse and buggy days a decade or two back. Does that make sense to you? After the nuclear facilities were built it took them just eighteen months to make the first bomb. Imagine that, just eighteen months. Yes, I realize the scientists were working on the plans before this time. But my question is who told them what to do and how to make that bomb? There is speculation that when these atomic denotations occur, some interesting things happen. And it's not good either. And I'm not just talking about the devastation that comes about in the aftermath of Hiroshima and Nagasaki either. I did not include these theories in this book for various reasons.

So how did they get this information to create this devastating device that can instantly wipe a whole town down to its foundations? When the bombs were dropped in Japan, some people became instantly vaporized if they were in the blast zone. And those outside the blast zone would become deadly sick with what is called radiation sickness. Most of them would die from that. And those that survive would realise their DNA was damaged and their ability to have healthy children would be minimized. So I again ask the question. Who gave them the information on how to construct and build this atomic bomb? As smart as we are, we are not that smart. We think we are, but we are not. We had help.

Now let's get back to the text in Enoch. Notice it states 'they sinned against birds, wild beasts, reptiles, and fish'. How do you sin against birds, wild beasts, etc.? These watcher angels and Nephilim were modifying or teaching man how to modify the DNA of these animals and eventually humans. Yep. Think I'm kidding? Do you think I have an over-active imagination? Really truly stretching it? Ok let's look in the Book of Jasher. This passage talks about the time right before the flood.

Book of Jasher, 4:17-18:
17 And every man made unto himself a god, and they robbed and plundered every man his neighbor as well as his relative, and they corrupted the earth, and the earth was filled with violence.
18 And their judges and rulers went to the daughters of men and took their wives by force from their husbands according to their choice, and the sons of men in those days took from the cattle of the earth, the beasts of the field and the fowls of the air, and taught the mixture of animals of one species with the other, in order therewith to provoke the LORD; and God saw the whole earth and it was corrupt, for all flesh had corrupted its ways upon earth, all men and all animals.

Remember, the book of Jasher was written thousands of years ago.

What is interesting is they mixed the species in that passage. That was not what the LORD did during creation. He wanted everything to reproduce after its own kind.

Genesis 1:11-13;
11 And God said, Let the earth bring forth grass, the herb yielding seed, and the fruit tree yielding fruit after his kind, whose seed is in itself, upon the earth: and it was so.
12 And the earth brought forth grass, and herb yielding seed after his kind, and the tree yielding fruit, whose seed was in itself, after his kind: and God saw that it was good.
13 And the evening and the morning were the third day. (King James Bible)

Genesis 1:21; *And God created great whales, and every living creature that moveth, which the waters brought forth abundantly, after their kind, and every winged fowl after his kind: and God saw that it was good.* (King James Bible)

Genesis 1:24-25;
24 And God said, Let the earth bring forth the living creature after his kind, cattle, and creeping thing, and beast of the earth after his kind: and it was so.
25 And God made the beast of the earth after his kind, and cattle after their kind, and every thing that creepeth upon the earth after his kind: and God saw that it was good. (King James Bible)

As you can tell, this mixing of species is a direct attack against the LORD and His creation. This is big time stuff, warfare with nothing being held back. As you get more into this book, you will see how these fallen angels and their offspring the Nephilim would attack everything.

In the above passage in Jasher it says, 'their judges and rulers'? Remember where it said in the following verse in the Bible;

Genesis 6:4; *The Nephilim were on the earth in those days—and also afterward—when the sons of God went to the daughters of* *men and had children by them. They were the heroes of old, men of renown.* (New International Version)

Notice the last part of the verse - "heroes of old, men of renown". They were politicians and rulers. Today they might be celebrities, senators or in Congress too. State or local judges. They might have been Presidents or Prime Ministers. They were also something more than those positions they held.

They taught the mixture of different breeds or species of animals. How about cloning of animals like sheep? How about this one for you? Combining man and an animal? That's way out there isn't it… or is it? Check out these pictures. Anything look familiar to you? Do these pictures remind you of any myths you were taught in school?

Centaur carrying off a nymp **Satyr**

Now you know what a 'Centaur' and a "Satyr" look like in ancient myth. A Centaur is a hybrid with the body of a horse with a neck and head of a human. A Satyr is another hybrid with two hind goat legs and the

rest of the body of a human. These are mythical Greek creatures. They are primarily hybrids; that is half man or woman and half horses, etc. Myths basically have some part of it as factual.

Sphinx of Giza, Egypt

Have you really noticed this stone carving? It has the head of a man and the body of a lion. Some other cravings have the head of a falcon on other statues. Why did they create this 'monument'?

After reading what the Bible says about these statues, you get the impression that the LORD does NOT want us to be genetically modifying anything. PERIOD. Actually, I believe it is an outright abomination to Him.

These Nephilim and their angel fathers were teaching men how to modify the creation of God before the flood. They were combining species to create a new race of beings. They taught things to men that turned them away from the love of the LORD into doing evil and kindling the anger of the LORD, the true and Living God. Their thinking was to modify and destroy His creation. They wanted to deceive you and I… man and woman. They wanted to deceive as many of us as possible so that we can join them (the fallen angels) in the Lake of Fire that burns with fire and brimstone for eternity.

So I'm going to ask the question. Why would we want to create a being that is half man/women and half animal?

Genetically Altered Animals / Men

2 Samuel 23:20; *And Benaiah the son of Jehoiada, the son of a valiant man, of Kabzeel, who had done many acts, he slew two lion like men of Moab: he went down also and slew a lion in the middle of a pit in time of snow:* (American King James Version)

1 Chronicles 11:22: *Benaiah the son of Jehoiada, the son of a valiant man of Kabzeel, who had done many acts; he slew two* *lionlike men of Moab: also he went down and slew a lion in a pit in a snowy day.* (King James Bible, Cambridge Edition)

Imagine that, the body of a man and the head of a lion. Here are the descendants of the Nephilim continuing to combine species. Doesn't it sound like a science fiction movie? Well it's right there in the Bible, literally right there in Scripture.

If you remember, Satyrs are beings which have goat like features. A man or woman could have a goat tail, goat ears, etc. Others are half man/women and half goat.

Isaiah 13:21; *But wild beasts of the desert shall lie there; and their houses shall be full of doleful creatures; and owls shall dwell there, and satyrs shall dance there.* (King James Bible Cambridge Edition)

Isaiah 34:14: *The wild beasts of the desert shall also meet with the wild beasts of the island, and the satyr shall cry to his fellow; the screech owl also shall rest there, and find for herself a place of rest.* (American King James Version)

First there are lion-like men and now satyrs. Remember seeing statues of them earlier in this book?

Now I'm going to ask - how did they combine the species? We have found no evidence of microscopes from the era so they could see what they were doing back then. We haven't stumbled upon some needles so they could extract some DNA from one species, alter it, and insert it into another. As best we can tell, there were no laboratories to perform these acts of sin either. Yet these ancient texts state it was done. These half human and half animal combination are taught in colleges as myths. My question is if the Greek, Roman, and other gods are considered 'myths', why are they spending so much energy and time making college and university students learn these things? What is so important that these 'higher' learning institutions teach these things? There are other things to learn about instead of these 'myths'. Yet could they be correct? Were these beings actually here on earth? So much is tied to Genesis 6. More than you might ever have imagined.

Different folklore and carvings on certain stone walls show the evidence that it was indeed done. Remember seeing the head of a falcon and the body of a man in Egyptian paintings from thousands of years ago?

So how did they do it? These descendants of these Nephilim tried to do everything they possibly could to corrupt, attack, and destroy God's creation.

Doesn't it start to make sense now why the LORD is going to judge mankind on earth during the tribulation period? They are repeating the same thing they did back in the days of Noah thousands of years ago. The challenge is they know the time is starting to run out. And I believe it will be worse right before and during the tribulation period than it was during the days of Noah.

Look what is on this FDA website. Can you tell how they are trying to spin the information, so you start to understand that this is OK? When it is not…

Genetic engineering is a targeted and powerful method of introducing desirable traits into animals using recombinant DNA (rDNA) technology. DNA is the chemical inside the nucleus of a cell that carries the genetic instructions for making living organisms.

In January, 2009, the Food and Drug Administration issued a final guidance for industry on the regulation of genetically engineered (GE) animals. The guidance explains the process by which FDA is regulating GE animals and provides a set of recommendations to producers of GE animals to help them meet their obligations and responsibilities under the law. While the guidance is intended for industry, FDA believes it may also help the public gain a better understanding of this important and developing area.

(http://www.fda.gov/animalveterinary/developmentapprovalprocess/geneticengineering/geneticallyengineeredanimals/default.htm)

Mark 13:22; *For false messiahs and false prophets will rise up and perform signs and wonders so as to deceive, if possible, even God's chosen ones.* (New Living Translation)

Now why did I place that Scripture right here? It shows you how much we are being deceived. Look at how they are creating a new animal species! That is a unique thing to do. It reveals how much we are oblivious as to what is truly happening around us. See the deception they are putting right before your very eyes? If you think it is OK to combine the species to make a new breed of an animal, you are blinded by the lie they are spinning for you. You do NOT understand what happened in Genesis 6. The LORD does NOT want us to tamper with His creation. Now they who are behind the scenes at the highest levels are orchestrating ways to make sure the truth remains hidden. They know these things are wrong. They know it is in deviance of the creation He formed.

The above verse in the Book of Mark talks about all of what is going to happen. Again, if you believe this cloning and combining of species are OK, then you believe the deception. You need to step back and reevaluate it. If you don't, then more than likely you will believe the LIE which is coming up in the great deception in the tribulation period. Because the deception will challenge your faith in the LORD God.

What I find interesting is the last part of that verse… deceiving God's chosen ones. Some translate "chosen" as the "elect". Jesus spend time actually talking about this and was strongly talking to his disciples about what to look for during that time. The time, the days we live in now. And those coming up shortly. At the Mount of Olives opposite from the temple Peter, James, John and Andrew talked with Jesus privately. I wonder why they were talking to Him privately. I suppose we all want to have our private time with Him. So what are the first words out of Jesus' mouth; "Watch out that no one deceives you…" And that starts way back in verse 6.

Mark 13:6; *Jesus said to them: "Watch out that no one deceives you.* (New International Version)

Matthew 24:37; *As it was in the days oj Noah, so it will be at the coming oj the Son oj Man.* (New International Version)

Just as in the days of Noah, so shall it be with the coming of the son of Man. I think we are already in the days of Noah. It is here and has started already. I believe so many people are feeling there is something wrong, and they are not getting the answers they need from most of the churches or other religious leaders. There are a growing number of people who want to know the truth so they can make better decisions.

Thousands of years ago, they were modifying the DNA of animals and humans. And today, man has and is still receiving the knowledge from the powers of darkness on how to do it again. And why? Why are they doing this again? So they can clone arms for us or organs to transplant into us if our present organ fails? Or are they cloning animals that will produce more meat for us to consume? Are they modifying the DNA so we can live much longer? Or is there something deeper? Or is there another agenda, a higher priority?

The LORD's people need to start thinking outside the box. The evidence of them trying to deceive us is all around. It's in books. The movies, the news, and television programs are secretly programming you to accept what they want you to know so you will not think twice when they unveil their plans. They are programming you to think a particular way.

Why do they call the different stations that control certain numbers on your TV dial or remote control 'channels'? Could it be they are 'channeling' a particular way they want you to think? Let's take the shows that are on any given 'channel'. If memory serves me correctly, didn't some public television stations use to start the evening by saying something like, "Tonight's programming schedule is…" Interesting how they use that word 'programming'. Now if you don't like the 'programming' on a certain 'channel', you change to a different 'channel.' Hopefully you will find some 'programming' you do want to watch. You may be more willing to accept and have them feed your mind with their programming. Generally speaking, people usually find something they want to watch, so that station is 'channeling' different 'programming' into your mind to their own end.

Let me ask the question. Why are you willing to let the powers that be, which control what programming comes on, have access to your mind in that matter? You know they sometimes spin different things so you will start thinking the way they want you to think. It's done very slowly too. Consider these possibilities.

1. They are putting uncertainty into your mind set.
2. They can strike fear and anxiety into you, so it makes it seemingly more difficult to cope with what is going on around you.
3. If you continually see and hear the same thing over and over again, they know sooner or later you will drop your guard and at least partially accept that there isn't much you can do about it. It hopeless so why bother doing anything about it.
4. They give you "positive" information such as, for example, there are benefits to eating this food. Then a week or a month later, they print, send out, and / or broadcast if you eat that certain food, it can have a negative effect on your health. They do this more and more, so you don't do anything at all.
5. They are masters of the art of disinformation information. That is what I call it when the powers that be give you information they know is completely false (a lie) or is mostly false (which is still a lie). Then when you investigate it, you realize it is a dead end.

They are willing to do whatever is necessary to accomplish their agendas. You would never have any lengthy type of conversation with someone you know lies to you, hides the truth, and spins things, so you think a certain way that doesn't uplift and enhance you. Yet you watch and listen to the TV programmes that spread outright lies, half truths, falsehoods and get right smack dab into your face about it, and then laugh at you because you are falling for the simple spin job they are giving you. They spread fear. They create a spirit of hopelessness. Then they reason with you, to convince you to give up your rights. It's for the better good, you are told. Or so they say. How often do you question anything you hear on the TV, or read in a newspaper or hear on the radio? If you don't you are being deceived, and you are not receiving the truth.

There are some folks who feel this might be a bit extreme. They may say or think; 'All I'm doing is really watching sports like football, basketball, and baseball games. Maybe some golf… on Saturday or Sunday.' And that is precisely my point.

They created an interest you are enjoying so they can divert your attention. Then they slowly begin to dismantle your freedoms, your liberties, and the freedom to worship the LORD.

Sometimes we as His people don't want to see the forest because of the trees are in it. They don't want to see or realize the reality around them is negative and will come up with any type of excuse to explain it away, so we don't have to deal with it then. This happened so many times with the Israelites. So do you think we would read it, gain wisdom and knowledge, and act accordingly? Nope. We come up with the same reasoning as the Israelites did. "I'm not accepting this. This isn't what I want to hear. It's negative."

Let's look at one example. Here is Jerusalem besieged by Nebuchadnezzar's army around October 10, 589 B.C. They are besieged because of the sin that is in their life which they haven't repented of yet. In some aspects, they wouldn't admit their sin either. They were in denial of not obeying the LORD and His calling and commandments. Now during this siege, a famine caused the food to run out in the city about eighteen months into this siege by Nebuchadnezzar's army. After about thirty months or so, his army broke through the gates in 586 B.C. (Source: Reese Chronological Bible). So here is Jerusalem besieged for some 30 months. The food had basically run out at the half way point, and horrific conditions are deteriorating by the day inside the walls. There were stories of cannibalism going on inside it. Do you think the King of Judea would take responsibility, repent, and surrender to Nebuchadnezzar to spare his people these horrific circumstances? Oh no. What about today? A Nebuchadnezzar like army is already inside our country. Do you think the LORD's people would take notice and turn back to Him? Do you think they would humble themselves, pray, seek His face, and turn from their wicked ways? No. They continue in their pagan sun god worship. Well that is exactly what is happening today, right here, right now in America. More about this later.

All of this certainly does remind me of this verse.

Ecclesiastes 1:9; *History merely repeats itself. It has all been done before. Nothing under the sun is truly new.* (New Living Translation)

You would think we would learn from history. You would think we would see the on the wall. The LORD sends His apostolic leaders, the prophets, and the seers into the land to warn people to turn back to Him, so He doesn't have to judge them. And do you think they are turning back to Him?

So what is the world deceiving us about? Let's start with what the LORD really hates that's being done here. One of them is genetically altering/combining food stuffs and the aforementioned altering/combining animal species. Let's start with the food stuffs.

What has been genetically engineered in our society today?

1. Corn, soy, cotton canola, and cottonseed.
2. Yeast, NutraSweet, Equal, diet drinks, medicines, vitamins, gum, candies, etc.
3. Tomatoes, potatoes, papaya, zucchini, beets, and squash.
4. New colors in plants. Lavender colored carnations is one of them.
5. Some types of carrots, tobacco, papaya,
6. Bacteria

Now what about animals?

1. Animals such as mice, rats, rabbits, sheep, goats, dairy cows, lions and tigers and pigs (plus the fluorescent ones).
2. Fruit flies and mosquitoes.
3. Fish, such as salmon, trout, and tilapia.
   (Source;
   http://en.wikipedia.org/wiki/Genetically_modified_organism#Plants)

The above is for starters. Wonder why cancer is rising higher and higher? Can you see what is starting to take shape? Do you still think your non-organic food is safe to consume?

Let's go back to Genesis 6. The corruption in the land was beyond measure. It was bringing out the worse part of man. But wait, there is more.

A few of the angels in heaven were observing what was happening on earth and approached the LORD our Most High

God. Because of the deeds that were done, Azaz'el was punished for it.

1st Book of Enoch, 10:4-8:
4 And secondly YAHWEH said to Raphael, "Bind Azaz'el hand and foot and throw him into the darkness!" And he made a hole in the desert which was in Duda'el and cast him there;
5 he threw on top of him rugged and sharp rocks. And he covered his face in order that he may not see light;
6 and in order that he may be sent into the fire on the great day of judgment.
7 And give life to the earth which the angels have corrupted. And he will proclaim life for the earth: that he is giving life to her. And all the children of the people will not perish through all the secrets of the angels, which they taught to their sons.
8 And the whole earth has been corrupted by Azaz'el's teaching of his own actions; and write upon him all sin.

Did you catch what is going on? By Azaz'el's actions, what he had done, it corrupted the whole earth. This watcher angel, the head angel, started a string of events that to this day is felt on earth. When you begin to understand the enormous corruption he and the other one hundred and ninety nine angels did, you will see why things became worse.

Which desert is Azaz'el in right now? Could he be under the Tigris and the Euphrates rivers perhaps? How about the one in Africa, the Sahara or out west maybe in Nevada? Remember, we need to read the Bible and those ancient texts from a middle-eastern view. Once we do this, everything becomes much clearer. I did find one possible place from the website listed below.

The sins of people would be conferred upon the goat for Azaz'el (the Scapegoat), and this goat would be taken into the wilderness a few miles southeast of Jerusalem and cast off the cliff of Haradan into an abyss at the bottom of which Azazel was believed to be imprisoned. The Bible does not mention this, but this was what the Jews did with the goat. There is an obvious parallel between the goat's being cast into an abyss and Azazel and the one hundred and ninety nine angels being judged and cast into the depths of Tartarus.

(Source; http://www.centralcal.com/jude.htm)

There can be some symbolism with what they did and what Jesus did on the cross by casting all our sin upon Himself for our payment for it.

Some scholars believe Tartarus is actually below Hades hell. I'm not sure I understand where that is, and I'm not sure I really want to know either.

Now, according to the Book of Enoch, there is further condemnation against the watcher angels.

Book of Enoch, 10:9-12:
9 And to Gabriel YAHWEH said, "Proceed against the bastards and the reprobates and against the children of adultery; and destroy the children of adultery and expel the children of the Watchers from among the people. And send them against one another so that they may be destroyed in the fight, for length of days have they not."
10 "They will beg you everything-for their fathers on behalf of themselves-because they hope to live an eternal life. They hope that each one of them will live a period of five hundred years."
11 And to Michael YAHWEH said, "Make known to Semyaza and the others who are with him, who fornicated with the women, that they will die together with them in all their defilement."
12 "And when they and all their children have battled with each other, and when they have seen the destruction of their beloved ones, bind them for seventy generations underneath the rocks of the ground until the day of their judgment and of their consummation, until the eternal judgment is concluded."

The Nephilim were hoping to live five hundred years. But I believe by the text above the LORD did not allow it. Some scholars believe He did let them live five hundred years. However, the timelines don't match up. If you remember, around 2439 B.C. is when Genesis 6:2 took place. Then the flood of Genesis 7 happened about 120 years later in 2319 B.C. Now these watcher angels had to watch their offspring die in battle. Exactly when they died, it is not stated. I believe they die either right before or during the flood of Genesis 7. If these Nephilim did die in battle, now you can understand the battles of the ancient Greek and Roman gods. Remember when we were taught that Apollo, Zeus, etc. battled and battled each other until someone was defeated? This could be exactly the time period these battles took place.

The next event was of the watcher angels being bound for seventy (70) generations. Guess when those seventy generations are complete? Could it be during the Tribulation? Or right before that period starts? In either case, it appears they will be let loose on the earth again. As in the days of Noah, so shall the coming of the son of man!

As I mentioned earlier, in the following text you will find, I believe, the origin of the demons that are roaming on the earth… disembodied spirits. When you see the word 'Kodesh', it means holy.

Book of Enoch, 15:8-12:
8 "But now the giants who are born from the union of the spirits and the flesh shall be called evil spirits upon the earth, because their dwelling shall be upon the earth and inside the earth."
9 "Evil spirits have come out of their bodies. Because from the day that they were created from the kodesh ones they became the Watchers; their first origin is the spiritual foundation. They will become evil upon the earth and shall be called evil spirits."
10 "The dwelling of the spiritual beings of heaven is heaven; but the dwelling of the spirits of the earth, which are born upon the earth, is in the earth."
11 "The spirits of the giants oppress each other; they will corrupt, fall, be excited, and fall upon the earth, and cause sorrow. They eat no food, nor become thirsty, nor find obstacles."
12 "And these spirits shall rise up against the children of the people and against the women, because they have proceeded forth from them."

According to this passage, because these descendants of the Nephilim were born here on earth, they are to remain on earth. These 'evil spirits' came out of their bodies. Therefore, they will remain here. And what will they do? They will corrupt what they can corrupt and cause sorrow. What they did (back then) and continue to do is cause the people of the earth as much pain, torment, suffering, anguish, and sorrow as they could.

Book of Jubilees, 5:6-7 & 9-10:
6 which He had created. But Noah found grace before the eyes of the Lord. And against the angels whom He had sent upon the earth, He was exceedingly wroth, and He gave commandment to root them out of all their dominion, and He bade us to bind them in the depths of the earth, and
7 behold they are bound in the midst of them, and are (kept) separate. And against their sons went forth a command from before His face that they should be smitten with the sword, and be removed
9 and their days shall be one hundred and twenty years'. And He sent His sword into their midst that each should slay his neighbour, and they began to slay each other till they all fell by the sword
10 and were destroyed from the earth. And their fathers were witnesses (of their destruction), and after this they were bound in the depths of the earth for ever, until the day of the great condemnation, when judgment is executed on all those who have corrupted their ways and their works before

Now you can see there is clear evidence of what happened in Genesis 6 with the union of women and the watcher angels. This is the reason why we are tormented and are tempted to be led astray, away from the Heavenly Father. It's because of the spirits of the Nephilim. And we give in to them. Most of the time, we don't realize it is happening to us. They are relentless. They hound us, they put in our paths temptations, they create paths of sorrow to engulf us if we allow them. They cause the temptation of a spirit of strife, they plan, re-plan, and go to plan C, then D, and E. We can be distracted from the dreams, goals, and aspirations we have in our life. This is the reason why we are to pray for each other. We are our brother's keeper. When we truly love people according to 1 Corinthians chapter 13, we can approach each other so we can assist them because we know what is happening to them. Then others will pray for us when these demons' spirits try to make us miserable and take us away from the path that serves others.

Are you starting to realize (a little bit better) what happened in Genesis 6? This evil is so horrific that it is affecting every person who was and is walking on this earth right now. As we dig deeper into this, you will see how mind blowing it is, to say the very least. This is what the church is not talking about enough. This concept, if taught, will allow other Christians to begin to understand what happened, why, and what we can do to overcome it. Why? Because greater is He that is within you, than he that is in the world. We are not the enemy. It's these fallen angels and the demonic spirits (disembodied spirits) of the Nephilim who are on the attack against us. They are the enemy.

1 John 4:4; *But you belong to God, my dear children. You have already won a victory over those people, because the Spirit who lives in you is greater than the spirit who lives in the world.* (New Living Translation)

I believe these disembodied spirits are probably the ones that Jesus cast out when He was on the earth.

I don't believe that an angel from the heaven has any reason to leave its body. Do you know of a reason? Could it be to enter another being? Why would they need to do that? I can't think of a reason. A heavenly angel knows that something more powerful than they already lives in the body of a believer. And that is the precious Holy Spirit. Now satan and his fallen angels have a reason to enter into a person. It is to lead us astray, away from the LORD. It occurred during the Last Supper when he influenced Judas to betray Jesus.

John 13:27; *As soon as Judas took the bread, Satan entered into him. "What you are about to do, do quickly," Jesus told him,* (New International Version)

I want to examine that word "entered". In Greek, it actually means to physically go into. Examples would be; they entered the house or they entered the building. That means satan actually entered into Judas. Why am I bringing this up? Some feel the fallen angels can inhabit us. I don't believe there is any other time when the Bible states an angel inhabited a person. Only in the above verse. So did the evil one have special power to do this? The answer is unknown at this time.

Eventually these watcher angels decide to petition God for mercy through Enoch. Enoch agrees to do such a thing and the LORD gives him an audience. The conclusion is interesting.

1st Book of Enoch, 16:1-3:
1 "From the days of the slaughter and destruction, and the death of the giants and the spiritual beings of the spirit, and the flesh, from which they have proceeded forth, which will corrupt without incurring judgment, they will corrupt until the day of the great conclusion, until the great age is consummated, until everything is concluded upon the Watchers and the wicked ones."
2 "And so to the Watchers on whose behalf you have been sent to intercede - who were formerly in heaven - say to them,"
3 '"You were once in heaven, but not all the mysteries of heaven are open to you, and you only know the rejected mysteries. Those ones you have broadcast to the women in the hardness of your hearts and by those mysteries the women and men multiply evil deeds upon the earth.'" Tell them, "Therefore, you will have no shalom!"

There it is again. "They will corrupt without incurring judgment. They will corrupt until the day of judgment." That is referring to the disembodied Nephilim evil spirits. Now why will they corrupt until the day of judgment? Because they came from the union of divine beings or angels and woman.

I find it fascinating the part that says; "mysteries of heaven are open to you, and you only know the rejected mysteries." I would say the LORD knows many things these fallen angels and the Nephilim do not know.

Enoch 68:2-3:
2 On that day, Michael addressed himself to Raphael, saying to him, "The power of the spirit grabs me and causes me to go up on account of the severity of the judgment concerning the

knowledge of the secrets. Who is able to endure the severity of the judgment which has been executed and before which one melts away?"
3 Michael continued to speak further, saying to Raphael, "Who is he whose heart does not become sordid in respect to this matter and whose reins do not become stirred up from the Word of the Judgment which has been pronounced against them."

If you stop and think about what is said in the above text, it seemingly says that Michael is surprised and extremely concerned for the judgment that was given out to those fallen angels and their descendants, the Nephilim.

Man is waiting for the Day of Judgment too. And when is that Day of Judgment?

Ecclesiastes 12:14; *For God will bring every deed into judgment, including every hidden thing, whether it is good or evil.* (New International Version)

Psalm 96:13; *Let all creation rejoice before the LORD, for he comes, he comes to judge the earth. He will judge the world in righteousness and the peoples in his faithfulness.* (New International Version)

Matthew 10:15; *Truly I tell you, it will be more bearable for Sodom and Gomorrah on the day of judgment than for that town.* (New International Version)

John 12:48; *The one who rejects me and does not receive my words has a judge; the word that I have spoken will judge him on the last day.* (English Standard Version)

Revelation 20:11-15;
11 Then I saw a great white throne and him who was seated on it. The earth and the heavens fled from his presence, and there was no place for them.
12 And I saw the dead, great and small, standing before the throne, and books were opened. Another book was opened, which is the book of life. The dead were judged according to what they had done as recorded in the books.

13 The sea gave up the dead that were in it, and death and Hades gave up the dead that were in them, and each person was judged according to what they had done.
14 Then death and Hades were thrown into the lake of fire. The lake of fire is the second death.
15 Anyone whose name was not found written in the book of life was thrown into the lake of fire. (New International Version)

The throne mentioned in the passage above is what we call the 'Great White Throne Judgment'. If your name is not found written in that book, it is eternal torment for you forever and ever in the lake of fire.

It's these watcher angels who married the daughters of men that caused a hybrid being, basically half man and half angel, to be born. They have tremendous strength and knowledge. The watcher angels and their offspring corrupted man to do evil continually. It didn't take long before they were able to corrupt man. It went from a "normal" wickedness to wickedness of unknown proportions.

Genesis 6:5; *The LORD saw that the wickedness of man was great in the earth, and that every intention of the thoughts of his heart was only evil continually.* (English Standard Version)

They taught man (generally speaking) things they shouldn't have taught them. They gave man information they were not mature enough to use correctly. Then the LORD stepped in and decided to put an end to this iniquity because it was threatening many things. Which was the plan satan and his fellow fallen angels had in mind all along.

Our God was filled with wrath at what was happening on the earth due to what these watcher angels had started and what these Nephilim were doing. He decided to have these Nephilim killed right before the watcher angels eyes. Then the watchers were cast into the depths of the earth.

Enoch

Enoch is a very interesting Bible character. He is the great grandfather of Noah. In the book of Jude, we are told Enoch prophesied. Yet not much is written about him in the Bible. I have often wondered why. Not that I'm questioning God about it necessarily, but I am wondering if there isn't more about him.

Genesis 5:21–24;
21 And Enoch lived sixty and five years, and begat Methuselah:
22 And Enoch walked with God after he begat Methuselah three hundred years, and begat sons and daughters:
23 And all the days of Enoch were three hundred sixty and five years:
24 And Enoch walked with God: and he was not; for God took him. (New International Version)

Notice it stated 365 years. Is there a connection between how many days are in a year and how long Enoch lived?

Here is a man who the Bible says; "Walked with God". How would you like that written in your resumé and have the Word of God mention that about you forever? The Bible references only one other person that walked with God. And it was Enoch's great grandson, Noah. With that said about Enoch, why so little written about his life or what he did or didn't do? Then he was taken.

I wondered if Enoch knew ahead of time that he was going to heaven that day. Or did it just happen? What were his wife's thoughts about that? Did she know ahead of time? Did he kiss her goodbye that morning? What were his last words to her? It's always best to make sure your last words with someone you love are nice and gentle… because you just might not be able to talk with them again. Maybe Enoch left home that day and maybe either of the following two happened.

"Dear, I'm going down into town. I should be back in time for dinner."

"OK Enoch." His wife quickly responded.

"Oh honey, I'm planning on cooking some lamb, just the way you like it."

"Oh, really. I love that lamb." He responded quickly.

"I know you do. I am getting some of that lettuce that is about six hundred cubits (about a quarter of a mile) down the path too." She said with a smile.

"Well that is something really special to come home to… But not even close to how special you are my darling wife."

"Oh Enoch. I'm not that young spring chicken I use to be any more. After all the children we have had and after some three hundred and thirty plus years of marriage, you still make me feel young and beautiful…"

"In my eyes, I think you are so much more now than way back then. And you were fantastic back then…"

She blushes a bit.

"Well I'm off dear. The LORD wants me to deliver a message or two to some people in the town. There is some wickedness there. I'll be talking with the LORD as to what He wants me to say to them…"

They probably kissed each other, and they embrace like they always do. Did she know that would be the last time she would see him on earth? Did she realize it would be the last time she would hug and kiss him, the man she loved being married to for centuries?

Later on that night, Enoch hadn't showed up yet. She goes out and checks to see if she can find him nearby. She looks around, but she doesn't see him. Does she start to worry when he doesn't come home? Does the LORD or an angel appear in a dream or in person to her explaining what happened to him? The Bible doesn't say.

Or did it happen this way?

Enoch gets up and says good morning to his wife. She says good morning back to him. She goes off and starts to make breakfast. He sits at the edge of the bed. He is both elated and joyous how the LORD spoke to him and explained the LORD

God wants him to come up to heaven. But he is also saddened slightly by it too.

He hears the sweet voice of her singing in the other room as he gets up and begins to help her with breakfast.

"So Enoch, where are you going today?"

"I'm going into town. The LORD wants me to deliver a message or two to some people in the town. There is some wickedness there. I'll be talking with the LORD as to what He wants me to say to them…"

"The way you walk with the LORD, I'm sure He looks forward to you talking with Him. I'm sure He will give you the words to say as you tell me He always did!"

Enoch shakes his head yes. But his heart is a little heavy.

They sit down to eat breakfast. She notices he is not talking as much as he usually does.

"OK honey, what's going on? You are not as talkative as you usually you are. You get this way when you are fasting and praying, which you are not doing right now. You have a heavy heart about something or the LORD gave you a vision. So out with it, unless you are not supposed to share it with me because the LORD told you to keep it to yourself…"

Enoch manages a smile. His wife for over three hundred and thirty years knows him very well. She has always been the person he loved the most. He didn't know that in the future Ezekiel and his wife would have the same relationship too. She was always a trusted confidant, a friend, a person he could go to when he needed an honest opinion about something. He quickly remembers all the years they had together and how much of a helpmate she has been to him.

He feels a nudge and he turns to her.

"Yes?" he asks her.

"Did you just get another vision? You zoned out like you usually do when the LORD shows you something. I almost didn't nudge you. But I thought I'd do it anyway…" she says with a smile.

He smiles back at her.

"The LORD told me what is going to happen today."

"Oh, really!?! Tell me about it, if you can…"

He looks into her eyes.

"The LORD God is taking me today."

"Oh really? Wow, another exciting adventure for you. If I remember correctly, the LORD God has taken you to other places before." Where is He taking you today?"

"Honey, He is taking me to heaven today."

"What a trip that will be. How long are you staying there? Are you going to be back for supper? I'm making lamb tonight, and I'm going down to get some of the lett…"

He touches her arm and she stops in the middle of the word.

"Honey, I'm not coming back…"

Her joy turned to tears. Her joyful heart turned to heaviness.

"Your… not… coming… back…?"

Her tears ran down her face.

"You mean you are going to… di???" She couldn't get the word out completely.

"Honey, I'm not going to die. The LORD God is going to take me to heaven."

"You mean, you are leaving me? The LORD is taking you away from me?"

Enoch didn't answer. He didn't need to answer it.

"Well that is great for you honey. But what about me?"

Enoch didn't say anything.

"We have been together for over three hundred and thirty years Enoch. We've had Methuselah and all the rest of our sons and daughters. We've had a great life together honey. And now this is it?"

Enoch shares a part of his heart with her.

"You are so special to me. It's hard to put into words how special you are to me. From the first time I saw you, I knew you were different. And I wanted to get to know you better back then, my love. You have been all that I hoped you would be to me and then so much more. The joy of being and seeing the LORD God whom I've talked with for so many centuries is somewhat diminished a bit because my mate, my confidant, my best of all my friends I must leave behind…"

They hug and embrace. Then they kiss each other like they always did.

"It's time for me to go now." Enoch said.

His wife gets up and puts on her sandals and walks with him out of the door. He continues to walk for about three hundred cubits (a little bit over six hundred feet) and then turns to her.

"Well dear, this is…" Enoch didn't say the last work. She gently placed her fore-finger on his lips she kissed so often. Then she whispers into his ear.

"I'm going with you on this journey. If this is indeed your last day on this earth, and our last day together, then I'm spending every last moment of it with you. Now you can go ahead and tell me that it isn't a good idea or you don't think I should be doing this. But I suggest you just accept the fact that I love you so deeply that I want to spend the very last moments with you while you are here."

She stands directly in front of him. She brushes his clothes slightly in a gentle caring fashion and place her hands on his chest. She looks into his eyes and continues;

"You know Enoch, I always wondered if we were going to die together. If we didn't, I know we will be together in heaven and continue our lives there, but at a much grander scale. So my dear man, allow me to be with you in these final moments. I've always wanted to be with you despite your moods that come about every once in a while…" she said with that grin that melts his heart. "I want to spend them together with you. We have shared so many things together, didn't we?"

He paused then smiled at her. She just knew what to say and how to say it most of the time.

"Don't concern yourself about me. God will take care of things for me. Before we leave, I want to say thank you for being the man that you are. I would not want my life to be any other way… well you did drive me crazy sometimes. But I love you. I appreciate the life we had together. Sooner or later we will be together again!"

"What a wonderful mate the LORD God had given me. Oh how great is the LORD God. Yes, we did share many things together."

They turn and begin to walk towards the town together. He grabs and holds her hand as the journey starts. Then she speaks up.

"Any last words for the kids dear? I'm sure they will ask if you have any last words for them…"

"Oh my dear, how did you know that I was thinking about that just this moment? As a matter of fact, I do.

Enoch pauses and continues.

"Please tell Methuselah to remember the things I taught him. Always walk in the ways of the LORD. Keep himself humble and pure before the sight of the LORD God and preach His righteous. Love is the greatest of all things. Make sure he teaches his children what we taught him."

"Now make sure you tell them to…"

My little story of what Mr. and Mrs. Enoch's last morning together might have been like is just that, a story. It may have happened that way.

But did Enoch know ahead of time that he was going to be taken to heaven that day? We really don't know because the Bible didn't say anything about this. Someday we will.

I really often wondered about his wife. What she felt, how she handled it when he didn't show up for supper that night. I really wonder what she thought when he never came home. Did an angel of the LORD come down and appear to her, telling her what had happened to him? Did an angel of the LORD appear to her in a dream? Or was she not told at all what happened to her husband?

There is some text in the Book of Jasher that addresses this event. It goes into great detail about what happened to Enoch.

Jasper 3:1-38

1 And Enoch lived sixty-five years and he begat Methuselah; and Enoch walked with God after having begot Methuselah, and he served the Lord, and despised the evil ways of men.

2 And the soul of Enoch was wrapped up in the instruction of the Lord, in knowledge and in understanding; and he wisely retired from the sons of men, and secreted himself from them for many days.

3 And it was at the expiration of many years, whilst he was serving the Lord, and praying before him in his house, that an

angel of the Lord called to him from Heaven, and he said, Here am I.
4 And he said, Rise, go forth from thy house and from the place where thou dost hide thyself, and appear to the sons of men, in order that thou mayest teach them the way in which they should go and the work which they must accomplish to enter in the ways of God.
5 And Enoch rose up according to the word of the Lord, and went forth from his house, from his place and from the chamber in which he was concealed; and he went to the sons of men and taught them the ways of the Lord, and at that time assembled the sons of men and acquainted them with the instruction of the Lord.
6 And he ordered it to be proclaimed in all places where the sons of men dwelt, saying, where is the man who wishes to know the ways of the Lord and good works? Let him come to Enoch.
7 And all the sons of men then assembled to him, for all who desired this thing went to Enoch, and Enoch reigned over the sons of men according to the word of the Lord, and they came and bowed to him and they heard his word.
8 And the spirit of God was upon Enoch, and he taught all his men the wisdom of God and his ways, and the sons of men served the Lord all the days of Enoch, and they came to hear his wisdom.
9 And all the kings of the sons of men, both first and last, together with their princes and judges, came to Enoch when they heard of his wisdom, and they bowed down to him, and they also required of Enoch to reign over them, to which he consented.
10 And they assembled in all, one hundred and thirty kings and princes, and they made Enoch king over them and they were all under his power and command.
11 And Enoch taught them wisdom, knowledge, and the ways of the Lord; and he made peace amongst them, and peace was throughout the earth during the life of Enoch.
12 And Enoch reigned over the sons of men two hundred and forty-three years, and he did justice and righteousness with all his people, and he led them in the ways of the Lord.
13 And these are the generations of Enoch, Methuselah, Elisha, and Elimelech, three sons; and their sisters were Melca and

Nahmah, and Methuselah lived eighty-seven years and he begat Lamech.
14 And it was in the fifty-sixth year of the life of Lamech when Adam died; nine hundred and thirty years old was he at his death, and his two sons, with Enoch and Methuselah his son, buried him with great pomp, as at the burial of kings, in the cave which God had told him.
15 And in that place all the sons of men made a great mourning and weeping on account of Adam; it has therefore become a custom among the sons of men to this day.
16 And Adam died because he ate of the tree of knowledge; he and his children after him, as the Lord God had spoken.
17 And it was in the year of Adam's death which was the two hundred and forty-third year of the reign of Enoch, in that time Enoch resolved to separate himself from the sons of men and to secret himself as at first in order to serve the Lord.
18 And Enoch did so, but did not entirely secret himself from them, but kept away from the sons of men three days and then went to them for one day.
19 And during the three days that he was in his chamber, he prayed to, and praised the Lord his God, and the day on which he went and appeared to his subjects he taught them the ways of the Lord, and all they asked him about the Lord he told them.
20 And he did in this manner for many years, and he afterward concealed himself for six days, and appeared to his people one day in seven; and after that once in a month, and then once in a year, until all the kings, princes and sons of men sought for him, and desired again to see the face of Enoch, and to hear his word; but they could not, as all the sons of men were greatly afraid of Enoch, and they feared to approach him on account of the Godlike awe that was seated upon his countenance; therefore no man could look at him, fearing he might be punished and die.
21 And all the kings and princes resolved to assemble the sons of men, and to come to Enoch, thinking that they might all speak to him at the time when he should come forth amongst them, and they did so.
22 And the day came when Enoch went forth and they all assembled and came to him, and Enoch spoke to them the words of the Lord and he taught them wisdom and knowledge, and they

bowed down before him and they said, May the king live! May the king live!
23 And in some time after, when the kings and princes and the sons of men were speaking to Enoch, and Enoch was teaching them the ways of God, behold an angel of the Lord then called unto Enoch from heaven, and wished to bring him up to heaven to make him reign there over the sons of God, as he had reigned over the sons of men upon earth.
24 When at that time Enoch heard this he went and assembled all the inhabitants of the earth, and taught them wisdom and knowledge and gave them divine instructions, and he said to them, I have been required to ascend into heaven, I therefore do not know the day of my going.
25 And now therefore I will teach you wisdom and knowledge and will give you instruction before I leave you, how to act upon earth whereby you may live; and he did so.
26 And he taught them wisdom and knowledge, and gave them instruction, and he reproved them, and he placed before them statutes and judgments to do upon earth, and he made peace amongst them, and he taught them everlasting life, and dwelt with them some time teaching them all these things.
27 And at that time the sons of men were with Enoch, and Enoch was speaking to them, and they lifted up their eyes and the likeness of a great horse descended from heaven, and the horse paced in the air;
28 And they told Enoch what they had seen, and Enoch said to them, On my account does this horse descend upon earth; the time is come when I must go from you and I shall no more be seen by you.
29 And the horse descended at that time and stood before Enoch, and all the sons of men that were with Enoch saw him.
30 And Enoch then again ordered a voice to be proclaimed, saying, Where is the man who delighteth to know the ways of the Lord his God, let him come this day to Enoch before he is taken from us.
31 And all the sons of men assembled and came to Enoch that day; and all the kings of the earth with their princes and counsellors remained with him that day; and Enoch then taught the sons of men wisdom and knowledge, and gave them divine

instruction; and he bade them serve the Lord and walk in his ways all the days of their lives, and he continued to make peace amongst them.
32 And it was after this that he rose up and rode upon the horse; and he went forth and all the sons of men went after him, about eight hundred thousand men; and they went with him one day's journey.
33 And the second day he said to them, Return home to your tents, why will you go? perhaps you may die; and some of them went from him, and those that remained went with him six day's journey; and Enoch said to them every day, Return to your tents, lest you may die; but they were not willing to return, and they went with him.
34 And on the sixth day some of the men remained and clung to him, and they said to him, We will go with thee to the place where thou goest; as the Lord liveth, death only shall separate us.
35 And they urged so much to go with him, that he ceased speaking to them; and they went after him and would not return;
36 And when the kings returned they caused a census to be taken, in order to know the number of remaining men that went with Enoch; and it was upon the seventh day that Enoch ascended into heaven in a whirlwind, with horses and chariots of fire.
37 And on the eighth day all the kings that had been with Enoch sent to bring back the number of men that were with Enoch, in that place from which he ascended into heaven.
38 And all those kings went to the place and they found the earth there filled with snow, and upon the snow were large stones of snow, and one said to the other, Come, let us break through the snow and see, perhaps the men that remained with Enoch are dead, and are now under the stones of snow, and they searched but could not find him, for he had ascended into heaven.

As you can tell, there appears to be a lot more about Enoch than what is mentioned in the Bible. I found it interesting he ruled the land righteously. It kind of reminds me of Moses. It also reminds me to what the coming Messiah is going to do during the one thousand year reign, which happens right after the horrible Tribulation period.

We know that Enoch did not die. There is only one other person in the Bible who didn't taste death either. And that was Elijah.

So much is written about Elijah in both the new and old Testaments in the Bible. He raised people from the dead.

1 Kings 17:17-24;
17 Some time later the son of the woman who owned the house became ill. He grew worse and worse, and finally stopped breathing.
18 She said to Elijah, "What do you have against me, man of God? Did you come to remind me of my sin and kill my son?"
19 "Give me your son," Elijah replied. He took him from her arms, carried him to the upper room where he was staying, and laid him on his bed.
20 Then he cried out to the LORD, "LORD my God, have you brought tragedy even on this widow I am staying with, by causing her son to die?"
21 Then he stretched himself out on the boy three times and cried out to the LORD, "LORD my God, let this boy's life return to him!"
22 The LORD heard Elijah's cry, and the boy's life returned to him, and he lived.
23 Elijah picked up the child and carried him down from the room into the house. He gave him to his mother and said, "Look, your son is alive!"
24 Then the woman said to Elijah, "Now I know that you are a man of God and that the word of the LORD from your mouth is the truth." (New International Version)

In another great event, Elijah made fun of the prophets of Baal openly and later God consumed Elijah's sacrificial offering. He mentored Elisha. Fifty other prophets followed both Elijah and Elisha because they were in training. He was taken up in ultimate style of the time, in a flaming chariot, with Elisha getting his mantle.

Just so you know, I believe the name of Elijah means "My God is the LORD".

Now here was the time Elijah had a bout with depression.

1 Kings 19:1-5; 12-14
1 Now Ahab told Jezebel everything Elijah had done and how he had killed all the prophets with the sword.
2 So Jezebel sent a messenger to Elijah to say, "May the gods deal with me, be it ever so severely, if by this time tomorrow I do not make your life like that of one of them."
3 Elijah was afraid and ran for his life. When he came to Beersheba in Judah, he left his servant there,
4 while he himself went a day's journey into the wilderness. He came to a broom bush, sat down under it and prayed that he might die. "I have had enough, LORD," he said. "Take my life; I am no better than my ancestors."
5 Then he lay down under the bush and fell asleep. All at once an angel touched him and said, "Get up and eat.""

12 After the earthquake came a fire, but the LORD was not in the fire. And after the fire came a gentle whisper.
13 When Elijah heard it, he pulled his cloak over his face and went out and stood at the mouth of the cave. Then a voice said to him, "What are you doing here, Elijah?"
14 He replied, "I have been very zealous for the LORD God Almighty. The Israelites have rejected your covenant, torn down your altars, and put your prophets to death with the sword. I am the only one left, and now they are trying to kill me too." (New International Version)

Despite Elijah's depression (it might have lasted for around forty days, but we are not sure), the LORD was gentle with him. He knew Elijah's heart. The LORD didn't condemn or rebuke him for what he said and felt. He fed Elijah and gave him water to drink. Interesting response isn't it? Maybe that should be our first response; to show compassion first.

Romans 12:10; *Love each other with genuine affection, and take delight in honoring each other.* (New Living Translation)

I suggest you read the rest of 1 Kings 19. It's very interesting reading.

With all that said about Elijah, hardly anything about Enoch is revealed. Yet Enoch is one of those we believe will be coming back during the tribulation period, along with Elijah. Of all the prophets mentioned by name in the Bible, few of them have very little told to us about their life.

There are other writings that are available. Some of them will be discussed here.

The 1st Book of Enoch gives accounts of different topics that the rest of the Bible doesn't talk much about actually. Interestingly enough, some parts of the New Testament (Book of Jude and the Gospel of Luke), to name a few, actually seemingly say almost the same thing as the 1st Book of Enoch.

Let me talk a bit about this Book of Enoch. We have books that are stories of Benjamin Franklin or George Washington. We have other books that contain information that we think about and say in our heads, "wow, I didn't know that..." So why shouldn't we consider this book, with that same mindset, as well?

Below are some verses from the Bible and the 1st Book of Enoch which basically say the same thing.

Matthew 5:5; *Blessed are the meek, for they shall inherit the earth.* (English Standard Version)

Enoch 5:7 But to the elect there shall be light, joy, and peace, and they shall inherit the earth. To you, wicked ones, on the contrary, there will be a curse.

Luke 6:24; *"What sorrow awaits you who are rich, for you have your only happiness now.* (New Living Translation)

Enoch 94:8; "Woe unto you, O rich people! For you have put your trust in your wealth. You shall ooze out of your riches, for you do not remember YAHWEH the Most High."

Matthew 19:28; *Jesus replied, "I assure you that when the world is made new and the Son of Man sits upon his glorious* *throne, you who have been my followers will also sit on twelve thrones, judging the twelve tribes of Israel.* (New Living Translation)

Enoch 108:12; "I shall bring them out into the bright light, those who have loved MY kodesh NAME, and seat them each one by one upon the throne of his honor."

Matthew 26:24; *The Son of Man will go just as it is written about him. But woe to that man who betrays the Son of Man! It would be better for him if he had not been born."* (New International Version)

Enoch 38:2; Where will the habitation of sinners be . . . who have rejected the Lord of spirits. It would have been better for them, had they never been born.

Luke 16:26; *And besides all this, between us and you a great chasm has been fixed, so that those who want to go from here to you cannot, nor can anyone cross over from there to us.'* (New International Version)

Enoch 22:9; And he replied and said to me, "These three have been made in order that the spirits of the dead might be separated. And in the manner in which the souls of the righteous are separated by this spring of water with light upon it,"

John 14:2; *In my Father's house are many mansions: if it were not so, I would have told you. I go to prepare a place for you.* (King James Version)

Enoch 45:3; In that day shall the Elect One sit upon a throne of glory, and shall choose their conditions and countless habitations.

John 12:36; *While ye have light, believe in the light, that ye may be the children of light. These things spoke Jesus, and departed, and concealed himself from them.* (Webster's Bible Translation)

Enoch 108:11; the good from the generation of light.

John 4:14; *but whoever drinks the water I give them will never thirst. Indeed, the water I give them will become in them a spring of water welling up to eternal life."* (New International Version)

Enoch 48:1; all the thirsty drank, and were filled with wisdom, having their habitation with the righteous, the elect, and the holy.

The verses above mean the same thing. I think that the 1st Book of Enoch has historical value that should be considered. In the end, isn't it the Holy Spirit of God that teaches us the things of God?

So why did I spend so much time talking about Enoch? So we get to understand the whole time frame right before and during the first part of Genesis chapter 6! That is our focal point, that is the time frame we need to know so we can be prepared for the onslaught that will take place; more than likely right before our very eyes. And if we are not carefully as Christians, we will be deceived just like the rest of the world will believe the lie.

Two Pairs Two By Two Onto the Ark Right? Not Exactly.

I find it interesting how people seem to believe that just two of all of the animals that lived and breathed on the land were taken aboard the Ark. Yet that is not completely correct. Actually it was more than that.

Genesis 7:2-3;
2 Take with you seven pairs of every kind of clean animal, a male and its mate, and one pair of every kind of unclean animal, a male and its mate,
3 and also seven pairs of every kind of bird, male and female, to keep their various kinds alive throughout the earth. (New International Version)

There were fourteen what the Bible calls clean animals and only two unclean which were brought aboard the ark. So there were seven male and seven females of clean. But just one male and one female of the unclean. Now the question is what is considered clean and unclean. Let's see what the Bible says about what was clean and unclean.

Clean

1. **Deuteronomy 14:4-6;**
   4 Here are the [kinds of] animals you may eat: oxen, sheep, goats,
   5 deer, gazelles, fallow deer, wild goats, mountain goats, antelope, and mountain sheep.
   6 You may eat all animals that have completely divided hoofs and that also chew their cud. (GOD'S WORD ® Translation)
2. **Deuteronomy 14:9-11;**
   9 Here's what you may eat of every creature that lives in the water: You may eat any creature that has fins and scales.
   10 But never eat anything that doesn't have fins and scales. It is unclean for you.
   11 You may eat any clean bird. (GOD'S WORD ® Translation)
3. **Deuteronomy 14:20;** *However, you may eat any [other kind of] flying creature that is clean.* (GOD'S WORD ® Translation)

Unclean

1. **Deuteronomy 14:7-8;**
   7 But some animals chew their cud, while others have completely divided hoofs. You may not eat these [kinds of] animals. They include camels, rabbits, and rock badgers. (Although they chew their cud, they don't have divided hoofs. They are unclean for you.)
   8 Also, you may not eat pigs. (Although their hoofs are divided, they don't chew their cud.) Never eat their meat or touch their dead bodies. (GOD'S WORD ® Translation)
2. **Deuteronomy 14:10;** *But never eat anything that doesn't have fins and scales. It is unclean for you.* (GOD'S WORD ® Translation)
3. **Deuteronomy 14:12-19;**
   12 But here are the birds that you should never eat: eagles, bearded vultures, black vultures,
   13 buzzards, all types of kites,
   14 all types of crows,
   15 ostriches, nighthawks, seagulls, all types of falcons,
   16 little owls, great owls, barn owls,
   17 pelicans, ospreys, cormorants,
   18 storks, all types of herons, hoopoes, and bats.
   19 Every swarming, winged insect is also unclean for you. They must never be eaten. (GOD'S WORD ® Translation)

This gives you an idea what is considered clean and unclean. The reasons why there was more clean animals than unclean was because it would be healthy for us to eat them. Those unclean animals were really considered more scavengers than anything else. God designed some of them to clean up after the clean animals which died or were diseased and/or weak. That would include those that lived in the sea too. Usually the dead fish floated to the bottom, and the scavengers moved in and cleaned up on the decaying flesh.

Let's ask the question. How did Noah know what is clean and unclean? That information wasn't given to us in the Bible until after the Israelites left Egypt. That was hundreds of years after the flood of Genesis 7 occurred.

Flood

I often wondered what those people thought moments when the water came down from the sky. Remember, I don't think water ever descended from the sky before. Today we call it rain...

Did Noah and his family hear the cries for help? Did those people start to pound on the side of the ark. Maybe they were clawing at the sides of it, trying to get in. Begging for mercy, pleading for help, saying they were sorry and asked to be forgiven because they believe now. Maybe they left fingernail indentations on the gopher wood. Did they recognize some of the voices of people they knew? Did they sit down and remember them? Did they mourn and weep because they were going to die? Did ALL those in the ark remember those they knew, those they loved? Did they mourn them and weep too? Did they wonder what would happen after the rain ended and they could leave the ark? Did they appreciate them being spared from that type of death? Did they understand the favor God had on their lives and act accordingly?

Actually the Book of Jasher gives an account of that very thing.

Jasher 6:9-33:
9 Two and two came to Noah into the ark, but from the clean animals, and clean fowls, he brought seven couples, as God had commanded him.
10 And all the animals, and beasts, and fowls, were still there, and they surrounded the ark at every place, and the rain had not descended till seven days after.
11 And on that day, the Lord caused the whole earth to shake, and the sun darkened, and the foundations of the world raged, and the whole earth was moved violently, and the lightning flashed, and the thunder roared, and all the fountains in the earth were broken up, such as was not known to the inhabitants before; and God did this mighty act, in order to terrify the sons of men, that there might be no more evil upon earth.

12 And still the sons of men would not return from their evil ways, and they increased the anger of the Lord at that time, and did not even direct their hearts to all this.
13 And at the end of seven days, in the six hundredth year of the life of Noah, the waters of the flood were upon the earth.
14 And all the fountains of the deep were broken up, and the windows of heaven were opened, and the rain was upon the earth forty days and forty nights.
15 And Noah and his household, and all the living creatures that were with him, came into the ark on account of the waters of the flood, and the Lord shut him in.
16 And all the sons of men that were left upon the earth, became exhausted through evil on account of the rain, for the waters were coming more violently upon the earth, and the animals and beasts were still surrounding the ark.
17 And the sons of men assembled together, about seven hundred thousand men and women, and they came unto Noah to the ark.
18 And they called to Noah, saying, Open for us that we may come to thee in the ark—and wherefore shall we die?
19 And Noah, with a loud voice, answered them from the ark, saying, Have you not all rebelled against the Lord, and said that he does not exist? and therefore the Lord brought upon you this evil, to destroy and cut you off from the face of the earth.
20 Is not this the thing that I spoke to you of one hundred and twenty years back, and you would not hearken to the voice of the Lord, and now do you desire to live upon earth?
21 And they said to Noah, We are ready to return to the Lord; only open for us that we may live and not die.
22 And Noah answered them, saying, Behold now that you see the trouble of your souls, you wish to return to the Lord; why did you not return during these hundred and twenty years, which the Lord granted you as the determined period?
23 But now you come and tell me this on account of the troubles of your souls, now also the Lord will not listen to you, neither will he give ear to you on this day, so that you will not now succeed in your wishes.

24 And the sons of men approached in order to break into the ark, to come in on account of the rain, for they could not bear the rain upon them.
25 And the Lord sent all the beasts and animals that stood round the ark. And the beasts overpowered them and drove them from that place, and every man went his way and they again scattered themselves upon the face of the earth.
26 And the rain was still descending upon the earth, and it descended forty days and forty nights, and the waters prevailed greatly upon the earth; and all flesh that was upon the earth or in the waters died, whether men, animals, beasts, creeping things or birds of the air, and there only remained Noah and those that were with him in the ark.
27 And the waters prevailed and they greatly increased upon the earth, and they lifted up the ark and it was raised from the earth.
28 And the ark floated upon the face of the waters, and it was tossed upon the waters so that all the living creatures within were turned about like pottage in a cauldron.
29 And great anxiety seized all the living creatures that were in the ark, and the ark was like to be broken.
30 And all the living creatures that were in the ark were terrified, and the lions roared, and the oxen lowed, and the wolves howled, and every living creature in the ark spoke and lamented in its own language, so that their voices reached to a great distance, and Noah and his sons cried and wept in their troubles; they were greatly afraid that they had reached the gates of death.
31 And Noah prayed unto the Lord, and cried unto him on account of this, and he said, O Lord help us, for we have no strength to bear this evil that has encompassed us, for the waves of the waters have surrounded us, mischievous torrents have terrified us, the snares of death have come before us; answer us, O Lord, answer us, light up thy countenance toward us and be gracious to us, redeem us and deliver us.
32 And the Lord hearkened to the voice of Noah, and the Lord remembered him.
33 And a wind passed over the earth, and the waters were still and the ark rested.

There are some good lessons to ponder. Don't wait too long before turning to the LORD God.

Through my research for this book, I noticed that all of the civilizations I read about referenced the flood of Genesis 7, in one way or another. Flavius Josephus makes mention of the flood in a, shall I say unique way.

Antiquities of the Jews - Book I
Chapter 3:6; Now all the writers of barbarian histories make mention of this flood, and of this ark; among whom is Berosus the Chaldean. For when he is describing the circumstances of the flood, he goes on thus: "It is said there is still some part of this ship in Armenia, at the mountain of the Cordyaeans; and that some people carry off pieces of the bitumen, which they take away, and use chiefly as amulets for the averting of mischiefs." Hieronymus the Egyptian also, who wrote the Phoenician Antiquities, and Mnaseas, and a great many more, make mention of the same. Nay, Nicolaus of Damascus, in his ninety-sixth book, hath a particular relation about them; where he speaks thus: "There is a great mountain in Armenia, over Minyas, called Baris, upon which it is reported that many who fled at the time of the Deluge were saved; and that one who was carried in an ark came on shore upon the top of it; and that the remains of the timber were a great while preserved. This might be the man about whom Moses the legislator of the Jews wrote."

Here is some interesting information about the flood. The rain fell from heaven but also came up from within the earth. Water had risen up to fifteen cubits above all the mountains.

Book of Jubilees 5:24-26
24 And the Lord opened seven flood-gates of heaven, And the mouths of the fountains of the great deep, seven mouths in number.
25 And the flood-gates began to pour down water from the heaven forty days and forty nights, And the fountains of the deep also sent up waters, until the whole world was full of water.

26 And the waters increased upon the earth: Fifteen cubits did the waters rise above all the high mountains, And the ark was lift up above the earth, And it moved upon the face of the waters.

Genesis 8:2-3;
2 Now the springs of the deep and the floodgates of the heavens had been closed, and the rain had stopped falling from the sky.
3 The water receded steadily from the earth. At the end of the hundred and fifty days the water had gone down, (New International Version)

There is quite a bit of information that supports the flood that God brought upon the earth. Here are some discovered locations of huge water storage aquifers that were probably used during the flood that God brought upon the earth.

1. **Ogallala Aquifer**
   This aquifer covers eight states. This is one of the biggest ones in the world. Many people believe that it was only the rain that caused the flood. These verses in the Bible prove some of the water came from beneath the earth too.
   (Source; http://www.waterencyclopedia.com/Oc-Po/Ogallala-Aquifer.html#b & http://en.wikipedia.org/wiki/Ogallala_Aquifer)
   Genesis 8:1-2;
   1 But God remembered Noah and all the wild animals and livestock with him in the boat. He sent a wind to blow across the earth, and the floodwaters began to recede.
   2 The underground waters stopped flowing, and the torrential rains from the sky were stopped. (New Living Translation)
   Keep in mind, God created a water like canopy in the sky during creation to shield us from the harmful radiation we get from the sun. It could have looked like a transparent bag. You could see through it. It could have been miles up in the atmosphere. It circled the globe. Now the exact thickness of it is up for discussion. But because of this canopy, many believe everything probably lived longer during that time.

Genesis 1:6-8;

6 And God said, "Let there be a vault between the waters to separate water from water."

7 So God made the vault and separated the water under the vault from the water above it. And it was so.

8 God called the vault "sky." And there was evening, and there was morning—the second day. (New Living Translation)

2. **Huge Underground Ocean.**

   There is a massive body of water in eastern Asia that is estimated to be located between 400 to 800 miles below the surface. It may still contain as much water as in the Arctic Ocean.

   (Source; http://news.nationalgeographic.com/news/2007/02/070227-ocean-asia.html

3. **The Blob**

   Located underneath the Caribbean Sea, there seems to be a location there of water that is 80 miles thick and 380 miles tall.

   (Source; http://thetruth-blog.blogspot.com/2011/01/what-were-waters-from-flood.html)

4. **Wadsleyite Deposit**

   Wadsleyite is a mineral in the earth's mantle which can hold a lot of water. It is believed that there is so much of this mineral that it is estimated it have enough water that can fill ten to thirty of our oceans.

   (Source; http://thetruth-blog.blogspot.com/2011/01/what-were-waters-from-flood.html)

   It is believed that the water from the flood receded into the ground. Because some of the water came from within the earth, that can account for some of it. The rest of the water, which came down, is believed to come down from the water canopy in the upper sky. That water also entered into the earth. It is believed that the mountains of the earth were pushed upwards by the LORD God so the water from the canopy can be stored within the earth. They continued to be pushed upwards until there was enough room for the water from the sky to be stored in it.

Psalm 104:6-9;
6 You covered the earth with an ocean as though it were a robe. Water stood above the mountains
7 and fled because of your threat. Water ran away at the sound of your thunder.
8 The mountains rose and the valleys sank to the place you appointed for them.
9 Water cannot cross the boundary you set and cannot come back to cover the earth. (GOD'S WORD® Translation)
These verses are awesome! For the longest time, I thought all the world's excess water from the flood was actually collected and stored at the north and south poles when it became ice. Now I believe part of it is up there, and most of it is within the earth itself. Why is part of it up at the poles? It's God's reminder for us that once the earth was flooded because of man's sin.

5. **Whale fossils**
   These were found high up in the Andes Mountain range. This range can rise up to 13,000 feet. So how would a whale make its way up there?
   (Source; http://www.nytimes.com/1987/03/12/us/whale-fossils-high-in-andes-show-how-mountains-rose-from-sea.html & http://en.wikipedia.org/wiki/Andes)
6. **Sea Shells on top of Mount Everest**
   So how would sea shells find their way up there?
   (Source; http://evolutionwiki.org/wiki/Seashells_on_mountains_are_evidence_of_a_flood)

Some more interesting facts about the flood are included in the Book of Baruch. Baruch was the prophet Jeremiah's scribe. His name means 'blessed.' it mentions four hundred and nine thousand giants died in the flood.

3rd Baruch 4:10:
And the angel said, "Rightly you ask; when God caused the Flood over the earth and destroyed all flesh and 409,000 giants, and the water rose over the heights 15 cubits, the water entered Paradise and killed every flower, but it removed the sprig of the vine completely and brought it outside."

Now that you know about how many of these giants had died, add to those numbers either a billion, five, ten or seventeen billion people to the total.

Interestingly enough, the next text states that the LORD brought home others that walked with Him.

Book of Jasher, 5;21; And all the sons of men who knew the Lord, died in that year before the Lord brought evil upon them; for the Lord willed them to die, so as not to behold the evil that God would bring upon their brothers and relatives, as he had so declared to do.

It appears Noah did some interesting things to try and persuade the LORD God not destroy the whole earth again in this manner. It's very interesting reading.

Antiquities of the Jews - Book I
Chapter 3:7-8;
7 But as for Noah, he was afraid, since God had determined to destroy mankind, lest he should drown the earth every year; so he offered burnt-offerings, and besought God that nature might hereafter go on in its former orderly course, and that he would not bring on so great a judgment any more, by which the whole race of creatures might be in danger of destruction: but that, having now punished the wicked, he would of his goodness spare the remainder, and such as he had hitherto judged fit to be delivered from so severe a calamity; for that otherwise these last must be more miserable than the first, and that they must be condemned to a worse condition than the others, unless they be suffered to escape entirely; that is, if they be reserved for another deluge; while they must be afflicted with the terror and sight of the first deluge, and must also be destroyed by a second. He also entreated God to accept of his sacrifice, and to grant that the earth might never again undergo the like effects of 'his wrath; that men might be permitted to go on cheerfully in cultivating the same; to build cities, and live happily in them; and that they might not be deprived of any of those good things which they enjoyed before the Flood; but might attain to the like length of

days, and old age, which the ancient people had arrived at before.
8 When Noah had made these supplications, God, who loved the man for his righteousness, granted entire success to his prayers, and said, that it was not he who brought the destruction on a polluted world, but that they underwent that vengeance on account of their own wickedness; and that he had not brought men into the world if he had himself determined to destroy them, it being an instance of greater wisdom not to have granted them life at all, than, after it was granted, to procure their destruction; "But the injuries," said he, "they offered to my holiness and virtue, forced me to bring this punishment upon them. But I will leave off for the time to come to require such punishments, the effects of so great wrath, for their future wicked actions, and especially on account of thy prayers. But if I shall at any time send tempests of rain, in an extraordinary manner, be not affrighted at the largeness of the showers; for the water shall no more overspread the earth. However, I require you to abstain from shedding the blood of men, and to keep yourselves pure from murder; and to punish those that commit any such thing. I permit you to make use of all the other living creatures at your pleasure, and as your appetites lead you; for I have made you lords of them all, both of those that walk on the land, and those that swim in the waters, and of those that fly in the regions of the air on high, excepting their blood, for therein is the life. But I will give you a sign that I have left off my anger by my bow [whereby is meant the rainbow, for they determined that the rainbow was the bow of God]. And when God had said and promised thus, he went away.

I just love it when other writings back up what God's Word says in the Bible! I find it interesting there is a possibility because Noah was praying and humbly asking the LORD God not to flood the earth again that He granted his request! It's apparent that Noah and his family were chosen to survive the flood. And for good reason too.

Noah's three sons names were Shem which means 'name', Ham which means 'raged' or 'hot', and Japheth which means 'let him spread out.' You will soon understand why Ham was given that name.

Immediate Post Flood

It is obvious the Nephilim came back into the land after the waters receded. The Bible talks about these Nephilim (by using this name) only one more time in **Numbers 13:33**.

Numbers 13:28; *But the people living there are powerful, and their towns are large and fortified. We even saw giants there, the descendants oj Anak!* (New Living Translation)

Numbers 13:32; *So they put out this false report to the Israelis about the land that they had explored: "The land that we've explored is one that devours its inhabitants. All the people whom we observed were giants.* (International Standard Version)

Numbers 13:33; *We saw the Nephilim there (the descendants of Anak come from the Nephilim). We seemed like grasshoppers in our own eyes, and we looked the same to them."* (New International Version)

So the Nephilim came back. They were killed in Genesis 7. Yet they found their way back into the land.

One of the reasons, why God flooded the earth was so all those people, animals, and human hybrids (half man, half animal) that lived on earth would be destroyed. Another reason so man can start fresh. If this is the case, then how did they come back and become a force for evil again?

That is the question. Here are some possibilities. One is more fallen angels married the daughters of men. But there is no Biblical basis for this theory. They came through one of the bloodlines. I'm referring to the wives of the sons of Noah. It is safe to say the Noah's bloodline was clean because it states this fact.

Genesis 6:9; *These [are] the generations of Noah: Noah was a just man [and] perfect in his generations, [and] Noah walked with God.* (King James Version)

That word "perfect" comes from the Hebrew word "tā·mîm". It means any of the following; blameless, complete, entire, full, intact, integrity, perfect, sincerity, unblemished, uprightly, who is perfect, whole, without blemish, without defect. In this context, it is better translated as unblemished, without blemish or without defect. It is not referring to a sinless life. It is referring to his genetics. He was not corrupted by the genetically engineered man, the fallen angels and the Nephilim were involved in at that time.

I believe Noah's wife also had a clean bloodline. The Bible never does state the name of Noah's wife. Other ancient texts state her name was Emzara. She was the daughter of Rake'el, who was the son of Methuselah. And Methuselah was the son of Enoch. I would say that family tree line should be pure. Then other texts speculate that Naamah was his wife too. The Bible mentions her by name but does not connect her to Noah.

Genesis 4:22; *Zillah also had a son, Tubal-Cain, who forged all kinds of tools out of bronze and iron. Tubal-Cain's sister was Naamah.* (New International Version)

So who is left? Could the Nephilim have reappeared from someone's blood line? Yes. So which one? Could it be from all three of the wives of Noah's three sons? These are excellent questions.

Genesis 7:13; *On that very day Noah and his sons, Shem, Ham and Japheth, together with his wife and the wives of his three sons, entered the ark.* (New International Version)

Jasher; 5:35; Then Noah took the three daughters of Eliakim, son of Methuselah, for wives for his sons, as the Lord had commanded Noah.

When you look at the genealogy of Ham, you will understand where almost all of the Nephilim reappeared and were descended from in that bloodline. But in the end, while it would be nice to know how they came back again, we need to recognize that they reappeared. Henceforth, no matter how they have reappeared and are manifesting themselves here today, we need to get ready so we can combat them with the power of the Holy Spirit of the LORD!

It does say Noah was unblemished, it does not state that the wives were unblemished. If we take the Bible literally, it does state the following;

Genesis 6:12; *God saw how corrupt the earth had become, for all the people on earth had corrupted their ways.* (New International Version)

"All" usually means "all". That could have included Ham's wife. Some get into a big discussion as to how they returned. They will give their opinions as to how and why.

There is another possibility. It appears the watcher angels decided to carve in rock some instructions. They basically left a paper trail… or in that day, a rock trail. Could they have left lessons how to clone or genetically engineer a Nephilim? Could that be what the carvings in the pyramids mean? These carvings survived the flood. What information did they leave behind? What topics did they write about? Here is some interesting text from the book of Jubilees.

Book of Jubilees 8:1-4
1 In the twenty-ninth jubilee, in the first week, in the beginning thereof Arpachshad took to himself a wife and her name was Rasu'eja, the daughter of Susan, the daughter of Elam, and she
2 bare him a son in the third year in this week, and he called his name Kainam. And the son grew, and his father taught him writing, and he went to seek for himself a place where he might seize for
3 himself a city. And he found a writing which former (generations) had carved on the rock, and he read what was thereon, and he transcribed it and sinned owing to it; for it contained the teaching of the Watchers in accordance with which they used to observe the omens of the sun and moon and

4 stars in all the signs of heaven. And he wrote it down and said nothing regarding it; for he was
5 afraid to speak to Noah about it lest he should be angry with him on account of it. And in the thirtieth jubilee

The Bible mentions many times these giants were all over in the Promised Land. When the Israelites entered into this land, they needed to do to get rid of them. But in the end, the bottom line is they returned to plague man again. While that discussion of how is exciting and compelling, it doesn't change the fact that they are here, and we need to know how to combat them.

Israel's Enemies Who Were Nephilim

King Og was said to be around twelve to eighteen feet tall. The exact height depends on which cubit measurement they used. His kingdom (in the land of Bashan) stretched from east of the Sea of Galilee, north into Syria and into Iraq.

Deuteronomy 3:3-14;
3 So the LORD our God also gave into our hands Og king of Bashan and all his army. We struck them down, leaving no survivors.
4 At that time we took all his cities. There was not one of the sixty cities that we did not take from them—the whole region of Argob, Og's kingdom in Bashan.
5 All these cities were fortified with high walls and with gates and bars, and there were also a great many unwalled villages.
6 We completely destroyed them, as we had done with Sihon king of Heshbon, destroying every city—men, women and children.
7 But all the livestock and the plunder from their cities we carried off for ourselves.
8 So at that time we took from these two kings of the Amorites the territory east of the Jordan, from the Arnon Gorge as far as Mount Hermon.
9 (Hermon is called Sirion by the Sidonians; the Amorites call it Senir.)

10 We took all the towns on the plateau, and all Gilead, and all Bashan as far as Salekah and Edrei, towns of Og's kingdom in Bashan.
11 (Og king of Bashan was the last of the Rephaites. His bed was decorated with iron and was more than nine cubits long and four cubits wide. It is still in Rabbah of the Ammonites.)
12 Of the land that we took over at that time, I gave the Reubenites and the Gadites the territory north of Aroer by the Arnon Gorge, including half the hill country of Gilead, together with its towns.
13 The rest of Gilead and also all of Bashan, the kingdom of Og, I gave to the half-tribe of Manasseh. (The whole region of Argob in Bashan used to be known as a land of the Rephaites.
14 Jair, a descendant of Manasseh, took the whole region of Argob as far as the border of the Geshurites and the Maakathites; it was named after him, so that to this day Bashan is called Havvoth Jair.) (New International Version)

Amos writes about how God talks about how big these beings were, and He destroyed them.

Amos 2:9; *"But as my people watched, I destroyed the Amorites, though they were as tall as cedars and as strong as oaks. I destroyed the fruit on their branches and dug out their roots.* (New Living Translation)

What is interesting is the cedar trees mentioned above rise to the height from 80 to 130 feet tall. Some species can grow up to 200 feet tall. Sometimes they get up to eight feet in diameter. (Source; http://en.wikipedia.org/wiki/Lebanon_Cedar)

King Sihon and his kingdom were located just south of the land of Bashan. If you will note the LORD told Moses to wipe them all out and leave no survivors.

Numbers 21:34-35;
34 But the LORD said to Moses, "Do not fear him, for I have given him into your hand, and all his people, and his land. And you shall do to him as you did to Sihon king of the Amorites, who lived at Heshbon."

35 So they defeated him and his sons and all his people, until he had no survivor left. And they possessed his land. (English Standard Version)

The Philistines were always troublesome to the Israelites. Goliath whom David battled was also a Philistine. They sometimes had six fingers and six toes.

1 Chronicles 20:5-6;
5 During another battle with the Philistines, Elhanan son of Jair killed Lahmi, the brother of Goliath of Gath. The handle of Lahmi's spear was as thick as a weaver's beam!
6 In another battle with the Philistines at Gath, they encountered a huge man with six fingers on each hand and six toes on each foot, twenty-four in all, who was also a descendant of the giants. (New Living Translation)

Then you have the Emites and the Anakites.

Deuteronomy 2:11; *Both the Emites and the Anakites are also known as the Rephaites, though the Moabites call them Emites* (New Living Translation)

It's interesting how the Bible gives an account about the Israelites checking out the land of Canaan. They came back stating the people who lived there devoured all living things. It's apparent they knew the Nephilim were cannibals. The 1st Book of Enoch mentions it.

Numbers 13:31-33;
31 But the other men who had explored the land with him disagreed. "We can't go up against them! They are stronger than we are!"
32 So they spread this bad report about the land among the Israelites: "The land we traveled through and explored will devour anyone who goes to live there. All the people we saw were huge.
33 We even saw giants there, the descendants oj Anak. Next to them we felt like grasshoppers, and that's what they thought, too!" (New Living Translation)

Here is evidence of an Egyptian who is believed to be another descendant Nephilim. He was a small one, by Nephilim standards. This takes place right after David becomes King of Israel, after the King Saul falls on his sword because his armor-bearer would not pierce him with his own sword as Saul commanded him to do.

1 Chronicles 11:22-23;
22 Benaiah son of Jehoiada, a valiant fighter from Kabzeel, performed great exploits. He struck down Moab's two mightiest warriors. He also went down into a pit on a snowy day and killed a lion.
23 And he struck down an Egyptian who was five cubits tall. Although the Egyptian had a spear like a weaver's rod in his hand, Benaiah went against him with a club. He snatched the spear from the Egyptian's hand and killed him with his own spear. (New International Version)

I find it interesting how the other translations didn't seem to translate 'deceased' to Rephaim. The name Rephaim means dead. If you read it with the word deceased in the sentence, it doesn't quite make sense. If you put the word 'Rephaim' in it, then you know what the writer is referring to here.

Isaiah 26:14; *Dead -- they live not, Rephaim, they rise not, Therefore Thou hast inspected and dost destroy them, Yea, thou destroyest all their memory.* (Young Literal Translation)

In this version, it is translated into giants.

Isaiah 26:14; *Let not the dead live, let not the giants rise again: therefore hast thou visited and destroyed them, and best destroyed all their memory.* (Douay-Rheims Bible)

The LORD explains who the additional enemies of Israel's enemies are in the verses below. The Book of Jasher gives you an account of who the descendants of Ham were.

Joshua 3:9-10;
9 Joshua said to the Israelites, "Come here and listen to the words of the LORD your God.
10 This is how you will know that the living God is among you and that he will certainly drive out before you the Canaanites, Hittites, Hivites, Perizzites, Girgashites, Amorites and Jebusites. (New International Version)

Book of Jasher 7:10
And these are the sons of Ham; Cush, Mitzraim, Phut and Canaan, four sons; and the sons of Cush were Seba, Havilah, Sabta, Raama and Satecha, and the sons of Raama were Sheba and Dedan.

I believe most of the civilizations who were Nephilim mostly has the following "ities" and "ines" after their names. There are some who believe that Gog and MaGog were these giants also. Here are the sons of Ham.

Why am I including his genealogy? You'll see in a few moments.

Genesis 10:6; *The sons of Ham: Cush, Mizraim, Put and Canaan.* (New International Version)

Genesis 10:8; *Cush was the father of Nimrod, who grew to be a mighty warrior on the earth.* (New International Version)

Genesis 10:8-9;
8 And Chus begot Nebrod: he began to be a giant upon the earth.
9 He was a giant hunter before the Lord God; therefore they say, As Nebrod the giant hunter before the Lord. (Greek Septuagint Bible)

Brenton, Sir Lancelot C. L. (2010-09-05). English Translation of the Greek Septuagint, Including the Apocrypha (Kindle Locations 335-337). E.C. Marsh. Kindle Edition.

This is the same Nimrod, who would rebel against the LORD God and build the tower at Babel that God would destroy. It's believed he was a giant too.

Genesis 10:8-20;
8 Cush was the father of Nimrod, who became a mighty warrior on the earth.
9 He was a mighty hunter before the LORD; that is why it is said, "Like Nimrod, a mighty hunter before the LORD."
10 The first centers of his kingdom were Babylon, Uruk, Akkad and Kalneh, in Shinar.
11 From that land he went to Assyria, where he built Nineveh, Rehoboth Ir, Calah
12 and Resen, which is between Nineveh and Calah—which is the great city.
13 Egypt was the father of the Ludites, Anamites, Lehabites, Naphtuhites,
14 Pathrusites, Kasluhites (from whom the Philistines came) and Caphtorites.
15 Canaan was the father of Sidon his firstborn,[g] and of the Hittites,
16 Jebusites, Amorites, Girgashites,
17 Hivites, Arkites, Sinites,
18 Arvadites, Zemarites and Hamathites. Later the Canaanite clans scattered
19 and the borders of Canaan reached from Sidon toward Gerar as far as Gaza, and then toward Sodom, Gomorrah, Admah and Zeboyim, as far as Lasha.
20 These are the sons of Ham by their clans and languages, in their territories and nations. (New International Version)

Notice the "ites" and the "ines". See where the Philistines bloodline came from? Remember Goliath was a Philistine. Now you can see why the genealogies are so important for many reasons. There it is! Isn't it so thoughtful and wonderful how the Lord God reveals things to us, so we have the knowledge we need to have to push forward! Glory to God!

Also keep in mind just because some people were enemies of Israel, it doesn't mean they were the descendant of the Nephilim either.

Here is where some of the above people settled in the land back in those days. The following listed below was taken from some ancient maps. These are the locations where I believe they settled.

Nimrod
In Iraq around the Tigress and Euphrates rivers and beyond.
Ludites
This is where we call eastern Turkey
Anamites
It's unclear where they settled. They were called Anamim. Some speculate they were in northern Egypt. Could it be the Egyptian culture was started at this time? Then their gods were fashioned and created?
Lehabites
This is what we call Libya today.
Nephtuhites
It's unclear where they settled.
Pathrusites
This is what is called Lower Egypt.
Casluhites
They settled in the Nile river basin. Goliath eventually would emerge from them.
Caphtorites
They presumably lived in Caphtor or what is known today as Crete. This is somewhat interesting. Were they, just like with the Anamites, the start of the Greek god's myth? The Nephilim would be able to fulfill the legendary myths of the Greek and Roman gods due to their gigantic size and strength. Some of it could be fulfilled before the Genesis 7 flood. These Titans, as they were called would cause wars and fight against each other. The time period would be just about right for this to happen.

Here are more verses of Israel's enemies who were either Nephilim or their descendants. I give you these so you can better understand the enormous battles they had when the Israelites entered into the land flowing with milk and honey, as the Bible states.

Here are more names of the descendants of the Nephilim and what they mean.

Genesis 14:5; *In the fourteenth year Chedorlaomer and the kings who were with him came and defeated the Rephaim in Ashteroth-karnaim, the Zuzim in Ham, the Emim in Shaveh-kiriathaim,* (English Standard Version*)*

Rephaim (also could be called Rephaites) means the dead, giants.

Genesis 14:5 above. Emim means, terror,

Genesis 14:5 above. Zuzim means, roving creatures

Numbers 13:22; *They went up through the Negev and came to Hebron, where Ahiman, Sheshai and Talmai, the descendants of Anak, lived. (Hebron had been built seven years before Zoan in Egypt.)* (New Living Translation)

Numbers 13:33; *We saw the Nephilim there (the descendants of Anak come from the Nephilim). We seemed like grasshoppers in our own eyes, and we looked the same to them."* (New International Version)

Anakim means; patronymic of preceding. Here is an interesting side note. The Israelites just left Egypt. They were there for some four hundred years. How would they know about the Nephilim and the Anakim? Yet it is very plain to see they knew about the Nephilim and what they are capable of doing.

Numbers 23:14; *So Balak took Balaam to the plateau of Zophim on Pisgah Peak. He built seven altars there and offered a young bull and a ram on each altar.* (New Living Translation)

Zophim means watchmen or watchers.

Deuteronomy 2:10-11;
10 (The Emites used to live there—a people strong and numerous, and as tall as the Anakites.
11 Like the Anakites, they too were considered Rephaites, but the Moabites called them Emites. (New International Version)

Deuteronomy 2:20-21;
20 (That too was considered a land of the Rephaites, who used to live there; but the Ammonites called them Zamzummites.
21 They were a people strong and numerous, and as tall as the Anakites. The LORD destroyed them from before the Ammonites, who drove them out and settled in their place. (New International Version)

Zamzummims means intriguers,

Deuteronomy 3:11; *(Og king of Bashan was the last of the Rephaites. His bed was decorated with iron and was more than nine cubits long and four cubits wide. It is still in Rabbah of the Ammonites.)* (New International Version)

Deuteronomy 9:2; *The people are strong and tall--Anakites! You know about them and have heard it said: "Who can stand up against the Anakites?"* (New International Version)

Joshua 11:21-22;
21 At that time Joshua went and destroyed the Anakites from the hill country: from Hebron, Debir and Anab, from all the hill country of Judah, and from all the hill country of Israel. Joshua totally destroyed them and their towns.
22 No Anakites were left in Israelite territory; only in Gaza, Gath and Ashdod did any survive. (New International Version)

Joshua 12:4-5;
4 And the territory of Og king of Bashan, one of the last of the Rephaites, who reigned in Ashtaroth and Edrei.
5 He ruled over Mount Hermon, Salekah, all of Bashan to the border of the people of Geshur and Maakah, and half of Gilead to the border of Sihon king of Heshbon. (New International Version)

Joshua 15:8; *Then it ran up the Valley of Ben Hinnom along the southern slope of the Jebusite city (that is, Jerusalem). From there it climbed to the top of the hill west of the Hinnom Valley at the northern end of the Valley of Rephaim.* (New International Version)

Joshua 18:16; *The boundary went down to the foot of the hill facing the Valley of Ben Hinnom, north of the Valley of Rephaim. It continued down the Hinnom Valley along the southern slope of the Jebusite city and so to En Rogel.* (New International Version)

1 Samuel 17:4-5;
4 A champion named Goliath, who was from Gath, came out of the Philistine camp. His height was six cubits and a span.
5 He had a bronze helmet on his head and wore a coat of scale armor of bronze weighing five thousand shekels ; (New International Version)

Five thousand shekels of brass weigh about one hundred and twenty five pounds.
(Source; http://wiki.answers.com/Q/What_is_the_weight_in_us_pounds_of_5000_shekels_of_brass)

1 Samuel 17:7; *His spear shaft was like a weaver's rod, and its iron point weighed six hundred shekels. His shield bearer went ahead of him.* (New International Version)

Six hundred shekels weigh about fifteen pounds. Just the point of the spear is about fifteen pounds.

2 Samuel 21:16; *And Ishbi-Benob, one of the descendants of Rapha, whose bronze spearhead weighed three hundred shekels and who was armed with a new sword, said he would kill David.* (New International Version)

2 Samuel 21:18-22;
18 In the course of time, there was another battle with the Philistines, at Gob. At that time Sibbekai the Hushathite killed Saph, one of the descendants of Rapha.
19 In another battle with the Philistines at Gob, Elhanan son of Jair[c] the Bethlehemite killed the brother of Goliath the Gittite, who had a spear with a shaft like a weaver's rod.
20 In still another battle, which took place at Gath, there was a huge man with six fingers on each hand and six toes on each foot—twenty-four in all. He also was descended from Rapha.

21 When he taunted Israel, Jonathan son of Shimeah, David's brother, killed him.
22 These four were descendants of Rapha in Gath, and they fell at the hands of David and his men. (New International Version)

Those are some incredible verses! As you can tell, all of the above verses talk about these descendants of the Nephilim.

Here is the question. With so, so many verses that show us how many of Israel's enemies were Nephilim or their descendants, why has the church ignored this subject?

Like the questions I asked earlier, how did the leaders of Israelites know who were the descendants of the Nephilim? Could it be there might have been stories of what the times were like back then… after the flood? Or could there have been talks around a campfire many years afterwards, as these stories were passed down through the generations.

I would like you to notice that almost all these counties are Islamic today. And they are or have been at war with Israel.

Evidence the Nephilim Were Here

All of the information I've provided to you up to this point comes from various sources. If you do a search on the Internet, you will find scores and scores of pictures of Nephilim bones. Some of them have been altered and doctored up. Yet even with the photos being changed, the truth remains they were here because the Bible states they were here.

The picture to the right is of a skeleton which was made by artist Gino De Dominicis. It was on display here at the

Cathedral Duomo in Milan, Italy.

The size of this skeleton would be similar to the giants in the Old Testament. Before and after the flood of Genesis 7.

This one was twenty-eight meters in length. That would be around ninety one (91) feet tall. If you will notice, for some reason, the artist decided to make a very long nose on it. Not sure why either. This skeleton has gone on a tour to different parts of the world. There are many other views of this sculpture on the internet. Do a search with the words; "giant skeleton sculpture" without the quotes.

In the National Museum of Baghdad, there were ten to twelve foot axes on display there. These axes were used by these Nephilim and their descendants. Hopefully the war didn't destroy the artifacts there in that museum.

In this picture, you can get a perspective on just how large this ninety one foot giant was and what the Nephilim and their descendants were like many years ago. The skull alone is almost twice the height of the people standing near it.

As you can tell, they are tall hybrids. Now you can understand why in the Bible the scouts that were sent out to check out the Promised Land came back with the report they did.

I want to interject a word about the grapes the scouts brought back with them. There is evidence these grapes were genetically modified (GM) food. In my research, so far I am not able to find any types of large clusters of grapes they brought back.

Numbers 13:23; *When they reached the Valley of Eshcol, they cut off a branch bearing a single cluster of grapes. Two of them* *carried it on a pole between them, along with some pomegranates and figs.* (New International Version)

The tribes listed below were to be destroyed. They were actually Nephilim.

Deuteronomy 7:1-4;
1 When the LORD your God brings you into the land you are entering to possess and drives out before you many nations—the Hittites, Girgashites, Amorites, Canaanites, Perizzites, Hivites and Jebusites, seven nations larger and stronger than you—
2 and when the LORD your God has delivered them over to you and you have defeated them, then you must destroy them totally. Make no treaty with them, and show them no mercy.
3 Do not intermarry with them. Do not give your daughters to their sons or take their daughters for your sons,
4 for they will turn your children away from following me to serve other gods, and the LORD's anger will burn against you and will quickly destroy you. (New American Standard Bible)

God didn't want His people to marry these Nephilim. But in the end, there are those that believed they did and had families with them.

Ezra 9:1-2;
1 After these things had been done, the leaders came to me and said, "The people of Israel, including the priests and the Levites, have not kept themselves separate from the neighboring peoples with their detestable practices, like those of the Canaanites, Hittites, Perizzites, Jebusites, Ammonites, Moabites, Egyptians and Amorites.
2 They have taken some of their daughters as wives for themselves and their sons, and have mingled the holy race with the peoples around them. And the leaders and officials have led the way in this unfaithfulness." (New International Version)

God told Israel to destroy all of these people listed in that verse. Obviously they didn't. Eventually, the Israelites were marrying these Nephilim women. Later it would become possible for these children to become rulers of Israel; thus threatening the pure blood line of the coming Messiah, Jesus Christ. Keep in mind, not all Nephilim were giants either. It's believed the purpose of the flood was to destroy all the wickedness on the face of the earth. However, some of those Nephilim survived… or should I say the spirit of those Nephilim survived. More on this in another part of this book.

Here is where it says some of the Nephilim hybrids actually have six fingers and six toes. Although not in the Bible, it is believed they found some of them had two rows of teeth.

Numbers 13:32–33;
32 So they spread this bad report about the land among the Israelites: "The land we traveled through and explored will devour anyone who goes to live there. All the people we saw were huge.
33 We even saw giants there, the descendants of Anak. Next to them we felt like grasshoppers, and that's what they thought, too!" (New International Version)

1 Chronicles 20:6; *In another battle with the Philistines at Gath, they encountered a huge man with six fingers on each hand and six toes on each foot, twenty-four in all, who was also a descendant of the giants.* (New Living Translation)

2 Samuel 21:20; *In another battle with the Philistines at Gath, they encountered a huge man with six fingers on each hand and six toes on each foot, twenty-four in all, who was also a descendant of the giants.* ((New Living Translation))

How would you like to try and conqueror people that were at least one and a half times your height and weight; or maybe taller?

According to the book 'Judaism' by Arthur Hertzberg (1962), the wicked emperor Hadrian, boasted how he had conquered Jerusalem. He was shown a cave by Rabbi Johanan ben Zakkai. In that cave were the bones of Amorites who were buried in it. The Rabbi explained to the emperor, we defeated these Amorites when we were deserving of it. It's only because of our sin that God allowed you to defeat us. As you can see, these skeletons measure 18 cubits.

Because those Amorites were 18 cubits, they were between 25 to 37 foot tall. I would be more inclined to the 37 foot tall because that is why it's called a Hebrew cubit.

When we see the actual history of what actually happened, we understand what and why it happened the way it did. Maybe next time we read those verses, we will not be so quick to judge their actions. Would you go and fight someone like that?

Now let's look at another story; David and Goliath. In 1st Samuel 17:4, it states how tall Goliath was. In Hebrew cubit would be between twelve and thirteen feet tall. A span is about half a cubit.

1 Samuel 17:4; *And there came out from the camp of the Philistines a champion named Goliath of Gath, whose height was six cubits and a span.* (English Standard Version)

When all the mighty soldiers in Israel would not fight Goliath, here is this teenager who steps up to the plate and says I'll kill him. Remember, David was never tested in battle.

Weight of the Nephilim & Their Descendants

It's been estimated by some these Nephilim and their descendants would have weighted millions and millions of lbs. That didn't seem right to me. So I decided to do a BMI (Body Mass Index) of weight to height ratio. This will give you an idea how much they weighted in relation to their height. I believe these Nephilim could have easily been able to carry their own weight and much more. How? Because the angels were their fathers.

The first chart is the ranges of underweight and overweight.

BMI Range	Verdict
Less than 16	Highly Underweight
16 - 18.5	Underweight
18.5 - 25	Normal
25 - 30	Overweight
30 and above	Obese

I kept the BMI between 23 and 25. You will see the weight I entered and the height. Then it will calculate the BMI for me.

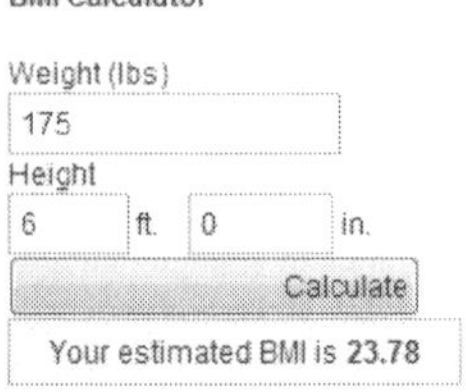

Let's place Goliath at 9' (ft) 6" tall and 12' tall. The two differences are the length of a cubit that it was measured by. Goliath probably weighted between 450 and 700 lbs.

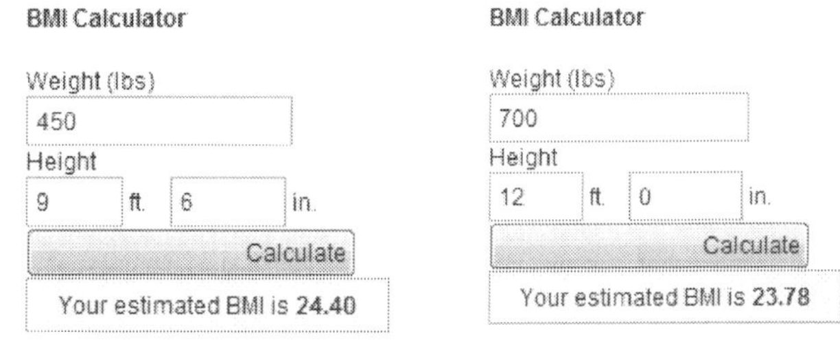

Let's look at King Og of Bashan. His bed was at least thirteen to eighteen feet long and six to eight feet wide. Let's pick his height at eighteen feet in length. King Og and his brother probably weighted about ¾ of a ton or 1,500 lbs.

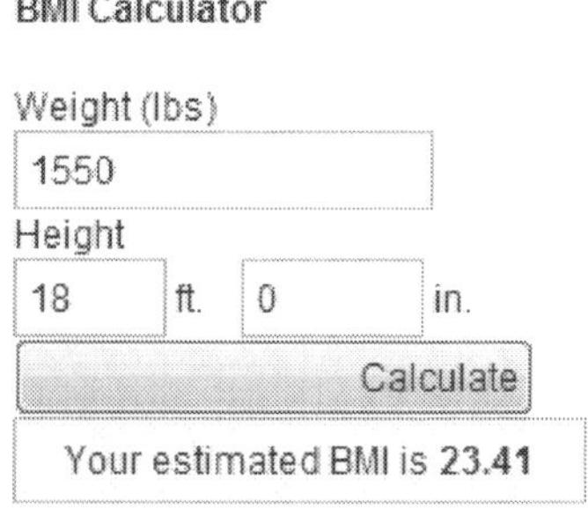

Now let's see how much a 30 ft Nephilim descendant would weigh.

BMI Calculator

Weight (lbs)
4300
Height
30 ft. 0 in.
Calculate
Your estimated BMI is **23.38**

Here is a 40 ft one.

BMI Calculator

Weight (lbs)
7600
Height
40 ft. 0 in.
Calculate
Your estimated BMI is **23.24**

The Bible talks about these Nephilim descendants being tall as cedars. Those cedars grew to be between 80 to 150 ft and more. I put below the 80 and the 150 ft. 80 ft would equal around 31,000 lbs. and 150 ft would equal around 110,000 lbs.

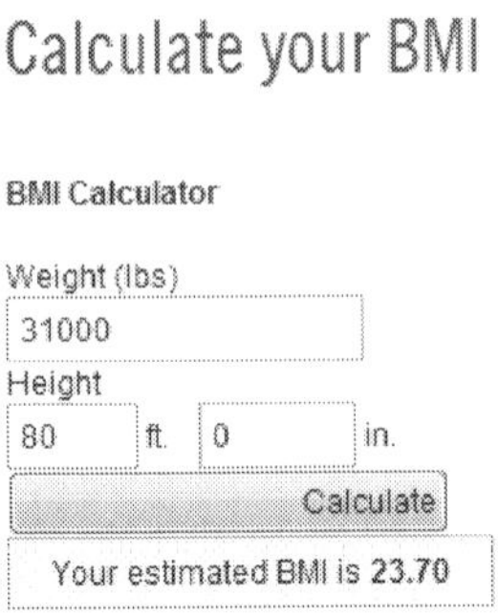

Calculate your BMI

BMI Calculator

Weight (lbs)
31000
Height
80 ft. 0 in.
Calculate
Your estimated BMI is 23.70

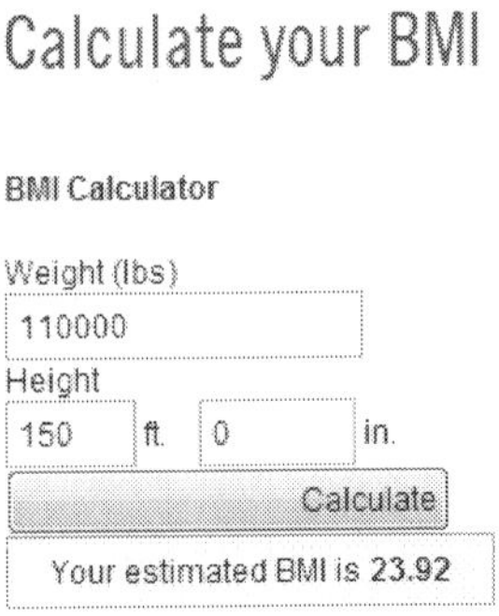

Calculate your BMI

BMI Calculator

Weight (lbs)
110000
Height
150 ft. 0 in.
Calculate
Your estimated BMI is 23.92

I will do two more comparisons. One Nephilim will be 450 ft (975,000 lbs) and the other will be 600 ft (1,700,000 lbs).

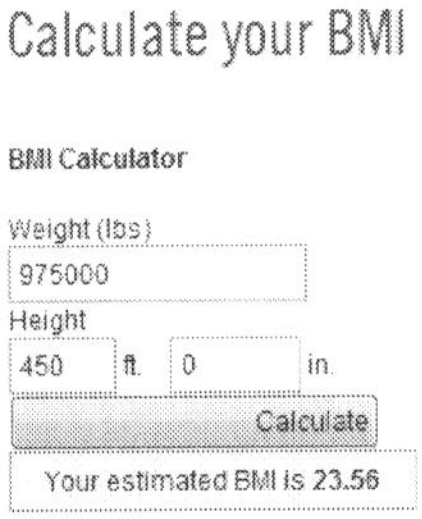

Calculate your BMI

BMI Calculator

Weight (lbs)
975000
Height
450 ft. 0 in.
Calculate
Your estimated BMI is 23.56

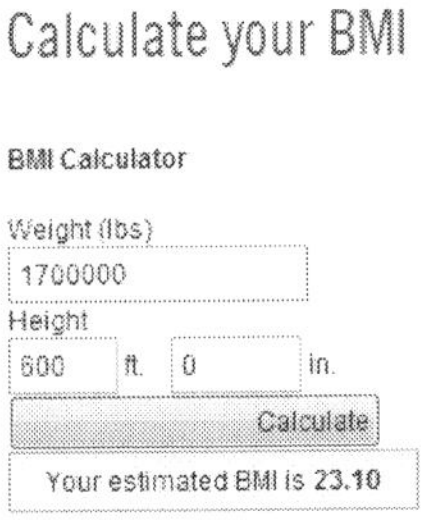

Calculate your BMI

BMI Calculator

Weight (lbs)
1700000
Height
600 ft. 0 in.
Calculate
Your estimated BMI is 23.10

(Source; BMI calculator; http://www.acefitness.org/acefit/healthy_living_tools_content.aspx?id=1)

Now I think you can see how these Nephilim could move around these huge, megalithic stones that man cannot move with modern day equipment. And add to that some of the angelic strength the angels had, you can now begin to understand how these megalithic structures were built.

This is the problem with the Egyptologist who has studied the pyramids and the other super structures in Egypt, for example. Some have spent a lifetime coming to certain conclusions. They conclude the Egyptians were smart enough to lay out these structures so perfectly. I don't believe anyone has come up with a viable plan that is reasonably accurate. This addresses how they were moved and put into place. The biggest challenge is moving, craving them out, removing them from the quarry, transporting them, and placing them on the site. Some of the best minds in the construction industry, from around the world, look at these structures and just humbly shake their heads. They don't have a clue how these were constructed. And quite frankly, I respect their admitting their lack of knowledge on the subject.

Nephilim / Giants Strength

Up to this point, with all of what the Bible says about the Nephilim and their descendants, there is one area I did not address yet. And that is their strength.

What is interesting is we pass onto our children certain qualities that we have within ourselves. And so did this union between the fallen angels and women. So what I'm going to cover right now is some information about angels that can describe how powerful they are in the physical sense. So with that in mind, you will begin to understand how they engineered, quarried, carried, and put into place these HUGE super structures.

Genesis 19:11; *Then they struck the men who were at the door of the house, young and old, with blindness so that they could not find the door.* (New International Version)

Psalm 103:20; B*less the LORD, you His angels, Mighty in strength, who perform His word, Obeying the voice oj His word!* (New American Standard Bible)

Psalm 104:4; *He makes the winds His messengers, Flaming fire His ministers.* (New American Standard Bible)

2 Chronicles 21:16; *David looked up and saw the angel of the LORD standing between heaven and earth, with a drawn sword in his hand extended over Jerusalem. Then David and the elders, clothed in sackcloth, fell facedown.* (New International Version)

2 Kings 19:35; *That night the angel of the LORD went out and put to death a hundred and eighty-five thousand in the Assyrian camp. When the people got up the next morning--there were all the dead bodies!* (New International Version)

Revelation 10:1; *Then I saw another mighty angel coming down from heaven. He was robed in a cloud, with a rainbow above his head; his face was like the sun, and his legs were like fiery pillars.* (New International Version)

Revelation 18:1; *After these things I saw another angel coming down from heaven, having great authority, and the earth was illumined with his glory.* (New American Standard Bible)

Revelation 18:21; *Then a mighty angel picked up a boulder the size of a large millstone and threw it into the sea, and said: "With such violence the great city of Babylon will be thrown down, never to be found again.* (New International Version)

Any soldier can understand what it would take for a man to kill 185,000 in one night. It really appears that these angels would have almost unlimited strength and focus.

Matthew 28:2-4;
2 There was a violent earthquake, for an angel of the Lord came down from heaven and, going to the tomb, rolled back the stone and sat on it.
3 His appearance was like lightning, and his clothes were white as snow.
4 The guards were so afraid of him that they shook and became like dead men. (New International Version)

One angel appeared on the scene. The guards saw the strength of what this one angel had as he rolled the stone away from the entrance of the tomb where the body of Jesus was laid. So what did the guards do? They just basically… fainted.

Acts 5:19; *But during the night an angel of the Lord opened the doors of the jail and brought them out.* (New International Version)

Acts 12:6-11;
6 On the very night when Herod was about to bring him forward, Peter was sleeping between two soldiers, bound with two chains, and guards in front of the door were watching over the prison.
7 And behold, an angel of the Lord suddenly appeared and a light shone in the cell; and he struck Peter's side and woke him up, saying, "Get up quickly." And his chains fell off his hands.
8 And the angel said to him, "Gird yourself and put on your sandals." And he did so. And he said to him, "Wrap your cloak around you and follow me."
9 And he went out and continued to follow, and he did not know that what was being done by the angel was real, but thought he was seeing a vision.
10 When they had passed the first and second guard, they came to the iron gate that leads into the city, which opened for them by itself; and they went out and went along one street, and immediately the angel departed from him.
11 When Peter came to himself, he said, "Now I know for sure that the Lord has sent forth His angel and rescued me from the hand of Herod and from all that the Jewish people were expecting." (New International Version)

This is fascinating. Here is Peter in jail going to be brought before King Herod. There are four squads of soldiers standing guard. There are two guards who are bound to Peter in his cell. The angel of the LORD struck Peter and woke him up. His chains fell off, and the angel led him out of the cell. All the while Peter is thinking he is seeing a vision or maybe just dreaming. Then he walks right by the first guard and then the second one. Then the gate to the city just opens up by itself, and he continues to walk right through it. The angel leaves and Peter notices this isn't a dream after all. This angel had the power to blind people's eyes to his and Peter's presence so they can just walk right past all those guards. Now are you starting to see what happened in Genesis 6 and what we are up against with all of these demonic angels? In the name of Jesus, we can defeat them!

2 Thessalonians 1:6-7;
6 God is just: He will pay back trouble to those who trouble you
7 and give relief to you who are troubled, and to us as well. This will happen when the Lord Jesus is revealed from heaven in blazing fire with his powerful angels. (New International Version)

2 Peter 2:11; *Angels, who have more strength and power than these teachers, don't bring an insulting judgment against them from the Lord.* (GOD'S WORD® Translation)

Revelation 5:2; *And I saw a mighty angel proclaiming in a loud voice, "Who is worthy to break the seals and open the scroll?"* (New International Version)

Now why did I include all these verses about angels? Because those fallen angels who rebelled against the LORD before we were born have the strength beyond what any of us will ever realize this side of heaven. We need to understand who they are and how they operate. Some of us say those words, but do we really understand how powerful the fallen ones of darkness are as they seem to destroy?

Some of the Nephilim were 450 foot tall according to the Book of Enoch. Then after the flood they were much smaller. The Nephilim descendants varied from twelve, eighteen, thirty to forty foot tall. As in the next verse in Amos, you see how some of them were between 80 and possibly up to 150 feet give or take.

Amos 2:9; "*But as my people watched, I destroyed the Amorites, though they were as tall as cedars and as strong as oaks. I destroyed the fruit on their branches and dug out their roots.* (New Living Translation)

Now you can get an idea how they can build these super structures. It appeared their height peeked out at maybe 200 foot in length after the flood. It would be nothing for them, with their muscle mass, to carry stone that was over 100,000 lbs and even beyond that weight. Maybe it would take two of them to handle a piece that is over 1,000,000 lbs.

It's been written the sound these Nephilim descendants made were fearful. Their eyes were so intimidating that hardly anyone could look into and fight them.

Some angels can be fearful to look upon or if you are touched by one. This is VERY Serious stuff.

Luke 2:9-10;
9 An angel of the Lord appeared to them, and the glory of the Lord shone around them, and they were terrified.
10 But the angel said to them, "Do not be afraid. I bring you good news that will cause great joy for all the people. (New International Version)

Judges 6:22-23;
22 When Gideon realized that it was the angel of the LORD, he exclaimed, "Alas, Sovereign LORD! I have seen the angel of the LORD face to face!"
23 But the LORD said to him, "Peace! Do not be afraid. You are not going to die." (New International Version)

Judges 12:6; *Then the woman came and told her husband, saying, "A man of God came to me and his appearance was like the appearance of the angel of God, very awesome. And I did not ask him where he came from, nor did he tell me his name.* (New American Standard Bible)

Daniel 8:15-17 & 27;
15 While I, Daniel, was watching the vision and trying to understand it, there before me stood one who looked like a man.
16 And I heard a man's voice from the Ulai calling, "Gabriel, tell this man the meaning of the vision."
17 As he came near the place where I was standing, I was terrified and fell prostrate. "Son of man,"

27 I, Daniel, was worn out. I lay exhausted for several days. Then I got up and went about the king's business. I was appalled by the vision; it was beyond understanding. (New International Version)

Here Daniel heard probably the voice of the living and true God from behind Gabriel (an angel), telling Gabriel to explain the vision to Daniel. As Gabriel approached Daniel, he's scared out of his mind, so to speak, and falls flat on his face before him. Then in verse twenty seven, he's telling us what he saw was so terrible, it took several days before he could come to grips with what he saw and was able to get back to his usual duties. That should make someone sit up and take notice of what is going to happen in the Tribulation period.

Luke 1:11-12;
11 Then an angel of the Lord appeared to him, standing at the right side of the altar of incense.
12 When Zechariah saw him, he was startled and was gripped with fear. (New International Version)

Acts 10:3-4;
3 One day at about three in the afternoon he had a vision. He distinctly saw an angel of God, who came to him and said, "Cornelius!"
4 Cornelius stared at him in fear. "What is it, Lord?" he asked. (New International Version)

Daniel 10:7-11;
7 I, Daniel, was the only one who saw the vision; those who were with me did not see it, but such terror overwhelmed them that they fled and hid themselves.
8 So I was left alone, gazing at this great vision; I had no strength left, my face turned deathly pale and I was helpless.
9 Then I heard him speaking, and as I listened to him, I fell into a deep sleep, my face to the ground.
10 A hand touched me and set me trembling on my hands and knees.
11 He said, "Daniel, you who are highly esteemed, consider carefully the words I am about to speak to you, and stand up, for I have now been sent to you." And when he said this to me, I stood up trembling. (New International Version)

The hand that touched Daniel is believed to be an angel of the LORD.

It's interesting that the LORD wanted all of the following people wiped out, completely eliminating them from Canaan. He commanded Israel to annihilate all the men, women, and children.

Deuteronomy 20:17; *Completely destroy them--the Hittites, Amorites, Canaanites, Perizzites, Hivites and Jebusites--as the LORD your God has commanded you.* (New International Version)

Why even the animals too? I'll cover that topic a little bit later.

1 Samuel 15:2-3;
2 This is what the LORD Almighty says: 'I will punish the Amalekites for what they did to Israel when they waylaid them as they came up from Egypt.
3 Now go, attack the Amalekites and totally destroy everything that belongs to them. Do not spare them; put to death men and women, children and infants, cattle and sheep, camels and donkeys.'" (New International Version)

This is interesting because in the above verse, I believe it is talking about destroying King Agag, a Nephilim. He fought Israel when they entered into the Promised Land from Egypt. Interestingly enough, one of the translations in verse 2 uses the word 'waylaid' instead of opposing or against.

When King Saul defeated King Agag, he didn't kill him, his people, and all of his cattle. This was the second time he disobeyed the LORD. As a result, He would take Saul's kingdom from him and eventually give it to David. Remember, the LORD allowed Saul to have a second chance when he didn't wait for Samuel to arrive and give him further instructions earlier.

While Saul had compassion for King Agag and also for his own men when they desperately needed meat, he didn't realize that following the LORD's commands were more important than showing compassion or feeding his men what he thought was good meat. Read 1 Samuel 15 to get a bit more understanding with what had happened.

What was not widely known and accepted during that time period was these people Saul just defeated were Nephilim. They had to be wiped out. Our Heavenly Father did not want them around on the earth to harass His people, Israel.

It's so important to understand and know that if we are called or felt the urge to do something for Him, it's so vitally important to carry it out. In some cases, when we don't, there is a price to pay for it down the road.

Joshua 13:13; *But the Israelites did not drive out the people of Geshur and Maacah, so they continue to live among the Israelites to this day.* (New International Version)

Geshur is believed to be up near the Golan Heights in northern Israel. Back in those days, it was considered to be in the Land of Bashan until Israel conquered it. Maacah or Abel Beth-maach is located further north than the Golan Heights. It's almost in the land of Syria.

Joshua 16:10; *However, they did not force out the Canaanites who lived in Gezer. So the Canaanites still live in Ephraim today, but they are required to do forced labor.* (GOD'S WORD® Translation)

Judges 1:27-36;

27 But Manasseh did not drive out the people of Beth Shan or Taanach or Dor or Ibleam or Megiddo and their surrounding settlements, for the Canaanites were determined to live in that land.

28 When Israel became strong, they pressed the Canaanites into forced labor but never drove them out completely.

29 Nor did Ephraim drive out the Canaanites living in Gezer, but the Canaanites continued to live there among them.

30 Neither did Zebulun drive out the Canaanites living in Kitron or Nahalol, so these Canaanites lived among them, but Zebulun did subject them to forced labor.

31 Nor did Asher drive out those living in Akko or Sidon or Ahlab or Akzib or Helbah or Aphek or Rehob.

32 The Asherites lived among the Canaanite inhabitants of the land because they did not drive them out.

33 Neither did Naphtali drive out those living in Beth Shemesh or Beth Anath; but the Naphtalites too lived among the Canaanite inhabitants of the land, and those living in Beth Shemesh and Beth Anath became forced laborers for them.
34 The Amorites confined the Danites to the hill country, not allowing them to come down into the plain.
35 And the Amorites were determined also to hold out in Mount Heres, Aijalon and Shaalbim, but when the power of the tribes of Joseph increased, they too were pressed into forced labor.
36 The boundary of the Amorites was from Scorpion Pass to Sela and beyond. (New International Version)

Joshua 11:22; *No Anakites were left in Israelite territory; only in Gaza, Gath and Ashdod did any survive.* (New Living Translation)

It appears, by the verses listed above, that Israel did not completely wipe out these Nephilim descendants as God commanded. As a result, the consequences of those actions will be felt for thousands of years. All of Israel's neighbors are still there around her like the Palestinian's, the Jordanians, etc. It's believed by some the United Nations changed the names of the Amalekites, who lived in Palestine, to the Palestinians years ago. The Ammonites are also believed to be Jordanians.

It's interesting where the location of these areas listed in Joshua 11:22 are on the map.

1. Gaza; Israel is on its western border, it's southern border is Egypt, and its western border is the Mediterranean Sea.
2. Gath; while there is considerable discussion as to the exact location of this place, it appears it might halfway between the Sea of Galilee and Bethlehem.
3. Ashdod; it appears to be west, slightly northwest, of Gath.

As you can imagine, as these people tried to eliminate Israel thousands of years ago, they are still continuing to do the same today. Why is that seemingly the case? Could it be because Israel wiped their ancestors out many centuries ago? Revenge possibly? The LORD did command His people Israel to wipe them out. But they didn't. The situation in and around Israel today, with all the fighting and unrest, is a result of them not obeying the above order. This appears to be the result. Interesting, isn't it, when we don't follow the commands of our Heavenly Father.

Were Some of the Pharisees Descendants of the Nephilim?

This question has been rattling around in my mind for quite a while. There were some verses in the New Testament that led me to think they were part of that lineage. When I was writing this book is when I realized that some of the Pharisees could have been Nephilim descendants.

I know the LORD God was always telling His people not to marry outside of their race just so they don't get them infected with the Nephilim descendant DNA in their bloodline. I believe you will find it interesting what God told them to do when Israel married outside of their race. Again, this is the Genesis 6 situation. Because churches and pastors haven't spoken out about this in the past for various reasons, we sometimes get a strange perspective of the stories in the Bible; why God did what He did, why He wanted things done a particular way, and when He wanted it done. God acted in love, so Jesus would go to the cross to redeem us. Once that is understood, the stories and the situations in the Bible take on a completely different meaning.

Remember when I mentioned that most of those who were descendants of the Nephilim had either the "ities" or "ians" after their names? When you see the names below, you can see the bigger picture. Remember when Noah cursed Canaan after the incident when he was drunk and was naked? The Canaanites were the first one listed.

Ezra 9:1-2;

1 After these things had been done, the leaders came to me and said, "The people of Israel, including the priests and Levites, have failed to keep themselves separate from the neighboring groups of people and from the disgusting practices of the

Canaanites, Hittites, Perizzites, Jebusites, Ammonites, Moabites, Egyptians, and Amorites.
2 The Israelites and their sons have married some of these foreign women. They have mixed our holy race with the neighboring groups of people. Furthermore, the leaders and officials have led the way in being unfaithful." (GOD'S WORD® Translation)

Ezra 10:1-4;
1 While Ezra was praying, confessing [these sins], crying, and throwing himself down in front of God's temple, a large crowd of Israelite men, women, and children gathered around him. They also began to cry bitterly.
2 Then Shecaniah, son of Jehiel, one of the descendants of Elam, interrupted by saying to Ezra, "We have been unfaithful to our God by marrying foreign women who came from the people around us. However, there is still hope for Israel.
3 So we must now make a promise to our God to get rid of all foreign women and the children born from them, as my lord [Ezra] and the others who tremble at the commandments of our God have advised us to do. We must do what Moses' Teachings tell us.
4 Get up! It's your duty to take action. We are with you, so be strong and take action." (GOD'S WORD® Translation)

Because of the threat of possibly corrupting the seed of the coming Messiah, Jesus, they decided to get rid of them.

Ezra 10:9-12;
9 Then all the men of Judah and Benjamin gathered within three days in Jerusalem. On the twentieth day of the ninth month, all the people sat in the courtyard of God's temple. They were trembling because of this matter and shivering because of the heavy rain.
10 Ezra the priest stood up and said to them, "You have been unfaithful by marrying foreign women, and now you have added to Israel's guilt.
11 Confess to the LORD God of your ancestors what you have done, and do what he wants. Separate yourselves from the people of this land and from your foreign wives."

12 Then the whole assembly shouted in reply, "Yes! We will do as you say. (GOD'S WORD® Translation)

Now you can begin to wonder about all the wives Solomon had. Were some of them descendant of the Nephilim? It is mentioned in different parts of the Old Testament the men inter-married with other races during times when they were not warring against them.

Here is a bit more history about these "foreign" women as mentioned above in Ezra. It is believed they were Samaritans who lived in the lower parts of Syria. Some of these Samaritans migrated south into northern Israel.

When the Assyrian army came and took the northern 10 tribes away into captivity, some of the Israelite men were left behind. Eventually, they married these Samaritan women who were in the land. These women influenced their husbands to worship their false gods. Keep in mind these Samaritan women were believed to be the descendant of the Nephilim. Now when you hear the names of Samaritan or Sumerian, you will get an understanding of whom they were. So that is why God told them to get rid of these foreign (Samaritan) women. They were known to be witches. The witch of Endor, however, was considered to be a Canaanite woman who might have been from that same area of Iraq. However, details are a little sketchy as to the exact location when Saul met that witch of Endor.

Some ancient information suggests that the LORD God did NOT accept the offerings from those who were inbred with these Samaritan or Sumerian women. Then that started a hatred towards the Jewish religious leaders… Pharisees, Sadducees, the Sanhedrin and the Scribes. They really spoke up against them even more. These descendants that came from the Jews and the Sumerian women were to be considered exiled and not accepted within Israel.

There is information which seems to reveal that Nazareth in Samaria was a hot bed of iniquity and nothing really good came out of it. Hence why Nathanael said the following when Philip came to him stating he found the Messiah Moses wrote about.

John 1:44-46;

44 Philip, like Andrew and Peter, was from the town of Bethsaida.
45 Philip found Nathanael and told him, "We have found the one Moses wrote about in the Law, and about whom the prophets also wrote—Jesus of Nazareth, the son of Joseph."
46 "Nazareth! Can anything good come from there?" Nathanael asked. (New International Version)

Wild isn't it? Kind of paints a picture as to what they meant when they said things like the above. Here is the time when Jesus was going through Samaria and meets a Samarian woman by the well. Now that we have a better understanding of what the Samarian situation is like, this passage takes on a slightly different meaning.

John 4:1-26 & 39-42
1 Now Jesus learned that the Pharisees had heard that he was gaining and baptizing more disciples than John—
2 although in fact it was not Jesus who baptized, but his disciples.
3 So he left Judea and went back once more to Galilee.
4 Now he had to go through Samaria.
5 So he came to a town in Samaria called Sychar, near the plot of ground Jacob had given to his son Joseph.
6 Jacob's well was there, and Jesus, tired as he was from the journey, sat down by the well. It was about noon.
7 When a Samaritan woman came to draw water, Jesus said to her, "Will you give me a drink?"
8 (His disciples had gone into the town to buy food.)
9 The Samaritan woman said to him, "You are a Jew and I am a Samaritan woman. How can you ask me for a drink?" (For Jews do not associate with Samaritans.)
10 Jesus answered her, "If you knew the gift of God and who it is that asks you for a drink, you would have asked him and he would have given you living water."
11 "Sir," the woman said, "you have nothing to draw with and the well is deep. Where can you get this living water?

12 Are you greater than our father Jacob, who gave us the well and drank from it himself, as did also his sons and his livestock?"
13 Jesus answered, "Everyone who drinks this water will be thirsty again,
14 but whoever drinks the water I give them will never thirst. Indeed, the water I give them will become in them a spring of water welling up to eternal life."
15 The woman said to him, "Sir, give me this water so that I won't get thirsty and have to keep coming here to draw water."
16 He told her, "Go, call your husband and come back."
17 "I have no husband," she replied. Jesus said to her, "You are right when you say you have no husband.
18 The fact is, you have had five husbands, and the man you now have is not your husband. What you have just said is quite true."
19 "Sir," the woman said, "I can see that you are a prophet.
20 Our ancestors worshiped on this mountain, but you Jews claim that the place where we must worship is in Jerusalem."
21 "Woman," Jesus replied, "believe me, a time is coming when you will worship the Father neither on this mountain nor in Jerusalem.
22 You Samaritans worship what you do not know; we worship what we do know, for salvation is from the Jews.
23 Yet a time is coming and has now come when the true worshipers will worship the Father in the Spirit and in truth, for they are the kind of worshipers the Father seeks.
24 God is spirit, and his worshipers must worship in the Spirit and in truth."
25 The woman said, "I know that Messiah" (called Christ) "is coming. When he comes, he will explain everything to us."
26 Then Jesus declared, "I, the one speaking to you—I am he."

39 Many of the Samaritans from that town believed in him because of the woman's testimony, "He told me everything I ever did."
40 So when the Samaritans came to him, they urged him to stay with them, and he stayed two days.
41 And because of his words many more became believers.

42 They said to the woman, "We no longer believe just because of what you said; now we have heard for ourselves, and we know that this man really is the Savior of the world." (New International Version)

What is interesting is despite the rift between the Samaritans and the other Jews, Jesus saw them as His people. Now look at this next passage with the Canaanite woman. Remember when I mentioned not all of the "ite" or "ines" were from the descendant of the Nephilim? This woman appears not to be one of them. And it appears she talked the LORD Jesus into helping her! When we are persistent, the LORD hears our crying out and reasoning!

Matthew 15:21-28;
21 Leaving that place, Jesus withdrew to the region of Tyre and Sidon.
22 A Canaanite woman from that vicinity came to him, crying out, "Lord, Son of David, have mercy on me! My daughter is demon-possessed and suffering terribly."
23 Jesus did not answer a word. So his disciples came to him and urged him, "Send her away, for she keeps crying out after us."
24 He answered, "I was sent only to the lost sheep of Israel."
25 The woman came and knelt before him. "Lord, help me!" she said.
26 He replied, "It is not right to take the children's bread and toss it to the dogs."
27 "Yes it is, Lord," she said. "Even the dogs eat the crumbs that fall from their master's table."
28 Then Jesus said to her, "Woman, you have great faith! Your request is granted." And her daughter was healed at that moment. (New International Version)

There are some texts that mention the father of Joseph and Mary were from Nazareth in Samaria -hence why the Jews asked Jesus the question in the verse below. They thought he was a Sumerian and possibly the son of a witch.

John 8:48; *The Jews answered him, "Aren't we right in saying that you are a Samaritan and demon-possessed?"* (New International Version)

Now back to the Pharisees... What does this have to do with some of the Pharisee's possibly being the descendant of the Nephilim? Here in this next passage are some verses for you to ponder.

John 8:39-45
38 I am telling you what I have seen in the Father's presence, and you are doing what you have heard from your father. "
39 "Abraham is our father," they answered. "If you were Abraham's children," said Jesus, "then you would do what Abraham did.
40 As it is, you are looking for a way to kill me, a man who has told you the truth that I heard from God. Abraham did not do such things.
41 You are doing the works of your own father." "We are not illegitimate children," they protested. "The only Father we have is God himself."
42 Jesus said to them, "If God were your Father, you would love me, for I have come here from God. I have not come on my own; God sent me.
43 Why is my language not clear to you? Because you are unable to hear what I say.
44 You belong to your father, the devil, and you want to carry out your father's desires. He was a murderer from the beginning, not holding to the truth, for there is no truth in him. When he lies, he speaks his native language, for he is a liar and the father of lies.
45 Yet because I tell the truth, you do not believe me! (New International Version)

As many times as I have read this passage, it never dawned on me (until now) these Jews were defending themselves against what Jesus was telling them. Was Jesus telling them they were of their father the devil? That they were part of the serpent seed line? That would be the descendants of the Nephilim. Some of their bloodlines were corrupted. That is evident because the

Roman army was battling the Nephilim descendants almost right up to the birth of Jesus.

Matthew 3:7; *But when he saw many of the Pharisees and Sadducees coming to where he was baptizing, he said to them: "You brood of vipers! Who warned you to flee from the coming wrath?* (New International Version)

What is interesting is this. John the Baptist was baptizing people in the Jordan River. Then these religious leaders came by when he was baptizing people. When John saw them coming, he said the above. Here is what that word "vipers" means in the Greek. According to the Strongs Concordance it is; 2191: properly, a poisonous snake; (figuratively) incisive words that deliver *deadly venom*, with the use of blasphemy. This *switches* the bitter for the sweet, light for darkness, etc. 2191/*exidna* ("viper") then suggests the venomous desire to *reverse* what is *true* for what is *false*.

Back in those days and centuries before that actually, it was considered very, VERY rude to call someone a viper due to the meaning behind it. So to be calling the religious leaders a viper that uses blasphemous words is a very serious situation. As it appears, John did not back down from that either. It is widely known that the descendants of the Nephilim and their disembodied spirits had made regular use of blasphemies against the LORD our God. Below is another verse that tells us what John said to them.

Luke 3:7; *John said to the crowds coming out to be baptized by him, "You brood of vipers! Who warned you to flee from the coming wrath?* (New International Version)

It appears Jesus agreed with John. While Jesus was teaching, the Pharisees got involved with the conversation. The subject of blasphemy and the Holy Spirit came up. That's when Jesus basically let those Pharisees have it as you can tell in the verses below.

Matthew 12:34;

You brood of vipers, how can you who are evil say anything good? For the mouth speaks what the heart is full of. (New International Version)

Matthew 23:33;
"You snakes! You brood of vipers! How will you escape being condemned to hell? (New International Version)

If you notice what Jesus said here, how will you escape being condemned to hell? As if they are already condemned. The fallen angels and the Nephilim spirits are already condemned. I believe that is what Jesus is referring to there.

So is there the possibility of the descendants that the Nephilim had a presence in the religious leadership of that day? It apparently seems so…

Did the Romans Battle the Nephilim Descendants?

For you history buffs, the Romans had actually engaged these Nephilim many times. One battle began around 400 B.C. The tribe was called the Senones, thought to be part of the Celtics civilization at one time. They were thought to be the same size as Goliath, who was between nine and a half to eleven feet tall.

Sometime around 390 B.C., these Nephilim descendants engaged the Roman army at the Battle of AT, soundly defeating some twenty four thousand (24,000) soldiers by outflanking them and pushed on to Rome, capturing and conquering it. Some texts state Rome was burned. They got these Nephilim descendants to leave by supposedly giving them one thousand pounds of gold.

In the Battle of Noreia in 113 B.C., four Roman armies engaged some three hundred thousand Cimbri and Teutone warriors, which were Nephilim descendants. The Roman armies were wiped out.

In 109 B. C, the Cimbri, Teutones, and Ambrones suddenly reappeared in Roman-occupied Provence. To check them, the

Senate sent an army out under the consul Silanus. The giants practically destroyed it while a few survivors escaped.

The Rhone River Battle in 105 B.C. two Roman armies engaged these Nephilim descendants. Of the two Roman armies, only ten soldiers and two generals escaped.

Ænotherus In his Annals of Bavaria, Aventine writes that a giant named Ænotherus, who threw down whole battalions like mowing grass, fought on the Emperor Charlemagne's side. The huge warrior hailed from Turgan, near the Lake of Constance.

Pusio and Secundilla. Caesar Augustus (27 B.C.-A.D. 14) assigned two giants who were over ten feet tall to lead the Roman armies into battle. The bodies of these two giants were preserved in a tomb, in Sallust's Gardens; their names were Pusio and Secundilla."

Battle of Telamon - This battle in 225 B.C., Roman troops caught seventy thousand invading Celts between their two armies. Forty thousand of the giant warriors were killed from across the Apennines. They captured another ten thousand.

In Morocco, a complete arsenal of hunting weapons including five hundred double-edged axes weighing seventeen and a half pounds, which were twenty times as heavy as would be convenient for modern man. To handle the axe at all one would need to have hands of a size appropriate to a giant with a stature of at least thirteen feet.

(Sources; http://en.wikipedia.org/wiki/Senones;
http://www.britannica.com/EBchecked/topic/534663/Senones;
http://www.freerepublic.com/focus/fr/830123/posts;
http://www.bibliotecapleyades.net/gigantes/WEurope3.html;

Roman Emperor Maximinus, the one who is thought to have defeated the offspring of the Nephilim was supposed to be over eight feet tall. (Source; The Complete Chronicle of the Emperors of Rome (Volume 1)

Why Don't We See More Nephilim Descendants' Bones?

Why is it that we don't see the bones of these people? They have dotted our landscape for thousands of years. Why the cover-up of these descendants' bones? Why do the government and its entities come and remove these bones when they are discovered? These bones are rarely seen in public.

Here are some thoughts to consider.

1. Because this proves the Darwinian Theory is false. And why don't they want to disprove this theory? It would prove the Bible is true, and the Darwinian Theory is utterly wrong.
2. There is reason to believe some who are in power have been and are continuing the funding of genetic engineering to reactivate the DNA from ancient people like King Ramses or possibly Nimrod. The question is how might they be able to do this. By using the DNA from the bones of Ramses. Think that is too farfetched? What do you think the movie Jurassic Park was all about? For you Star Trek® fans of the original series, remember Space Seed? How all those genetically engineered leaders on earth came to power and ruled? When they were defeated, they escaped in a space ship called the Botany Bay. Then some two hundred years later, the Enterprise picked them up. Khan was their leader. In that episode, Khan boasted he had five times the strength of Captain Kirk!
3. How about Minority Report? In that movie, there are people who can predict when a crime (called PreCrime) is going to happen and send people there to stop it before it happens.
4. Here is some more evidence for your consideration. Why do you think all of this cloning of animals is taking place? Why are they mixing breeds to see if they can make another type of animal?
5. Here is another point to consider. Remember the research projects and movies that portray people ceasing to get older. If we can reprogram this gene or these sets of genes, you will live a longer and healthy life. Doesn't that sound great?
6. They now believe they have found the gene in the DNA that controls your weight. Another that can control your height, your hair color, etc. Sounds wonderful doesn't it?

While it does sound interesting, we are not supposed to be doing these things. Again, this is all pointing back to the days of Noah and Genesis 6. These fallen angels had taught man how to change these things in the LORD's creation that are not to be tampered with. Starting to see the picture now? The LORD our God made us and everything else in a particular way. He knows what is best as He tells us in the verse below.

Isaiah 55:8-9;
8 *"My thoughts are nothing like your thoughts," says the LORD.*
"And my ways are far beyond anything you could imagine.
9 *For just as the heavens are higher than the earth, so my ways are higher than your ways and my thoughts higher than your thoughts.* (New Living Translation)

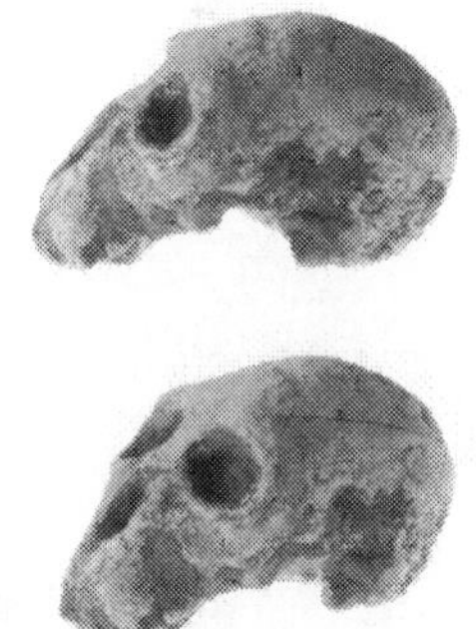

These giant bones still exist throughout the whole world. How about cone heads? A certain late night comedy show had done skits about these cone heads in the past, many times again and again. They sometimes made it sound as they were from outer space, and other times like they were royalty. There are many of these heads that are shaped like a cone in the ancient world. You can find them in South America. There is reason to believe that these skeletal heads come from the Egyptian Pharaohs. They possibly could be Nephilim. Remember, not all the Nephilim were giants. This is important to note.

What I find interesting is I'm told there are many anthropologists in America (people who study humankind) who will not talk about these oddly shaped skulls or the skeletons of these huge giants, despite the evidence that is before them. Why is that? Are they really searching for the truth about what they are finding and yielding to their common sense that these giants did exist? Are they finding/discoveries and making the conscious choice to reveal evidence that only fits the Darwinian Theory? Are they not willing to consider evidence which states they are in error? What does that mean? Let's look at the picture below. Notice "supposedly" the progression of man.

The powers of darkness are trying to deceive us into believing a lie, into believing half-truths that they slant into a falsehood. They have been lying to us ever since the Garden of Eden. It started with the following verse. There are so many lies, so much deception, and questioning throughout history that it brings confusion into our lives.

Genesis 3:4-5;
4 "You will not certainly die," the serpent said to the woman.
5 "For God knows that when you eat from it your eyes will be opened, and you will be like God, knowing good and evil." (New International Version)

Adam and Eve were already like the LORD. Just when your friends or co-workers might look at your children and say; "Wow, you look just like your mom." Or "you're a spitting image of your dad."

I remember when I was watching the news on a Christian channel. I couldn't believe what my eyes were seeing, and my ears were hearing. What's going on here? I just couldn't believe I was watching the news that the other 'worldly' news was spewing out, chuck-full of negativity and deception.

I remember hearing about and seeing old newspapers where they were covering positive events. If a church service had a revival taking place, it was in the newspaper. If a revival was going on in the area, it would be covered. It would mention how many people professed their faith in the Messiah. How many people walked down the aisle rededicating their life to Jesus. If a service had healings, it would be in the newspaper.

Nephilim and Their Control in our World Today

It is believed satan is going to do the same thing in the end time as he did in the Garden of Eden. He will use the same smooth talking words at the end as he did in the beginning. He will question you about what you believe, what is right in front of you and twist it ever so slightly and slowly until you are not sure what to believe. He will give those smooth reasonings as to what you think you see and what is actually there.

Everything that is evil does not mean it was caused by or comes from these Nephilim descendants. Keep in mind, governments don't lie. The people who run the government can and sometimes do lie. Corporations don't lie. It is the officers and the employees who can and sometimes do lie. They, at times, just simply don't reveal or just simply hide the truth. This has been going on for hundreds, or thousands of years. Our country is no different. Look at all the Freemasons and Illuminati symbols in our government buildings. Then you have Skull and Bones and the Bilderberg Group. It's all about power and making the way possible so satan can sit on the throne in Israel and be worshipped as god.

A mentor of mine made a statement which I remember so very clearly today. I didn't understand it at the time. It actually took almost nine years until I began to realize what the following means.

There is no difference between Communism and Democracy.

He was great at giving me these one-liners. It made me think. I thought so long and hard on the above from time to time. But then about nine years later that Ah… Ahhhh… moment came. Then it made sense. I added to that; Fascism, Socialism, Corporatism, and Islamism.

But the bottom line is this is an Ephesians 6 battle.

Ephesians 6:12; *This is not a wrestling match against a human opponent. We are wrestling with rulers, authorities, the powers who govern this world of darkness, and spiritual forces that control evil in the heavenly world.* (GOD'S WORD® Translation)

Whom are we wrestling with? It's satan, the fallen angels and the spirit of the Nephilim who are still here today.

2 Corinthians 4:4; *Satan, who is the god of this world, has blinded the minds of those who don't believe. They are unable to see the glorious light of the Good News. They don't understand this message about the glory of Christ, who is the exact likeness of God.* (New Living Translation)

The very concept of Communism is a rebellion against the LORD. It takes away the freedom that each and every person on this earth should have. The millions upon millions upon millions of Christians who have been tortured and murdered is a complete rebellion against Him who made them, who created them.

They stir up hate between one another. It could be between the Left (Liberals) and the Right (Conservatives). They love to divert our attention away from the real answers. The truth, the real truth that will set everyone free.

2 Corinthians 3:17; *Now the Lord is the Spirit, and where the Spirit of the Lord is, there is freedom.* (New International Version)

When people are fighting against one another, they sometimes don't see the truth. They try to hold onto a belief and might take it to the grave without noticing what has been gained and what has been lost. The importance of being right all the time permeates them to the point where they are not teachable to a better way. It doesn't enter into their thoughts that they may not be correct in their conclusions.

Maybe they are not open-minded enough to see if there is a better way, a higher plane of thought, or a more profound way to look and view the situation and solution.

The talk shows stir up controversy between both sides. It's their attempt to keep both sides off-balanced and their attention diverted from the real issue and solution. One talks about what is wrong from their viewpoint and the other side does the same. They debate about it. And what happens? Nothing new happens. Neither side budges from their position. In the end, nothing is solved, and usually nothing is gained. Time was wasted and again our attention is diverted away from solving the issues, rather than just sitting around and giving their opinions. This happens over and over and yet over again. Do you think we would have caught on by now? Nope. Those who are in agreement with their viewpoint feel good for a little while because someone is speaking what's on their mind. But does it get solved? Not at all. At times, each side spins the results and claims a victory. Then maybe the media spins it one particular way so as to influence people to lean to the other side. The media bombards you with their propaganda, and sometimes try to sway you when you don't have answers.

Then there is the disinformation they pass around. Most people think whatever they see on TV, read in the newspaper or read on their website, hear on the radio must be true and should be followed. Yet that information is slanted too. If that is true and correct, why bother watching it? Why bother reading or listening to it on radio? Here is an example. There are articles on how to live a longer life by taking this or using that. Then a month or two later, an article is published or appears on TV on if they take what was suggested before, it might harm you. They keep on doing this over and over again. What happens then is people do not know what to do and they wind up doing nothing.

These attacks against the LORD's people are nothing new. It's been going on for thousands of years. It's been happening before our precious Jesus walked on this earth over two thousand years ago.

The powers that be want to eliminate most of the population. satan's plan is much grander. He wants us to end up in the Lake of Fire with him and the other fallen angels and their offspring, the Nephilim along with their descendants.

Revelation 21:8; *But the cowardly, the unbelieving, the vile, the murderers, the sexually immoral, those who practice magic arts, the idolaters and all liars--their place will be in the fiery lake of burning sulfur. This is the second death."* (New International Version)

They stir up race riots. They fan the flames of hatred. They find some little crack in a situation that maybe they can turn a molehill into a mountain. Then they talk about it and really remind people what happened in the past. When will this end? You would have figured we grew beyond race hatred. Next is all the 'phobic's' they are creating. But you won't hear the phrase

Christa-phobic or Jew-phobic. Oh no… That's because the powers of darkness hate anything of, by, with, or that which pertains to the Most High the LORD. Yet at the mention of His name, the devils tremble.

James 2:19; *You believe that there is one God. That's fine! Even the demons believe that and tremble with fear.* (International Standard Version)

Matthew 8:29; *"What do you want with us, Son of God?" they shouted. "Have you come here to torture us before the appointed time?"* (New International Version)

In this next passage, ask the Holy Spirit to reveal the truth about what is being said here. To add to that, there was almost a fist fight at the end of it.

1 Kings 22:19-25;
19 Micaiah added, "Then hear the word of the LORD. I saw the LORD sitting on his throne, and the entire army of heaven was standing near him on his right and his left.
20 The LORD asked, 'Who will deceive Ahab so that he will attack and be killed at Ramoth in Gilead?' Some answered one way, while others said something else.
21 "Then the Spirit stepped forward, stood in front of the LORD, and said, 'I will deceive him.' " 'How?' the LORD asked.
22 "The Spirit answered, 'I will go out and be a spirit that tells lies through the mouths of all of Ahab's prophets.' "The LORD said, 'You will succeed in deceiving him. Go and do it.'
23 "So, the LORD has put into the mouths of all these prophets of yours a spirit that makes them tell lies. The LORD has spoken evil about you."
24 Then Zedekiah, son of Chenaanah, went to Micaiah and struck him on the cheek. "How did the LORD's Spirit leave me to talk to you?" he asked.
25 Micaiah answered, "You will find out on the day you go into an inner room to hide." (GOD'S WORD® Translation)

Woooo… isn't that fascinating. Zedekiah either slapped Micaiah on the cheek or hauled off and hit him with his fist because he was angry. As to that first part of this passage, I'll let the Spirit of God teach you about it. You may wish to read it slowly a couple of times. You should walk away with what I call a healthy fear of the LORD.

After King Ahab died, his son Ahaziah became King in Samaria for two years. He was just as evil as his father.

1 Kings 22:51-53;

51 Ahaziah, son of Ahab, became king of Israel in Samaria during Jehoshaphat's seventeenth year as king of Judah. Ahaziah ruled Israel for two years.
52 He did what the LORD considered evil. He followed the example of his father and mother and of Jeroboam (Nebat's son) who led Israel to sin.
53 Ahaziah served Baal, worshiped him, and made the LORD God of Israel furious, as his father had done. (GOD'S WORD® Translation)

The Difference Between demons and the fallen angels

Many people wonder what the difference is between a demon and a fallen angel. While most people believe they are one and the same, they can actually be quite different.

This topic again will take us back to Genesis 6. As you are beginning to see and understand, the first part of that chapter holds the answers to so many questions. So let's take a look at this passage of texts.

Enoch 15:6-12:
6 "Indeed you, formerly you were spiritual, having eternal life; and immortal in all the generations of the world."
7 "That is why formerly I did not make wives for you, for the dwelling of the spiritual beings of heaven is heaven.'"
8 "But now the giants who are born from the union of the spirits and the flesh shall be called evil spirits upon the earth, because their dwelling shall be upon the earth and inside the earth."
9 "Evil spirits have come out of their bodies. Because from the day that they were created from the kodesh ones they became the

Watchers; their first origin is the spiritual foundation. They will become evil upon the earth and shall be called evil spirits."
10 "The dwelling of the spiritual beings of heaven is heaven; but the dwelling of the spirits of the earth, which are born upon the earth, is in the earth."
11 "The spirits of the giants oppress each other; they will corrupt, fall, be excited, and fall upon the earth, and cause sorrow. They eat no food, nor become thirsty, nor find obstacles."
12 "And these spirits shall rise up against the children of the people and against the women, because they have proceeded forth from them."

As you have just read, it appears that because of this unholy union between the fallen angels and woman, a hybrid race was created and lived contrary to God's plan. With the birth of these giants and eventual death of their bodies, their spirit that was within them has nowhere to go but roam the earth. So now you know where the term 'evil spirits' had come from. They actually roam the earth. They want a body to possess, to inhabit. They try to create terror, hardship, and sorrow on the human race. Now when you hear the following term or terms from time to time (and there are many more of them), you will have a different understanding of them now;

1. He or she has an evil spirit.
2. He or she has a demon.
3. He or she is possessed.

Now the fallen angels can inhabit people too. Well there is a reference to one such fallen angel who did so.

John 13:27; *As soon as Judas took the bread, Satan entered into him. So Jesus told him, "What you are about to do, do quickly."* (New International Version)

Now what satan did with his body while he was in Judas is a mystery. Now whether other of the fallen angels can do this is unknown at this time.

In Jasher chapter 4, these Nephilim were raising havoc all over the land so the LORD would be provoked by what they did.

Jasher Chapter 4:16-18:
16 And all the sons of men departed from the ways of the Lord in those days as they multiplied upon the face of the earth with sons and daughters, and they taught one another their evil practices and they continued sinning against the Lord.
17 And every man made unto himself a god, and they robbed and plundered every man his neighbor as well as his relative, and they corrupted the earth, and the earth was filled with violence.
18 And their judges and rulers went to the daughters of men and took their wives by force from their husbands according to their choice, and the sons of men in those days took from the cattle of the earth, the beasts of the field and the fowls of the air, and taught the mixture of animals of one species with the other, in order therewith to provoke the Lord; and God saw the whole earth and it was corrupt, for all flesh had corrupted its ways upon earth, all men and all animals.

Jubilee 10:1-14:
1 And in the third week of this jubilee the unclean demons began to lead astray the children of
2 the sons of Noah, and to make to err and destroy them. And the sons of Noah came to Noah their father, and they told him concerning the demons which were leading astray and blinding and
3 slaying his sons' sons. And he prayed before the Lord his God, and said: 'God of the spirits of all flesh, who hast shown mercy unto me And hast saved me and my sons from the waters of the flood, And hast not caused me to perish as Thou didst the sons of perdition; For Thy grace has been great towards me, And great has been Thy mercy to my soul; Let Thy grace be lift up upon my sons, And let not wicked spirits rule over them Lest they should destroy them from the earth.
4 But do Thou bless me and my sons, that we may increase and Multiply and replenish the earth.
5 And Thou knowest how Thy Watchers, the fathers of these spirits, acted in my day: and as for these spirits which are living,

imprison them and hold them fast in the place of condemnation,
and let them not bring destruction on the sons of thy servant, my
God; for these are malignant, and
6 created in order to destroy. And let them not rule over the
spirits of the living; for Thou alone canst exercise dominion over
them. And let them not have power over the sons of the
righteous
7 ,8 from henceforth and for evermore.' And the Lord our God
bade us to bind all. And the chief of the spirits, Mastema, came
and said: 'Lord, Creator, let some of them remain before me, and
let them harken to my voice, and do all that I shall say unto
them; for if some of them are not left to me, I shall not be able to
execute the power of my will on the sons of men; for these are
for corruption and leading astray before my judgment, for great
is the wickedness of the sons of men.'
9 And He said: Let the tenth part of them remain before him, and
let nine parts descend into the
10 place of condemnation.' And one of us He commanded that
we should teach Noah all their
11 medicines; for He knew that they would not walk in
uprightness, nor strive in righteousness. And we did according to
all His words: all the malignant evil ones we bound in the place
of condemna-
12 tion and a tenth part of them we left that they might be subject
before Satan on the earth. And we explained to Noah all the
medicines of their diseases, together with their seductions, how
he
13 might heal them with herbs of the earth. And Noah wrote
down all things in a book as we instructed him concerning every
kind of medicine. Thus the evil spirits were precluded from
14 (hurting) the sons of Noah. And he gave all that he had
written to Shem, his eldest son; for he

It said; 'and the sons of men in those days took from the cattle of the earth, the beasts of the field and the fowls of the air, and taught the mixture of animals of one species with the other, in order therewith to provoke the LORD.' This is what demons do. It's an attack against the LORD God.

I find this an interesting passage of text in Jubilees. Here are the sons of Noah coming to their father and asking for help because the demon spirits are leading astray, blinding, and slaying his sons' sons. So that would make them Noah's grandchildren. So what does Noah do when he hears this information? What any godly father would do. He prays and talks with the LORD God about this situation. In that prayer, in that conversation with God, he humbly acknowledges to God that the Watcher angels were here on the earth and what they and their descendant had done. He actually acknowledges they were separate, meaning one was the fallen angels, and the other were these evil spirits.

When you read that text, you begin to realize this is what's causing all the temptation among mankind today. These disembodied spirits of these Nephilim giants (demons) are tempting mankind to wander away from the LORD. All the sorrow, pain, suffering are mainly caused by what they are doing and trying to do to us. That includes those who are around us. To our family, our friends, our fellow church members, to our government leaders, to our fellow workers, to our spouses, and our friends. The list can go on and on. This is where the battle is raging. These demons try to get each and every one of us fighting, bickering, arguing, and complaining against each other. Are we going to allow this to happen to us?

Sometimes the LORD creates these situations to test us or judge us for our sins.

Psalm 78:49; *He cast on them the fierceness of his anger, wrath, and indignation, and trouble, by sending evil angels among them.* (American King James Version)

Judges 9:23; *God sent an evil spirit between Abimelech and the citizens of Shechem, who acted treacherously against Abimelech.* (New International Version)

1 Samuel 16:14; *Now the Spirit of the LORD had left Saul, and the LORD sent a tormenting spirit that filled him with depression and fear.* (New Living Translation)

Doesn't this make you think?

A Nine King Regional War

I bring this into the picture because of what one man had done.

Genesis 14:1-12;
1 At that time [four kings]-King Amraphel of Shinar, King Arioch of Ellasar, King Chedorlaomer of Elam, and King Tidal of Goiim-2 went to war against [five kings]-King Bera of Sodom, King Birsha of Gomorrah, King Shinab of Admah, King Shemeber of Zeboiim, and the king of Bela (that is, Zoar).
3 The five kings joined forces and met in the valley of Siddim (that is, the Dead Sea).
4 For 12 years they had been subject to Chedorlaomer, but in the thirteenth year they rebelled.
5 In the fourteenth year Chedorlaomer and his allies came and defeated the Rephaim at Ashteroth Karnaim, the Zuzim at Ham, the Emim at Shaveh Kiriathaim,
6 and the Horites in the hill country of Seir, going as far as El Paran on the edge of the desert.
7 On their way back, they came to En Mishpat (that is, Kadesh), and they conquered the whole territory of the Amalekites and also the Amorites who were living at Hazazon Tamar.
8 Then the kings of Sodom, Gomorrah, Admah, Zeboiim, and Bela (that is, Zoar) marched out and prepared for battle in the valley of Siddim.
9 They fought against King Chedorlaomer of Elam, King Tidal of Goiim, King Amraphel of Shinar, and King Arioch of Ellasar-four kings against five.
10 The valley of Siddim was full of tar pits. As the kings of Sodom and Gomorrah fled, they fell because of the tar pits, but the other kings fled to the hills.
11 So the four kings took all the possessions of Sodom and Gomorrah, as well as all their food, and left.
12 They also took Abram's nephew Lot and his possessions since he was living in Sodom. (GOD'S WORD® Translation)

Here are four kings who are going to attack five kings. This is a major battle that took place. You should find the following interesting.

1. King Amraphel is Nimrod. He controlled what is now Iraq between the Tigris and the Euphrates Rivers.
2. King Arioch of Ellasar is about one hundred and twenty miles south and slightly east along the Euphrates river. Just north of Ur.
3. King Chedorlaomer of Elam is basically part of Iran.
4. King Tidal of Goiim ruled in what is thought to be the mountain range of Zagros in modern day Iran.

There are many names for Nimrod.
Egyptians, Nimrod = Osiris. Horus, Ra & Semiramis = Isis
Greeks; Nimrod = Adonis, Semiramis = Aphrodite
Phoenese, (Lebanon area) Nimrod = Baal, Semiramis = Ashtoreth
Persia, Nimrod = Mithras
Romans, Nimrod = Venus, Attis, Semiramis = Cupid

So the four kings were from what the other parts of Iraq and Iran today. The five kings were as follows;

1. King Bera of Sodom & King Birsha of Gomorrah were on the south side of the Dead Sea. King of Bela (that is, Zoar) was located between them both.
2. King Shinab of Admah and King Shemeber of Zeboiim were just south of Zoar.

It is believed the five kings were right along the south side of the Dead Sea. The exact location of Sodom and Gomorrah is questionable due to God destroying it. However, go to the website below. They make a compelling statement with evidence backing up their belief that they found the location of Sodom and Gomorrah. http://www.arkdiscovery.com/sodom_&_gomorrah.htm

Once they defeated the Kings of Sodom and Gomorrah, they plundered their possessions and took with them Lot, Abram's nephew. Once Abram heard of this, He gathered up three hundred and eighteen men and went after the four kings and met up with them at Dan. That could be a distance of possibly one hundred miles.

Genesis 14:13-16;

13 Then a soldier who had escaped came and told Abram the Hebrew what had happened. He was living next to the oak trees belonging to Mamre the Amorite, a brother oj Eshcol and Aner. (These men were Abram's allies.)
14 When Abram heard that his nephew had been captured, he armed his 318 trained men, born in his own household, and pursued the four kings all the way to Dan.
15 He split up his men to attack them at night. He defeated them, pursuing them all the way to Hobah, which is north of Damascus.
16 He brought back everything they had, including women and soldiers. He also brought back his relative Lot and his possessions. (GOD'S WORD® Translation)

The reason why I bring up the previous battle is that Nimrod, King Arioch, King Chedorlaomer, and King Tidal were considered the descendants of the Nephilim. Interesting how when we hear this story, the part that Abram defeated these giants gets omitted. Hmmm… three hundred and eighteen men against the mighty armies of these giants who just defeated five other kings? Isn't that fascinating?

Then when Abram was on his way back from this battle, along with Lot and his family with their possessions, they met King Melchizedek of Salem, who was the priest of the LORD God.

Genesis 14:17-20;

17 After Abram came back from defeating Chedorlaomer and his allies, the king of Sodom came out to meet him in the Shaveh Valley (that is, the King's Valley).
18 Then King Melchizedek of Salem brought out bread and wine. He was a priest of God Most High.
19 He blessed Abram, and said, "Blessed is Abram by God Most High, maker of heaven and earth.
20 Blessed is God Most High, who has handed your enemies over to you." Then Abram gave him a tenth of everything. (GOD'S WORD® Translation)

That is when Abram gave a tenth of all that he had. Isn't it interesting how with just a little bit of digging and having a chronological Bible at your side works to make the Bible come alive?

God Wants Us to Be Full of Knowledge

1 **Thessalonians 4:13**; *But we do not want you to be ignorant, brothers, about those who have died, so that you may not grieve like other people who have no hope.* (International Standard Version)

The Bible tells us God does not want us to be ignorant. If anyone lacks and wants wisdom, let him ask God for it.

James 1:5; *If any of you needs wisdom to know what you should do, you should ask God, and he will give it to you. God is generous to everyone and doesn't find fault with them.* (GOD'S WORD® Translation)

Why is it the Lord Jesus Christ does not want us to be ignorant? There are many reasons actually.

Despite what is going on around us in the world, we are supposed to see beyond these events. We are supposed to see the lies, the deceit, the deception that satan, the fallen angels, and the demons are mounting against us in this world. Look beyond the events which are occurring with more and more frequency.

Turn off the news and some of the non-Christian programming. They don't enhance your life. They cause, (on purpose) confusion, uncertainty, drama, anxiety, stress, worry, and fear.

2 Timothy 1:7; *For God did not give us a spirit of timidity, but a spirit of power, of love and of self-discipline.* (New International Version)

In the different translations, that word "timidity" has also been translated as "fear". The Yahoo online dictionary states fear is; 1. To be afraid or frightened of. 2. To be uneasy or apprehensive about: feared the test results. 3. To be in awe of; revere. 4. To consider probable; expect: I fear you are wrong. I fear I have bad news for you.

Romans 8:15; *So you have not received a spirit that makes you fearful slaves. Instead, you received God's Spirit when he adopted you as his own children. Now we call him, "Abba, Father."* (New Living Translation)

Here are some scientific reasons for being careful with what you are watching, what you place in front of you. When events are happening, here is what is really going on within you;

1. When we watch TV or watch a lot of news from the Internet, we are opening up the avenues of our sight and our hearing to what they are trying to programs us with their agenda. It is touching two senses.
2. When we read the newspaper or magazines, it is feeding it into our minds through our eyes. It is touching two senses also. We are seeing it and touching the paper it is written on.
3. When we listen to the radio, it is just touching the senses of our ears.
4. If we are there experiencing the whole event live on the scene, it is touching our eyes because we are seeing it without delay, our ears because we are listening to the event without delay, our touch because we are possibly helping those in need, and we are also feeling the extreme negative energy that is happening without delay. Add to them the smells that are unique to that time and place. When we are there at the scene, we can't shut if off. When we are on the Internet, radio, and TV, we can. Being there is causing us to get more and more senses involved within us.

Too many people watch too much TV. They say it doesn't affect them, but it does. Like the old saying goes, if you tell someone a lie long enough, sooner or later people will start believing it slowly and surely.

The TV commercials and programming use subliminal messages to shift your thinking to their agenda. Unless a person is trained to watch out for it, it will affect you. That's why they do it. Did you ever ask yourself why you watch television? Seriously? Have you asked yourself that question? Some reasons are;

1. You want background noise.
2. You want to pass your time up.
3. You believe you don't want to think, just relax.
4. You want to be entertained.

The list can go on and on. The Bible teaches us we are not to be fearful. The reason why we not suppose to be fearful is because it can spread division with thoughts about what God can do for us. Isn't fear, partially, a lack of faith in what God can and will do for us? If we stay in that state, are we showing our lack of faith in Him? Yes, we are supposed to have a healthy fear of God.

Job 28:28; *So he told humans, 'The fear of the Lord is wisdom! To stay away from evil is understanding.'"* (GOD'S WORD® Translation)

Proverbs 9:8; *Do not rebuke mockers or they will hate you; rebuke the wise and they will love you.* (New International Version)

Proverbs 1:7; *The fear of the LORD is the beginning of knowledge, but fools despise wisdom and discipline.* (New International Version)

Proverbs 3:7; *Do not consider yourself wise. Fear the LORD, and turn away from evil.* (GOD'S WORD® Translation)

Proverbs 9:10; *Fear of the LORD is the foundation of wisdom. Knowledge of the Holy One results in good judgment.* (New Living Translation)

Proverbs 15:33; *The fear of the LORD is the instruction for wisdom, And before honor comes humility.* (New American Standard Bible)

Psalm 111:10; *Fear of the LORD is the foundation of true wisdom. All who obey his commandments will grow in wisdom. Praise him forever!* (New Living Translation)

We are also supposed to fear Him and the second death. But anything other than that is not of God, but of the evil one. The 'evil one' is satan.

John 17:15; *My prayer is not that you take them out of the world but that you protect them from the evil one.* (New International Version)

A side note here. I can spend so much time on this very verse. It is so profound. Of course, that is how the whole Bible is just simply profound! So here is Our Lord Jesus talking with the Father on our behalf. He doesn't want His disciples to be removed from the earth. Does that mean He doesn't want us in heaven? Of course not. He wants us to be protected and enlightened about what the 'evil one' can and might do so we can make a conscious choice of not falling into one of his traps. Jesus already knew this. He doesn't want us to be ignorant.

Let's look at this in another way. The term 'evil one' appears about fifty seven times in the Bible. Almost all of them are in the New Testament. Of those fifty seven, twenty of them were spoken by our Precious Lord and Savior Jesus Christ. So be watchful and observe. We are NOT supposed to have the mentality that the world is so bad, and it's going to get worse by the moment, and we can't do anything about it. I'm really wanting the Lord to come back so I can get out of here. While most sincere Christians believe this, that's not what we are supposed to do. Sometimes we might think about it, but there are so many other people that need our Lord and Savior Jesus Christ that it's imperative that we reach them for Christ! And believe it or not, they are looking for the truth which is in Jesus Christ.

We are to let our light shine among others in this world so they can see what the Lord Jesus is all about... through you as well as other Christians. This is why our testimony is important. When you share it, you say this is what I was, but after I got saved and received the Lord Jesus as my Savior and Lord, this is what I am now.

Matthew 10:28; *Do not be afraid of those who kill the body but cannot kill the soul. Rather, be afraid of the One who can destroy both soul and body in hell.* (New International Version)

Revelation 20:14; *Then death and Hades were thrown into the lake of fire. The lake of fire is the second death.* (New International Version)

Hades in the above verse is hell. This is the place where people go who haven't trusted the Jesus for their only way to heaven. There they wait for the final sentencing and are thrown in the Lake of Fire. That is the second death that lasts for eternity.

"They' (I'll cover who 'they' are later) are spreading as much fear as possible. Between almost all the news programs, almost all the TV programs, nearly all the movies being produced today are programming you to fear and create uncertainty. What the government is or is NOT doing for us. 'They' have mounted a carefully planned attack against mankind. 'They' are distracting our attention away from this attack by using events like professional baseball, football, hockey, basketball, etc. Let's include the college level sports too.

Let's talk about a few of these distractions. People sit around on a Sunday night and watch "programming" like The Academy Awards (Oscars). Here is an event that gives awards to various categories for cinematic achievements. These movies that are nominated take the names of our precious Lord and Saviour and our Heavenly Father in vain. Most movies show one or more of the following; violence, death, destruction, nudity, sex, drinking, drug abuse and filthy language for starters. 'They' produce movies that show the darkness of things to come, so you become disengaged from the truth of what's awaiting satan and the fallen ones. Those on the television laugh and think they are enjoying themselves now. 'They' spend thousands and thousands of dollars on attire that clothe them so everyone will notice them on the "red carpet" and especially if they receive the Oscar, a graven image. Yet there are people in need of clothes and food who don't have much of either or both. This ceremony feeds their over-active EGO (Edging God Out). Then they get up and give their speeches and let slip out a swear word or two once in a while. Now the latest craze is a wardrobe malfunction. Yet there will come a time when they will regret their words, their actions. This rich man did.

Luke 16:19-28;
19 "There was a rich man who was dressed in purple and fine linen and lived in luxury every day.
20 At his gate was laid a beggar named Lazarus, covered with sores
21 and longing to eat what fell from the rich man's table. Even the dogs came and licked his sores.
22 "The time came when the beggar died and the angels carried him to Abraham's side. The rich man also died and was buried.
23 In Hades, where he was in torment, he looked up and saw Abraham far away, with Lazarus by his side.
24 So he called to him, 'Father Abraham, have pity on me and send Lazarus to dip the tip of his finger in water and cool my tongue, because I am in agony in this fire.'
25 "But Abraham replied, 'Son, remember that in your lifetime you received your good things, while Lazarus received bad things, but now he is comforted here and you are in agony.
26 And besides all this, between us and you a great chasm has been set in place, so that those who want to go from here to you cannot, nor can anyone cross over from there to us.'
27 "He answered, 'Then I beg you, father, send Lazarus to my family,
28 for I have five brothers. Let him warn them, so that they will not also come to this place of torment.' (New International Version)

Yet this is what the Bible says about this;

Matthew 6:16; *"When you fast, do not look somber as the hypocrites do, for they disfigure their faces to show men they are fasting. I tell you the truth, they have received their reward in full.* (New International Version)

Matthew 6:25; *"So I tell you to stop worrying about what you will eat, drink, or wear. Isn't life more than food and the body more than clothes?* (GOD'S WORD® Translation)

Colossians 3:8; *But now you must rid yourselves of all such things as these: anger, rage, malice, slander, and filthy language from your lips.* (New International Version)

Luke 6:25; *How terrible it will be for you who are full now, because you will be hungry! How terrible it will be for you who are laughing now, because you will mourn and cry!* (International Standard Version)

Let's look at the various music awards shows. They have their special effects. Most of them are dark and demonic. You will notice some of them have all these flames that go on and off all around and in the background. What does that remind you of? Hell perhaps? Why do they do this? To try and desensitize us to the hell that's awaiting all those who do not believe in Jesus Christ as their personal Savior and Lord. The deception that hell is not something to fear, it's one big party, or as some have said 'hell is right here on earth.' That is NOT the truth. satan is very crafty as you can see below. You would think we would have learned by his tricks and gimmicks how he is trying to deceive us. Are you seeing the great deception all around you now?

Genesis 3:1-7;
1 The snake was more clever than all the wild animals the LORD God had made. He asked the woman, "Did God really say, 'You must never eat the fruit of any tree in the garden'?"
2 The woman answered the snake, "We're allowed to eat the fruit from any tree in the garden
3 except the tree in the middle of the garden. God said, 'You must never eat it or touch it. If you do, you will die!'"
4 "You certainly won't die!" the snake told the woman.
5 God knows that when you eat it your eyes will be opened. You'll be like God, knowing good and evil."
6 The woman saw that the tree had fruit that was good to eat, nice to look at, and desirable for making someone wise. So she took some of the fruit and ate it. She also gave some to her husband, who was with her, and he ate it.
7 Then their eyes were opened, and they both realized that they were naked. They sewed fig leaves together and made clothes for themselves. (GOD'S WORD® Translation)

What about the elaborate costumes that are replicas of the ancient empires of Egypt and Assyrians, to name a few. Those empires worshipped false gods. There are more reasons than you realize why they are using those empires to entertain you. They are paraded out in such splendor for all to look at in awe… You see symbols of the Illuminati, the Masons and other secret societies during these events. And why do we watch them? So we know who got an award? Because we want to be entertained? So we know what to talk about at work the next day…

Sporting events. Let's say you go to a professional football game. You sit there watching a bunch of guys trying to get an oblong shaped ball across a line at either end of the field. Sometimes they try to kick it through some upright pipes that are at each end of the field. Sometimes the other team takes it away, and the players get mad and upset about it; expressing themselves with some "choice" words and some pushing and shoving sometimes. Then you have some referees that are dressed like zebras that break up the pushing and shoving that sometimes goes on. Players push and shove each other. Then these referees will throw up a big handkerchief and the clock stops. Then one team or another get yards taken away from their team. Let's not forget the Superbowl and all the wardrobe malfunctions at half time. Then those swear words at the end of the game from the players from the winning team being interviewed on live TV. That is always worth sticking around for. Let's not forget hockey. It's one of the few sports, other than boxing that the referees let a fight continue for a bit. Doesn't this seem like violence to you that the Bible says will happen in the end time?

'They' are trying and in many cases succeeding in dividing mankind so they can conqueror us individually. They are isolating people against people. Almost all of the game shows now are set up as individual events rather than team. Why is that a problem? Because when someone isolated, they are vulnerable to attack by the enemy. The Bible actually talks about this.

Ecclesiastes 4:10-12;

10 If they stumble, the first will lift up his friend—but woe to anyone who is alone when he falls and there is no one to help him get up.
11 Again, if two lie close together, they will keep warm, but how can only one stay warm?
12 If someone attacks one of them, the two of them together will resist. Furthermore, the tri-braided cord is not soon broken. (International Standard Version)

One of the most powerful pairings on this earth 'they" are attacking is the husband and a wife unit. After God created everything in six days, (including man) and then He rested on the seventh. Eventually, He created Eve. While we know this story very well, sometimes we don't really understand the reasoning behind this. Here is that verse about being alone or isolated.

Genesis 2:18-23;
18 Then the LORD God said, "It is not good for the man to be alone. I will make a helper who is right for him."
19 The LORD God had formed all the wild animals and all the birds out of the ground. Then he brought them to the man to see what he would call them. Whatever the man called each creature became its name.
20 So the man named all the domestic animals, all the birds, and all the wild animals. But the man found no helper who was right for him.
21 So the LORD God caused him to fall into a deep sleep. While the man was sleeping, the LORD God took out one of the man's ribs and closed up the flesh at that place.
22 Then the LORD God formed a woman from the rib that he had taken from the man. He brought her to the man.
23 The man said, "This is now bone of my bones and flesh of my flesh. She will be named [woman] because she was taken from man." (GOD'S WORD® Translation)

Consider this point I present to you. God created everything from nothing or from the dust of the ground. However, God made the woman from a rib He took it from Adams side. Ponder this for a few moments. That was something special, a unique moment in time. I absolutely love the 18th verse. *I will make a helper who is right for him.* It seems to me that makes a woman so extremely unique in a great way!

The LORD God did not do that for any other animal, just Adam. And I believe that is passed down to us. So the husband and wife are actually one in his sight.

Now why is this so significant in the power of agreement between two people? When two people agree on anything and push forward with it, the possibilities are endless as to what can happen.

Matthew 18:19; *"Again, I tell you that if two of you on earth agree about anything you ask for, it will be done for you by my Father in heaven.* (New International Version)

'They' are increasing the level of attacks against the husband and wife unit. 'They' are increasing the level of attacks against our minds, so we don't push forward in doing what we need to accomplish in our lives.

Don't just take my word for it. Look at these things yourself. While you are watching or after you watch anything I've just talked about, do you feel it enhanced your life and made you feel empowered and strengthened?

This is the reason why I'm writing this book. Not to cast fear, but to inform you of all that is going on all around you. Then, you can empower yourself to fighting the ways of the evil one and overcome; just like Jesus did when He walked here on earth.

Matthew 10:16: *"Behold, I am sending you out as sheep in the midst of wolves, so be wise as serpents and innocent as doves.* (English Standard Version)

Romans 8:37; *No, in all these things we are more than conquerors through him who loved us.* (English Standard Version)

We are the light of the world.

Matthew 5:14; *"You are the light of the world. A city on a hill cannot be hidden.* (New International Version)

Acts 13:47; *For the Lord gave us this command when he said, 'I have made you a light to the Gentiles, to bring salvation to the farthest corners of the earth.'"* (New Living Translation)

God's word is eternal. He takes His word extremely seriously. The Bible has many verses that address this concept.

Matthew 5:18; *because I tell all of you with certainty that until heaven and earth disappear, not one letter or one stroke of a letter will disappear from the Law until everything has been accomplished.* (International Standard Version)

Psalm 12:6-7;
6 The promises of the LORD are pure, like silver refined in a furnace and purified seven times.
7 O LORD, you will protect them. You will keep each one safe from those people forever. (King James Version)

Deuteronomy 4:2; *Never add anything to what I command you, or take anything away from it. Then you will be able to obey the commands of the LORD your God that I give you.* (GOD'S WORD® Translation)

Mark 13:31; *Heaven and earth will pass away, but my words will never pass away.* (New International Version)

Revelation 22:18-19;
18 I warn everyone who hears the words of the prophecy in this book: If anyone adds anything to this, God will strike him with the plagues that are written in this book.
19 If anyone takes away any words from this book of prophecy, God will take away his portion of the tree of life and the holy city that are described in this book. (International Standard Version)

I can keep talking and writing chapters on these verses alone. The thoughts and ideas laid in them reach deep and wide if someone wants to explore them with the Holy Spirit's revelation. The Word of God is pure! It is like silver that is purified seven times!

Movies & Television Shows

Do you realize how many movies are being made that are about murders based on a person's life? They are making movies based on tragedy, heartache, heartbreak, and how it affected other people. Why do they do this? The answer is really very simple. More on this later.

I realized many years ago that whatever you see in movies eventually you will probably see it happen in real life or has happened many hundreds or thousands of years ago. A lot of themes in movies can come from ancient times and 'myths'. Let me show you some examples.

Stargate© SG1 by MGM Studio©

According to the show, basically a portal was discovered that will take them to different worlds. They built a mechanism that allows them to walk into this 'wormhole', I'll call it, and be transported within a matter of minutes to a world hundreds or thousands of light years away.

Now what is interesting is an ancient legend from the local Indians in Southern Peru, Hayu Marca that describes what looks like a door-like opening that is carved out of the rock. This is supposed to be a gateway to the gods. (Source; History Channel)

Star Trek©, all the series and movies by Paramount Studios©

Supposedly scientists have now figured out the theory of dematerialization and can move sub-atomic particles from one place to another. That is what the transporter did on the starships and the star bases that were throughout the galaxy in the shows and movies.

Indiana Jones, early movies by Paramount Pictures©

Some of them actually mirrored Nazi Germany obsession with finding the Ark of the Covenant. Many of the items that Indiana Jones went after were based on myth and ancient writings.

2001 A Space Odyssey & 2010 the Year We Make Contact

When did we land the rover on Mars? How about a Monolith that was discovered in southern Utah in the Saint John area? I find it interesting they called something a monolith. Could there be a connection between these super structures and a monolith…

Remember one of the moons of Jupiter was named Europa? Do you know what Europa means? In Greek myth, she was a person carried off by Zeus who disguised himself as a bull… And supposedly, the area of land that stretches from Portugal through Germany was named after her… Europe.

Alien

All the movies portray us as not being alone, and we are fighting for our lives. Where do they get or should I say from whom do they receive the ideas for the design for the costumes in all these movies?

Paul

This one is not about the apostle either.

Terminator

"Skynet" was created by men who created a piece of machinery that ultimately turned against its creator. And subsequently attempts to destroy all humans on our planet. Sounds familiar? The series is about trying to stop it from being created in the first place.

Day the Earth Stood Still

Here is an alien who has come back to earth to see how humans have progressed. They see all what they perceive is wrong and determine that all the humans must die. Interestingly enough, the Bible mentions when God made the sun stand still.

Joshua 10:13; *So the sun stood still, and the moon stopped, till the nation avenged itself on its enemies, as it is written in the Book of Jashar. The sun stopped in the middle of the sky and delayed going down about a full day.* (New International Version)

Star Wars

In Cambodian myth, a god named Perra Pissncar had a sword that was made of light. Does that remind of you the light saber in this movie?

Below is only part of a list of movies that have had aliens in them in one form or another. Again, keep in mind, these movies are made and planned to reprogram our minds to accept the 'great deception' that is coming, regardless of what the writers and directors say that it was not their intention.

Abyss
Alien Nation
Alien vs. Predator
Avatar
Battlefield Earth
Battleship Galactica
Body Snatchers
Close Encounters of a Third Kind
Coneheads
Cowboys and Aliens
Ghost and Mrs Muir
Doom
District 9
ET
Fantastic Four, Rise of the Silver Surfer
Fifth Element
Flash Gordon
Forbidden Planet
Frankenstein
Hanger 18
Highlander
Indiana Jones and the Kingdom of the Crystal Skull
Invasion of the Body Snatchers
It came from Outer Space
Jurassic Park
K-PAX
Keep (1983)
Last Starfighter
Lost in Space

Men in Black
My Stepmother is an Alien
My Favorite Martian
Nightmare on Elm Street
Pitch Black
Possession
Predator
Project ELF
Race to Witch Mountain
Signs
Spaceballs
Starship Troopers
Super 8
Supergirl
Superman
Thing
Transformers
Twilight
True Blood
U.F.O
Visitor
Wall-e
War of the Worlds

Let's not forget mummies that come back to life. Many themes in movies vary depending on the genre. But one thing does stand out. It almost always ends up being a battle between right and wrong. More and more, the ending leaning towards the dark side is winning. Most of the films are now dark, gloomy, about death, mummies, aliens that attack us or want to help us. Do you see a pattern?

Television Shows

3rd Rock from the Sun
Babylon 5
Batman
Buck Rogers in the 25th Century
Dark Shadows
Doctor Who

Earth: Final Conflict
Exorcist
Farscape
Hitchhiker's Guide to the Galaxy
Mork & Mindy
Outer Limits
Roswell
Space Rangers
Taken
Them
Tommyknockers

Now do you see the deception that is all around you?

Legends of Yesterday

Many legends are part of our culture, many of which we don't give a second thought about. We see it in print and on the silver screen. If they are myths, why do we participate in watching some of these? Here are some examples.

- Superman
- Batman
- Football or baseball team names;
    - Giants
    - Vikings
    - Titans
    - Lake Monsters
    - SeaWolves
    - Flying Tigers
    - Las Vegas 51s
- Big Foot
- Cyclops
- Frankenstein
- Goliath
- Hercules, god of strength.
- King Kong
- Paul Bunyan

- Green Giant by Birds Eye®
- Think of all the Greek and Roman gods they had.

Let's discuss false gods, pagan rulers and fallen angels. I'm going to start off with part of the verse from Genesis 6. You will understand why as you read on.

Genesis 6:4; *The Nephilim were on the earth in those days—and also afterward—when the sons of God went to the daughters of humans and had children by them. They were the heroes of old, men of renown.* (New International Version)

Here is a partial list of the heroes of old and men of renown. Check out the names of the planets in our solar system too.

1. Heracles
2. Jason (of the Argonauts)
3. Achilles (as in Achilles heel)
4. Odysseus
5. Pelops
6. Atalanta (could the city of Atlanta be named after a false god?)
7. Europe (Interesting how Europe was named after a false god; just like the planet of Europa, one of Jupiter's moons)
8. Helen
9. Pandora (Don't open Pandora's box…)
10. Psyche
11. The Titans. These date back to just before the flood.
12. Zeus, king of the gods, the ruler of Mount Olympus and the god of the sky, weather, thunder, lightning, law, order, and fate.
13. Aphrodite, goddess of love, beauty and desire.
14. Apollo, god of music, healing, plague, the sun, prophecies, and poetry; associated with light, truth and the sun.
15. Ares, god of war, bloodshed, violence, manly courage, and civil order.

16. Pluto, god of the underworld. Saturn, god of time; Vulcan, smith god, of fire. Isn't it also a planet?
17. Artemis, virgin goddess of hunt, wilderness, animals, young girls, childbirth and plague.
18. Azazel, supposed to be the head of the fallen 200 watcher angels, was a half goat and half man. Still think you haven't been deceived yet?
19. Gaia, goddess of mother earth. Does 'earth day' mean anything to you? How about the term 'mother earth'? Now how about this one, 'mother nature'? Those who started earth day openly admit that it has nothing really to do with recycling. It has to do with praying to and worshipping mother earth. I'm all for recycling etc. because the Bible tells us to care for the earth.

    Genesis 1:28; *And God blessed them, and God said unto them, Be fruitful, and multiply, and replenish the earth, and subdue it: and have dominion over the fish of the sea, and over the fowl of the air, and over every living thing that moveth upon the earth.* (King James Bible (Cambridge Ed.)

    Genesis 2:15; *The LORD God took the man and put him in the Garden of Eden to work it and take care of it.* (New International Version)

    Anything more than recycling is pagan worship. Do tree huggers, among other ones, mean anything to you? I saw a video with people sincerely crying because a tree was cut down. How about those who worship nature?

    Revelation 9:20; *The rest of mankind who were not killed by these plagues still did not repent of the work of their hands; they did not stop worshiping demons, and idols of gold, silver, bronze, stone and wood--idols that cannot see or hear or walk.* (New International Version)
20. Mithra, one of the Iranian mythical gods. But it has its roots as far back as Nimrod's time. It is one of the names of Nimrod. Various sources state the Romans eventually made it one of their gods they worshipped somewhere around 300 to 200 B.C. It is said that Mithra was born on the twenty fifth day of the twelfth month of the year. Some sources state that the Romans sacrificed Jews to this god by way of the crucifixions on a cross.

Some Christians make the sign of the cross when they enter into a church or go through some rituals. Sometimes they may say; "in the name of the Father, and of the Son, and of the Holy Spirit, amen. However, it isn't required to say those words all the time when they make the sign of the cross. Actually, the reason why that was started was so people will know they are a member of the Mithra secret society. If one person makes this sign as does the other, each will know they are fellow members. Eventually, some religions incorporated this sign as part of their religion. To this very day, it is widely used.

It is believed one of the designs of the old Roman battle shield that is pictured in so many movies have what looks like a cross on it. You sometimes see it in the crusades which stretched all across Europe all the way to Jerusalem. However, it really isn't a cross.

If you will notice the picture on the right, it actually is a plus sign and coincides with the making of the sign of the cross. It was used long before the birth of Jesus the Messiah.

21. Hades, god of the underworld. According to some writings, he rules over the dead and wants to increase those he calls his subjects. Interesting name of this god.
22. Poseidon, god of the sea, protector of all waters. Hmmm, how about the movie "Poseidon adventure"?
23. Athena, Greek virgin goddess of reason, intelligent activity, arts and literature
24. Jupiter, king of the gods. Isn't it also a planet?
25. Jupiter's moons.
    a. Metis = First wife of Zeus.
    b. Adrastea = Daughter of Jupiter.
    c. Amalthea = Nymph nursed Zeus with goats milk.

d. Thebe = Nymph who was daughter of a river god Asopus.

26. Saturn's moons. It is believed that the moons of Saturn are named for the titans of Genesis 6. Others were named for Gaul (France), Norse, and other giants. The moons of the other planets, except for earth's moons, are named after Roman or Greek gods, goddesses, etc.
27. Mars, god of war. Another planet.
28. Mercury, messenger of the gods. Yet another one planet.
29. Neptune, god of the sea.
30. See a pattern with the naming of our planets after false gods too?
31. Orion Constellation = Greek myth known as the Hunter god.
32. Andromeda Constellation = Princess in Greek mythology.
33. Hercules Constellation = A Roman god but was renamed from the Greek god Heracles.
34. santa. I put him in here. He actually dates back to the days of Nimrod. More on this later on in this book. If you change the letters, you get satan. His name is not capitalized on purpose. Why is this fallen angel on the list? The Bible teaches God is our supply, not santa. The act of sitting on his lap or writing him a letter asking for what you want for christmas should be reserved for God the Father.

According to Greek mythology, their gods used 'powerful' weapons that were called Poseidon and Trident. Interesting to note the United States Navy developed nuclear missiles for its submarines calling them by those names.

There is a star system called Sirius. What else is Sirius? A satellite radio program.

There seems to be evidence that ancient civilizations had accurate mappings of the stars. Where did they get this information?

How did the Atlantic Ocean get its name? There are two possibilities. One is that the Atlantic was named after the

supposedly lost city of Atlantis. There are many sources that believe the name comes from the Greek god Atlas.
http://wiki.answers.com/Q/How_did_the_Atlantic_Ocean_get_its_name

Let's talk about the months in our calendar.

Names of the Months & Days of the Week

1. January, god of doors. Also Janus.
2. February, Roman month of sacrifices and purification.
3. March, god of war. Beginning of the year for soldiers.
4. April, when trees open their leaves. Also Tammuz.
5. May, goddess of growth when plants really start to grow. Interesting how this coincides with easter…
6. June, queen of the gods.
7. July, Julius Caesar, ruler of Rome. He renamed the calendar so he had a month named after him. Also Tishri.
8. August, Augustus, ruler of Rome. Augustus wanted a month named after himself too.
9. September, seventh month from March. Also seventh.
10. October, eighth month from March. Also octagon.
11. November, ninth month from March. Also Novas.
12. December, tenth month from March. Also Deca.

Do you see the pattern that is taking place? There are other origins and names of gods they gave. How about the deception now? Do you see it? Let's continue.

1. Monday; the moon god.
2. Tuesday; god of war.
3. Wednesday; cunning god.
4. Thursday; thunder god.
5. Friday; goddess of love. Also Dagon the fish or fishing (meaning multiple) god. So when those of you who are giving up meat on Friday and are eating fish, you are paying homage to this god. This tradition appears to go all the way back to the time of Nimrod. I am sure most people at one time or another have said; "doggone it" or "dagon it". Well guess where that came from? Yep, the

pagan fish god Dagon. This is another word we need to stop using.

6. Saturday; god of time.
7. Sunday; sun god.

As you can see, the names of false gods, pagan rulers, or fallen angels have made their way into our society in many ways. The LORD God has clearly told us we are not to know about them. We are not to even speak their names.

Exodus 23:13; *"Pay attention to all that I have said to you, and make no mention of the names of other gods, nor let it be heard on your lips.* (English Standard Version)

Does it say anywhere in the Bible we are to name the days of the week? There are some translations of the Bible that do not use the words Sunday, Monday, Tuesday, etc. The New International Version (NIV) and some other versions do not use those words to describe those days of the week. I believe Monday through Thursday is not mentioned in the Bible at all. Friday is not mentioned in most of the versions. Saturday is only mentioned in the New Living Translation version. So why does the NIV and a few others go to great lengths not to use the names of the days of the week? More on that later.

What about the months of the year? January is mentioned six times. But not in the NIV and a few other versions. Same thing for the month of February. March is mentioned, but I don't believe it was mentioned as a month. I believe you will find the same thing. So why does the Bible go to great lengths not to mention them by name? Let's look at how the NIV translation is wording the day and month.

Daniel 10:4; *On the twenty-fourth day of the first month, as I was standing on the bank of the great river, the Tigris,* (New International Version)

This is how the LORD wants it worded, in the above manner. So why is it that way? Because if we say those names, we will be saying the names of other gods. And we are forbidden to say their names, period. That is why the LORD wants it communicated in this fashion. Let's start with how we changed when each day starts. Where in the Bible does it give us permission to change that also?

So if the Bible words it that way, then we should too. That includes all correspondence and communication with others. I am changing the way I express the days of the week on the rare occasion I need to identify each. Seems wild isn't it? Do you think it is taking things too far now? I've really lost it now?

Genesis 1:5; *God called the light "day," and the darkness he called "night." And there was evening, and there was morning--the first day.* (New International Version)

Psalms 16:4; *Troubles multiply for those who chase after other gods. I will not take part in their sacrifices of blood or even speak the names of their gods.* (New Living Translation)

Exodus 23:13; *"Now concerning everything which I have said to you, be on your guard; and do not mention the name of other gods, nor let them be heard from your mouth.* (New American Standard Bible)

Deuteronomy 12:29-31;
29 The Lord your God will cut off before you the nations you are about to invade and dispossess. But when you have driven them out and settled in their land,
30 and after they have been destroyed before you, be careful not to be ensnared by inquiring about their gods, saying, "How do these nations serve their gods? We will do the same."
31 You must not worship the Lord your God in their way, because in worshiping their gods, they do all kinds of detestable things the Lord hates. They even burn their sons and daughters in the fire as sacrifices to their gods. (New International Version)

We are not to say, speak, utter, etc. the names of other gods from our mouth… period. I don't see any fine print there which allows us to speak the names of gods that are in the days or months so named. Well do you think this is going too far. You don't want to believe this is correct?

Some will say "Well, that's not what it means to me." The point is, you are not being worshipped. The LORD God is the one being worshipped. He makes up the rules we are to follow. Do you realize the Ten Commandments are split up in this way? The first four commandments are focused on how we are to love the LORD. The other six commandments are focused on how we are to love others.

Judges 17:6; *In those days Israel had no king; all the people did whatever seemed right in their own eyes.* (New Living Translation)

Judges 21:25; *In those days Israel had no king; all the people did whatever seemed right in their own eyes.* (New Living Translation)

Psalm 81:8-14;
8 "Listen to me, O my people, while I give you stern warnings. O Israel, if you would only listen to me!
9 You must never have a foreign god; you must not bow down before a false god.
10 For it was I, the LORD your God, who rescued you from the land of Egypt. Open your mouth wide, and I will fill it with good things.
11 "But no, my people wouldn't listen. Israel did not want me around.
12 So I let them follow their own stubborn desires, living according to their own ideas.
13 Oh, that my people would listen to me! Oh, that Israel would follow me, walking in my paths!
14 How quickly I would then subdue their enemies! How soon my hands would be upon their foes! (New Living Translation)

Parallels in the Different Civilizations

During my research, I looked at some of the different civilizations from the past. I've discovered four things that seemingly were consistent with almost all of them.

1. They wrote they received instructions as to what to do, where to do it, and how to do certain things that were

corrupt. And when they, the gods, got angry with the people, they sought to destroy them. This seems to fit those ancient writings which stated these 'gods' these civilizations talk about, are these 'watcher angels'. And some of them were their Nephilim offspring too.
Enoch 7:2-6;
2 And the women became pregnant and gave birth to great giants whose heights were three hundred cubits.
3 These giants consumed the produce of all the people until the people detested feeding them.
4 So the giants turned against the people in order to eat them.
5 And they began to sin against birds, wild beasts, reptiles, and fish. And their flesh was devoured the one by the other, and they drank blood.
6 And then the earth brought an accusation against the oppressors.
Jubilees 5:1-3;
1 And it came to pass when the children of men began to multiply on the face of the earth and daughters were born unto them, that the angels of God saw them on a certain year of this jubilee, that they were beautiful to look upon; and they took themselves wives of all whom they
2 chose, and they bare unto them sons and they were giants. And lawlessness increased on the earth and all flesh corrupted its way, alike men and cattle and beasts and birds and everything that walks on the earth -all of them corrupted their ways and their orders, and they began to devour each other, and lawlessness increased on the earth and every imagination of the thoughts of all men
3 (was) thus evil continually. And God looked upon the earth, and behold it was corrupt, and all flesh had corrupted its orders, and all that were upon the earth had wrought all manner of evil

2. They are all expecting their god to return some day.

John 14:3; *"If I go and prepare a place for you, I will come again and receive you to Myself, that where I am, there you may be also.* (New American Standard Bible)
Acts 1:11; *"Men of Galilee," they said, "why do you stand here looking into the sky? This same Jesus, who has been taken from you into heaven, will come back in the same way you have seen him go into heaven."* (New International Version)

3. Many of these same civilizations usually had some type of human sacrifice that was performed to satisfy their gods they were offering it to. Isn't it interesting that man realizes blood must be shed for redemption and entrance into eternal life??? It reminds me of the following verse below.
   Hebrews 9:22; *In fact, according to the law of Moses, nearly everything was purified with blood. For without the shedding of blood, there is no forgiveness.* (New Living Translation)
4. They expect a huge battle of global epic proportions towards the end of time.
   Revelation 16:16; *And the demonic spirits gathered all the rulers and their armies to a place with the Hebrew name [Armageddon].* (New Living Translation)

While others might find other similarities, the bottom line is it's interesting to see the above commonality between all of the civilizations.

Now you might begin to see what was happening on the earth with these Nephilim running around and creating havoc before and after the flood. There were male and female Nephilim. And they mated also.

Now the cries of the people on earth had ascended into heaven because of what these Nephilim were doing on earth before the flood of Genesis 7.

Azaz'al was the head watcher (of fallen angels). He was like a supervisor I would guess. The following paragraph is supposedly Michael, Surafel, and Gabriel observing the earth and noticed what was happening here.

Enoch 9:6-11;

6 "YOU see what Azaz'el has done; how he has taught all forms of oppression upon the earth. And they revealed eternal secrets which are performed in heaven and which man learned."
7 "Moreover Semyaz, to whom YOU have given power to rule over his companions, co-operating, they went in unto the daughters of the people on earth;"
8 "and they lay together with them-with those women-and defiled themselves, and revealed to them every kind of sin."
9 "As for the women, they gave birth to giants to the degree that the whole earth was filled with blood and oppression."
10 "And now behold, the Kodesh One will cry, and those who have died will bring their suit up to the gate of heaven. Their groaning has ascended into heaven, but they could not get out from before the face of the oppression that is being wrought on earth."
11 "And YOU know everything even before it came to existence, and YOU see this thing but YOU do not tell us what is proper for us that we may do regarding it."

Today, some people look back at these giants and called them gods, ancient aliens, you name it. As I mentioned before, there were two hundred of them assigned to do certain tasks here on this planet.

Enoch 6:5; And they were altogether two hundred; and they descended into 'Ardos, which is the summit of Hermon.

Then these 'sons of God' married the women on earth as it states in Genesis 6:4.

Enoch 6:2**;** And the angels, the children of heaven, saw them and desired them; and they said to one another, "Come, let us choose wives for ourselves from among the daughters of man and beget us children."

Why would these angels want to have children? Stop and think about it. As I mentioned earlier, it could be so they could figure out a way to get to the Tree of Life in the Garden of Eden.

It's believed some of these angels taught men how to do various things. I'm mentioning all this for a very good reason. It will soon make sense so you will see things differently and not be fearful. Some of them taught these women how to prepare magic potions, perform medicine dances, how to get ready the magic potion from plants and identify which plants were good for healing. Where do you see medicine dances performed? Voodoo???

Others taught how to make swords, knives, shields, and breastplates. Then there were jewelry, how to wear makeup.

Enoch 7:1-2;
1 And they took wives unto themselves, and everyone respectively chose one woman for himself, and they began to go unto them. And they taught them magical medicine, incantations, the cutting of roots, and taught them about plants.
2 And the women became pregnant and gave birth to great giants whose heights were three hundred cubits.

Then these Nephilim were born. They were giants. They did the work of men for a while. Sound familiar? They were three hundred cubits. To get an idea, Goliath's *height was six cubits and a span.*

Enoch 8:1; And Azaz'el taught the people the art of making swords and knives, and shields, and breastplates; and he showed to their chosen ones bracelets, decorations, shadowing of the eye with antimony, ornamentation, the beautifying of the eyelids, all kinds of precious stones, and all coloring tinctures and alchemy.

Shape Shifting Angels

There is reason to believe that angels can be shape-shifters. Abraham was visited by three angels as you will read in the verses below.

Genesis 18:1-8;
1 The LORD appeared to Abraham by the oak trees belonging to Mamre as he was sitting at the entrance of his tent during the hottest part of the day.

2 Abraham looked up, and suddenly he saw three men standing near him. When he saw them, he ran to meet them, and he bowed with his face touching the ground.
3 "Please, sir," Abraham said, "stop by to visit me for a while.
4 Why don't we let someone bring a little water? After you wash your feet, you can stretch out and rest under the tree.
5 Let me bring some bread so that you can regain your strength. After that you can leave, since this is why you stopped by to visit me." They answered, "That's fine. Do as you say."
6 So Abraham hurried into the tent to find Sarah. "Quick," he said, "get three measures of flour, knead it, and make bread."
7 Then Abraham ran to the herd and took one of his best calves. He gave it to his servant, who prepared it quickly.
8 Abraham took cheese and milk, as well as the meat, and set these in front of them. Then he stood by them under the tree as they ate. (GOD'S WORD® Translation)

Here is another example of shape-shifting in the following verse.

Hebrews 13:2; *Do not forget to show hospitality to strangers, for by so doing some people have shown hospitality to angels without knowing it.* (New International Version)

The Expansion of Knowledge

Daniel 12:4; *But you, Daniel, keep this prophecy a secret; seal up the book until the time of the end, when many will rush here and there, and knowledge will increase."* (New Living Translation)

Have you sat down and thought about why knowledge has increased and will continue to increase? For thousands of years, we have walked or rode on some animal to get wherever we need to go.

Yet in the mid 1800's, steel mills sprang up.

The first train might had been made in 1807. (Source; http://www.chacha.com/question/when-was-the-first-train-made%3F-and-when-was-the-first-train-ride)

It appears the first wind car might have been built in the 1300's. Later in the 1600's and early 1700's the steam car made it appearance. It was during the 1890's the first internal combustion engine was designed and actually worked. In 1903, Henry Ford offered the first car for sale which he made. At the time of this writing, the automobile has been around for sale for about one hundred and ten (110) years.
(Source; http://www.ausbcomp.com/~bbott/cars/carhist.htm)

Sometime around 1900, the Wright brothers flew the first airplane. Within a few years, they tweaked the design and was able to produce sustained flight!

Then there is the atomic weapon that was developed in the 1940's. Two of them were dropped on Japan, to get them to surrender so it would save hundreds of thousands of American lives. There is the fission, fusion, thermonuclear, neutron, and others.

The first genetically modified organism (GMO) was probably produced in the 1970's. You hear of cloning and stem cell research in the media from time to time. Doesn't this sound familiar? As in the days of Noah…

We went from horse and buggy days with limited understanding to building huge monuments and buildings. Yet as hard as they have tried, they still can't build a duplicate of the Great Pyramid in Giza. We have gone to the moon and sent robots to other planets to send us back pictures and results of data it discovered in space and on other planets. We fly across the world in an airplane in about a day depending on where your destination is located. Yet we don't really think it's out of the ordinary.

So why do we have all of this knowledge and understanding? How did we get it so quickly?

Life of the Prophets

Sometimes prophets and seers have short life spans. They give a good word from the LORD most of the time. However, when he or she has words which are less than "positive", shall I say, people get upset or get mad. Sometimes they stone and kill them. Other times they are sawn in half, burned at the stake, or hanged on a cross to die. Why? Because the people they were told to give a message to don't like what was said. The world hated Jesus because He told them their works were wrong.

John 7:7; *The world cannot hate you, but it hates me because I say that what everyone does is evil.* (GOD'S WORD® Translation)

Others simply are not going to receive it. Sometimes people don't listen to the voice of the Heavenly Father talking to them, tugging at their heart. Sometimes He sends someone to give them a word of instruction or rebuke. Sometimes they still don't want to hear it. Then sickness might come, or other things that cause calamity in their lives will show up so they will heed His voice. Yet sometimes they still don't care or pay attention to it. It happened to Israel, it's happening in America, and it's going to happen during the Tribulation period. Here is what's going to happen during that time.

Revelation 9:20-21;
20 The rest of mankind who were not killed by these plagues still did not repent of the work of their hands; they did not stop worshiping demons, and idols of gold, silver, bronze, stone and wood—idols that cannot see or hear or walk.
21 Nor did they repent of their murders, their magic arts, their sexual immorality or their thefts. (New International Version)

Jesus in Matthew actually mentions the killing of prophets in the past and the future when He was talking to the teachers of the law and Pharisees. The teachers of the law are primarily scribes.

Matthew 23:29-34;
29 "Woe to you, teachers of the law and Pharisees, you hypocrites! You build tombs for the prophets and decorate the graves of the righteous.
30 And you say, 'If we had lived in the days of our ancestors, we would not have taken part with them in shedding the blood of the prophets.'

31 So you testify against yourselves that you are the descendants of those who murdered the prophets.
32 Go ahead, then, and complete what your ancestors started!
33 "You snakes! You brood of vipers! How will you escape being condemned to hell?
34 Therefore I am sending you prophets and sages and teachers. Some of them you will kill and crucify; others you will flog in your synagogues and pursue from town to town. (New International Version)

In 2 Kings 1, King Ahaziah fell and injured himself during a rebellion. This is where Elijah had met the King's messengers and told them convey to the king he was going to die. The king didn't like that answer and summoned Elijah. So he sent two sets of fifty men and two officers. All of them were burned up.

2 Kings 1:9-12;
9 Then he sent to Elijah a captain with his company of fifty men. The captain went up to Elijah, who was sitting on the top of a hill, and said to him, "Man of God, the king says, 'Come down!'"
10 Elijah answered the captain, "If I am a man of God, may fire come down from heaven and consume you and your fifty men!" Then fire fell from heaven and consumed the captain and his men.
11 At this the king sent to Elijah another captain with his fifty men. The captain said to him, "Man of God, this is what the king says, 'Come down at once!'"
12 "If I am a man of God," Elijah replied, "may fire come down from heaven and consume you and your fifty men!" Then the fire of God fell from heaven and consumed him and his fifty men. (New International Version)

They were trying to get Elijah to come down the hill to see the king. The third set of fifty men and their officer were spared, and Elijah went to see King Ahaziah.

Why did I mention these situations? First, respect the prophets, seers, those in the apostolic. Secondly, keep in mind the devils fear our God much more than we do. Don't think so? Do you actually tremble when you hear the LORD our God's name spoken? Do you actually become somewhat fearful when you stop to think all the things you have done that were wrong and the judgment that can fall upon you? The angels rebelled just one time. And they were sentenced to the Lake of Fire burning with fire and brimstone. Let me repeat that. The angels rebelled just one time. And they were sentenced to the Lake of Fire burning with fire and brimstone. The Bible says the fear of the LORD is the beginning of wisdom. If you don't fear Him, then you are hardly out of first grade.

2 Chronicles 19:7; *"Now then let the fear of the LORD be upon you; be very careful what you do, for the LORD our God will have no part in unrighteousness or partiality or the taking of a bribe."* (New American Standard Bible)

Proverbs 15:33; *The fear of the LORD is instruction in wisdom, and humility comes before honor.* (English Standard Version)

Proverbs 16:6; *Unfailing love and faithfulness make atonement for sin. By fearing the LORD, people avoid evil.* (New Living Translation)

Time Travel

Is this possible today? Most people would answer it with a yes. Why? Maybe because several movies, talk shows, project such a scenario. Now a hundred years ago, probably not. But would those same people think (practically) they or anyone else could travel to a different time? Most of those people would answer no.

The reason why I'm sharing this with you is if you are presented with something long enough, more than likely you will believe it. They have been shoving down our throats the concepts of aliens, zombies, and time travel for many years since probably the 1960's, possibly even before that.

As I was writing this book and contemplating this concept, I did some research and formulated some thoughts about it. So the question is what does God have to say about time travel? Is it possible? Can it be done? Has it been done? Let's discuss what we do know about this topic.

As you will see in the verses below, it certainly does seem that God sees what has happened and what will happen.

Isaiah 46:10; *I make known the end from the beginning, from ancient times, what is still to come. I say: My purpose will stand, and I will do all that I please.* (New International Version)

Romans 4:17; *As it is written: "I have made you a father of many nations." He is our father in the sight of God, in whom he believed--the God who gives life to the dead and calls things that are not as though they were.* (New International Version)

Our God looks at time differently than we do.

2 Peter 3:8; *Dear friends, don't ignore this fact: One day with the Lord is like a thousand years, and a thousand years are like one day.* (GOD'S WORD® Translation)

Our God is omnipotent meaning 'all ruling' or 'almighty.'

Revelation 19:6; *And I heard as it were the voice of a great multitude, and as the voice of many waters, and as the voice of mighty thunderings, saying, Alleluia: for the Lord God omnipotent reigns.* (King James 2000 Bible 2003)

God is omnipresent.

Psalm 139:7–11;
7 Where can I go from your Spirit? Where can I flee from your presence?
8 If I go up to the heavens, you are there; if I make my bed in the depths, you are there.
9 If I rise on the wings of the dawn, if I settle on the far side of the sea,
10 even there your hand will guide me, your right hand will hold me fast.
11 If I say, "Surely the darkness will hide me and the light become night around me," (New International Version)

God is omniscient!

Psalm 44:20-21;
20 If we forgot the name of our God or stretched out our hands to pray to another god,
21 wouldn't God find out, since he knows the secrets in our hearts? (GOD'S WORD® Translation)

Hebrews 4:12-13;
12 God's word is living and active. It is sharper than any two-edged sword and cuts as deep as the place where soul and spirit meet, the place where joints and marrow meet. God's word judges a person's thoughts and intentions.
13 No creature can hide from God. Everything is uncovered and exposed for him to see. We must answer to him. (GOD'S WORD® Translation)

1 Corinthians 2:10; *but God has revealed it to us by his Spirit. The Spirit searches all things, even the deep things of God.* (New International Version)
(Source: How is God Omnipotent, Omnipresent, and Omniscient? http://www.cogwriter.com/god-omnipotent-omniscient-omnipresent.htm)

Here is an instance about Philip and the Ethiopian eunuch. The eunuch was reading from the prophet Isaiah's writings. Philip approached him asking if he understood what he was reading. He said not unless someone taught him. Philip sat down with him and explained that this passage was all about Jesus, the Messiah, and what He (Jesus) was going to do for us for the forgiveness of sins. And already did. Then the eunuch received the LORD and was baptized. Then right after the baptism, Philip was physically taken to another city.

Acts 8:26-40;
26 As for Philip, an angel of the Lord said to him, "Go south down the desert road that runs from Jerusalem to Gaza."
27 So he started out, and he met the treasurer of Ethiopia, a eunuch of great authority under the Kandake, the queen of Ethiopia. The eunuch had gone to Jerusalem to worship,

28 and he was now returning. Seated in his carriage, he was
reading aloud from the book of the prophet Isaiah.
29 The Holy Spirit said to Philip, "Go over and walk along
beside the carriage."
30 Philip ran over and heard the man reading from the prophet
Isaiah. Philip asked, "Do you understand what you are
reading?"
31 The man replied, "How can I, unless someone instructs me?"
And he urged Philip to come up into the carriage and sit with
him.
32 The passage of Scripture he had been reading was this: "He
was led like a sheep to the slaughter. And as a lamb is silent
before the shearers, he did not open his mouth.
33 He was humiliated and received no justice. Who can speak of
his descendants? For his life was taken from the earth."
34 The eunuch asked Philip, "Tell me, was the prophet talking
about himself or someone else?"
35 So beginning with this same Scripture, Philip told him the
Good News about Jesus.
36 As they rode along, they came to some water, and the eunuch
said, "Look! There's some water! Why can't I be baptized?"
38 He ordered the carriage to stop, and they went down into the
water, and Philip baptized him.
39 When they came up out of the water, the Spirit of the Lord
snatched Philip away. The eunuch never saw him again but went
on his way rejoicing.
40 Meanwhile, Philip found himself farther north at the town of
Azotus. He preached the Good News there and in every town
along the way until he came to Caesarea. (New Living Translation)

Isaiah had what I believe is a journey through time. Or should I say, to a different location on the timeline. What do I mean by that? He went to be where the throne of God was located. Notice there was no mention of a vision. He said, "I saw".

Isaiah 6:1-3:

1 In the year that King Uzziah died, I saw the Lord, high and exalted, seated on a throne; and the train of his robe filled the temple.
2 Above him were seraphim, each with six wings: With two wings they covered their faces, with two they covered their feet, and with two they were flying.
3 And they were calling to one another: (New International Version)

Ezekiel had that very interesting event described to him and then saw it. That great end time battle of Gog in the land of MaGog. I find it interesting how the LORD tells him to turn to Gog in the land of MaGog and prophesy against him.

Ezekiel 38:1-3;
1 The LORD spoke his word to me. He said,
2 "Son of man, turn to Gog from the land of Magog. He is the chief prince of [the nations of] Meshech and Tubal. Prophesy against him.
3 Tell him, 'This is what the Almighty LORD says: I am against you, Gog, chief prince of Meshech and Tubal. (GOD'S WORD® Translation)

I would assume that in order to turn to something, you need to be there to do it.

Another time Ezekiel was taken to Jerusalem.

Ezekiel 40:1; *It was the tenth day of the month in the beginning of the twenty-fifth year of our captivity and fourteen years after Jerusalem was captured. At that time the LORD's power came over me, and he brought me to Jerusalem.* (GOD'S WORD® Translation)

Ezekiel 40:17; *Then the man brought me into the outer courtyard. I saw rooms there and pavement all around the courtyard. There were 30 rooms along the edge of the pavement.* (GOD'S WORD® Translation)

Ezekiel 40:24; *Then the man led me to the south side, and I saw a gateway that faced south. He measured its recessed walls and* *its entrance hall. They were the same size as those of the other gateways.* (GOD'S WORD® Translation)

Ezekiel 40:28; *Then the man brought me to the inner courtyard through the south gateway. He measured the south gateway. It was the same size as the others.* (GOD'S WORD® Translation)

Ezekiel 40:32; *Then the man brought me to the east side of the inner courtyard. He measured the gateway. It was the same size as the others.* (GOD'S WORD® Translation)

Ezekiel 40:35; *Then the man brought me to the north gateway. He measured it. It was the same size as the others.* (GOD'S WORD® Translation)

Isn't this interesting? The LORD's tour continues. Now they go into the sanctuary.

Ezekiel 41:1; *After that, the man brought me into the sanctuary of the Temple. He measured the walls on either side of its doorway, and they were 101/2 feet thick. The doorway was 171/2 feet wide, and the walls on each side of it were 83/4 feet long. The sanctuary itself was 70 feet long and 35 feet wide.* (New Living Translation)

Ezekiel 42:1; *Then the man led me out of the Temple courtyard by way of the north gateway. We entered the outer courtyard and came to a group of rooms against the north wall of the inner courtyard.* (New Living Translation)

Talk about time travel? Wow… It continues.

Ezekiel 43:1 & 5;
1 After this, the man brought me back around to the east gateway.

5 Then the Spirit took me up and brought me into the inner courtyard, and the glory of the LORD filled the Temple. (New Living Translation)

The LORD our God just took Ezekiel on a tour to the coming third temple.

Ezekiel 44:1; *Then the man brought me back to the east gateway in the outer wall of the Temple area, but it was closed.* (New Living Translation)

Ezekiel 44:4; *Then the man brought me through the north gateway to the front of the Temple. I looked and saw that the glory of the LORD filled the Temple of the LORD, and I fell face down on the ground.* (New Living Translation)

John was taken in the Spirit and commanded to write down what he saw. He was commanded twice to write the things he saw. So his spirit was taken, and he was shown what eventually would become 'The Book of Revelation of Jesus Christ'. It's usually abbreviated to 'The Book of Revelation'. You never thought about looking at it in that way before have you?

Revelation 1:9-19;
9 I, John, your brother and companion in the suffering and kingdom and patient endurance that are ours in Jesus, was on the island of Patmos because of the word of God and the testimony of Jesus.
10 On the Lord's Day I was in the Spirit, and I heard behind me a loud voice like a trumpet,
11 which said: "Write on a scroll what you see and send it to the seven churches: to Ephesus, Smyrna, Pergamum, Thyatira, Sardis, Philadelphia and Laodicea."
12 I turned around to see the voice that was speaking to me. And when I turned I saw seven golden lampstands,
13 and among the lampstands was someone like a son of man, dressed in a robe reaching down to his feet and with a golden sash around his chest.
14 The hair on his head was white like wool, as white as snow, and his eyes were like blazing fire.
15 His feet were like bronze glowing in a furnace, and his voice was like the sound of rushing waters.

16 In his right hand he held seven stars, and coming out of his mouth was a sharp, double-edged sword. His face was like the sun shining in all its brilliance.
17 When I saw him, I fell at his feet as though dead. Then he placed his right hand on me and said: "Do not be afraid. I am the First and the Last.
18 I am the Living One; I was dead, and now look, I am alive for ever and ever! And I hold the keys of death and Hades.
19 "Write, therefore, what you have seen, what is now and what will take place later. (New International Version)

Also in the following verse John again was taken up.

Revelation 4:1-2;
1 After this I looked, and there before me was a door standing open in heaven. And the voice I had first heard speaking to me like a trumpet said, "Come up here, and I will show you what must take place after this."
2 At once I was in the Spirit, and there before me was a throne in heaven with someone sitting on it. (New International Version)

In this next event, Paul speaks about a follower of Christ, as he puts it, who was taken up to the third heaven. Some believe that this follower of Christ was Paul himself.

2 Corinthians 12:1-5;
1 I must brag, although it doesn't do any good. I'll go on to visions and revelations from the Lord.
2 I know a follower of Christ who was snatched away to the third heaven fourteen years ago. I don't know whether this happened to him physically or spiritually. Only God knows.
3 I know that this person
4 was snatched away to paradise where he heard things that can't be expressed in words, things that humans cannot put into words. I don't know whether this happened to him physically or spiritually. Only God knows.
5 I'll brag about this person, but I won't brag about myself unless it's about my weaknesses. (GOD'S WORD® Translation)

Displacing Time and Space

Let's look at a few things Jesus had done.

Matthew 4:4-7;
5 Then the devil took him to the holy city and had him stand on the highest point of the temple.
6 "If you are the Son of God," he said, "throw yourself down. For it is written: "'He will command his angels concerning you, and they will lift you up in their hands, so that you will not strike your foot against a stone.'"
7 Jesus answered him, "It is also written: 'Do not put the Lord your God to the test.'" (New International Version)

Then the devil took Him and had Him stand… or should I say maybe carried Him to the highest point of the temple. Remember, this is the very beginning of His ministry. He had just been baptized, and the Holy Spirit sent Him into the wilderness to fast and pray and be tempted of the devil.

Matthew 4:8-10;
8 Again, the devil took him to a very high mountain and showed him all the kingdoms of the world and their splendor.
9 "All this I will give you," he said, "if you will bow down and worship me."
10 Jesus said to him, "Away from me, Satan! For it is written: 'Worship the Lord your God, and serve him only.'" (New International Version)

The significance of the devil taking the Lord up to the top of the mountain was to let Jesus know he had control over all of this land. The devil has dominion over the earth just like we have dominion here too.

Luke 4:28-30;
28 All the people in the synagogue were furious when they heard this.
29 They got up, drove him out of the town, and took him to the brow of the hill on which the town was built, in order to throw him down the cliff.

30 But he walked right through the crowd and went on his way. (New International Version)

This is so incredible what Jesus had done in this passage. Here you have those that were in the synagogue and were really mad; furious enough to take Jesus up to the top of the cliff and throw him off of it for what He said to them. So what happened? Jesus turned around and walked right through them and went about His way. I don't know about you, but I don't think I can walk through an angry crowd who are trying to throw me off a cliff. So how did Jesus accomplish this?

If you check the verb 'through' in Greek, it actually means passing through them without pushing them aside. He walked through the crowd like we walk through the air all day long. Does that make sense? Jesus walked right through those people. That brings up a few other thoughts. How did that happen? Did Jesus make himself invisible? Or did He just walk right through them while they watched? Imagine seeing that for the first time. Try going home and explaining that to your spouse…

"Honey, you should have see what happened today. I'm not sure I believe it. This Jesus was talking in the synagogue and got us all mad and upset. So we forced him up the cliff to throw him off it. When we got to the top, he turned around and walked right through us. Honestly, he passed right through us…"

The spouse looks at him strangely and ponders her answer. She leans closer to him and says;

"Have you been drinking the wine again?"

While that is a little bit of humor, how do you explain what happened there?

There is another instance where Jesus did something similar.

John 8:58-59;
58 "I tell you the truth," Jesus answered, "before Abraham was born, I am!"
59 At this, they picked up stones to stone him, but Jesus hid himself, slipping away from the temple grounds. (New International Version)

Where this passage took place is believed in the temple. Keep in mind the temple was made of stone. If that be the case, where did Jesus hide Himself? Did He do something similar here like He did with the crowd that wanted to throw Him off the cliff? This is definitely something to ponder.

Here is another verse where Paul is discussing the love of Jesus. Could this be the fourth dimension? You will read how wide, how long, how high it is. Then he adds how deep it is. Deep?

Ephesians 3:18; *This way, with all of God's people you will be able to understand how wide, long, high, and deep his love is.* (GOD'S WORD® Translation)

Let's not forget the event with Philip and the Ethiopian Eunuch. I mentioned him elsewhere in this book. The eunuch is believed to have a position similar to what we would call here in the U.S. the Secretary of the Treasury Department.

Jacob's Ladder

**enesis 28:10-17;**
10 Jacob left Beersheba and traveled toward Haran.
11 When he came to a certain place, he stopped for the night because the sun had gone down. He took one of the stones from that place, put it under his head, and lay down there.
12 He had a dream in which he saw a stairway set up on the earth with its top reaching up to heaven. He saw the angels of God going up and coming down on it.
13 The LORD was standing above it, saying, "I am the LORD, the God of your grandfather Abraham and the God of Isaac. I will give the land on which you are lying to you and your descendants.
14 Your descendants will be like the dust on the earth. You will spread out to the west and to the east, to the north and to the south. Through you and through your descendant every family on earth will be blessed.

15 Remember, I am with you and will watch over you wherever you go. I will also bring you back to this land because I will not leave you until I do what I've promised you."
16 Then Jacob woke up from his sleep and exclaimed, "Certainly, the LORD is in this place, and I didn't know it!"
17 Filled with awe, he said, "How awe-inspiring this place is! Certainly, this is the house of God and the gateway to heaven!"
(GOD'S WORD® Translation)

This passage gives us such a fascinating account of many things.

1. God was above the ladder.
2. He addresses Jacob directly.
3. God identifies himself.
4. God is going to give Jacob this land to him and his off spring.
5. God tells him how many descendants he will have and for generations to come.
6. God will watch over him. Now keep in mind what happened previously to him. Jacob stole Esau's birthright from him. And then he stole Esau's blessing. Today, most of us do not understand the importance of the firstborn and the blessings that accompany it. It's obvious here the LORD showed mercy and favor towards Jacob despite what he had done in the past.

Did you notice the last three words of that passage? It said; "gateway to heaven." Sometimes Christians glaze over parts of Scripture that say things of this nature. However, what we do know is it is written right there. It was presented to us in that fashion. With that said, could it be at that exact place is where a travel gateway is located so the angels from heaven can move quickly up and down it? That could be one of these gateways the angels from heaven use to deliver messages from the LORD God. Could angels use it to carry out the commands of God? Could these gateways be used to transport the souls of believers in Christ to heaven when they die? Could there be other portals that take the souls of men who do not believe in the Lord Jesus down into Hades Hell?

Let's examine this in another light. Have you ever thought how the angels ascend and descend back and forth from heaven so fast?

Outside of our solar system, the closest star to earth is around 4.3 light years away from earth. One light year is equal to about 5.88 trillion miles. That is, give or take. That star would be over twenty trillion miles away. That is trillion with a "t". That is what we believe to be the closest one. How about farthest one away from earth? Some say they are as far away as billions of "light years" away.

Regardless how far away the furthest planet is, the question is where is heaven located. Is it outside the universe or inside it? If it is located in the extreme parts of our universe, then how do these physical beings (angels) get back and forth from heaven so quickly? Are they using vortexes or portals?

These are obviously interesting topics of discussions.

One Continent into Seven Continents

There are those who believe the earth was one giant land mass. If you were to look at a map of the world, and lay it flat, you can see how it could have been one huge land mass at one time.

I believe that the division of the continents happened after the event of the Tower of Babel. There could have been an earthquake which split the continents up and slowly they could have drifted apart over some months or even several years. Or the LORD could have had it done rapidly without an earthquake.

Whatever the method He chose, He divided the continents. It was done during the lifetime a man called Peleg. The name of Peleg actually means 'dividing' or 'division'. He was the 50th generation too. Isn't that fascinating?

It is estimated that Peleg was born around 2218 B.C.

Genesis 10:25; *Two sons were born to Eber: One was named Peleg, because in his time the earth was divided; his brother was named Joktan.* (New International Version)

1 Chronicles 1:19; *Two sons were born to Eber: One was named Peleg, because in his time the earth was divided; his brother was named Joktan.* (New International Version)

Did you notice anything special about the two verses above? They were translated exactly word for word. One came from Genesis, and the other one came from 1 Chronicles.

"In his time" is somewhat general. So we know that at some time during the life of Peleg, the division of the land occurred. The Book of Jasher also tells us the land was divided during Peleg's lifetime.

Jasher 7:19; These are the generations of Shem; Shem begat Arpachshad and Arpachshad begat Shelach, and Shelach begat Eber and to Eber were born two children, the name of one was Peleg, for in his days the sons of men were divided, and in the latter days, the earth was divided.

We know the Peleg lived at least 239 years.

Genesis 11:18-19;
18 When Peleg had lived 30 years, he became the father of Reu.
19 And after he became the father of Reu, Peleg lived 209 years and had other sons and daughters. (New International Version)

Jasher 10:1; And Peleg the son of Eber died in those days, in the forty-eighth year of the life of Abram son of Terah, and all the days of Peleg were two hundred and thirty-nine years.

I believe that sometime between 2218 B.C. and 2009 B.C. our heavenly Father divided up the continents. It was during the period Peleg lived here on earth.

I believe around 2144 B.C. they started building the Tower of Babel. Some scholars believe the tower incident occurred around 2240 B.C. Following my timeline, sometime between 2144 B.C. to 1979 B.C., is when the LORD divided one land mass into seven continents.

As an afterthought, I find it interesting that our Heavenly Father chose to separate one land mass into seven continents. And what does the number seven mean in the Bible?

Atlantis

There are some who believe there were civilizations that once thrived but suddenly just disappeared without a trace. One example is the ancient city of Atlantis. Some believe the Mayan civilization just seemed to have just vanished without a trace too. Many people are puzzled why these civilizations just disappeared. They should consider what the Bible says. The earth was flooded during the time of Noah. Some scientists believe the ocean levels are higher now than pre-flood days. If this were true then that could be one explanation as to why some civilizations like Atlantis are believed to have been underwater. This makes sense if you think about it. Yet there is another theory about Atlantis I found that is very interesting.

During some finds in Antarctica, scientists discovered some fossils of the woolly Mammoth's. They also found fossils of tigers and other animals which were remarkably preserved. They discovered some of these animals still had the remnants of an undigested meal in their bellies not completely digested. How does that happen? They froze very quickly in a very few short hours. So how does that happen? There are two possibilities.

The first one would be a pole shift of the earth's magnetic poles. That would mean where the poles are now would be basically warm, just like where the equator is now. That would also mean the earth would have rotated differently. So if the poles changed, it might have gone through Mexico at one end to Egypt at the other end as an example.

The other possibility is when the LORD broke apart the continents (after our languages were changed at the Tower of Babel) and placed them where they are now. Small parts of these continents broke apart during the move and today we call them islands. Because the land mass shifted suddenly and quickly, this would explain how these animals got frozen so quickly.

What is interesting is if the LORD indeed separated the continents in this way, how did these ancient structures survive the enormous shock that took place when this event occurred.

What is also interesting is why it's not recorded in the Bible… or is it? The answer would be a 'yes'. I've narrowed down when the LORD split the continents apart. This event most definitely has had an impact on life on the continents that were separated away from the main body of land.

Graham Hancock, a British author and journalist, believes that that the ancient city of Atlantis could actually be on Antarctica. Just as an observation, the similarities between the name of Atlantis and Antarctica are thought-provoking.

The Dominion Mandate

We have a mandate from the LORD God.

Genesis 1:26-28;
26 Then God said, "Let us make man in our image, after our likeness. And let them have dominion over the fish of the sea and over the birds of the heavens and over the livestock and over all the earth and over every creeping thing that creeps on the earth."
27 So God created man in his own image, in the image of God he created him; male and female he created them.
28 And God blessed them. And God said to them, "Be fruitful and multiply and fill the earth and subdue it, and have dominion over the fish of the sea and over the birds of the heavens and over every living thing that moves on the earth." (English Standard Version)

God reaffirms to Noah the dominion mandate.

Genesis 9:1-3;
1 God blessed Noah and his sons and said to them, "Be fertile, increase in number, and fill the earth.
2 All the wild animals and all the birds will fear you and be terrified of you. Every creature that crawls on the ground and all the fish in the sea have been put under your control.
3 Everything that lives and moves will be your food. I gave you green plants as food; I now give you everything else. (GOD'S WORD® Translation)

David confirms this mandate in this psalm!

Psalm 8:3-8;
3 When I look at your heavens, the work of your fingers, the moon and the stars, which you have set in place,
4 what is man that you are mindful of him, and the son of man that you care for him?
5 Yet you have made him a little lower than the heavenly beings and crowned him with glory and honor.
6 You have given him dominion over the works of your hands; you have put all things under his feet,
7 all sheep and oxen, and also the beasts of the field,
8 the birds of the heavens, and the fish of the sea, whatever passes along the paths of the seas. (English Standard Version)

Jesus gives us a dominion mandate.

Matthew 28:18-20;
18 Then Jesus came to them and said, "All authority in heaven and on earth has been given to me.
19 Therefore go and make disciples of all nations, baptizing them in the name of the Father and of the Son and of the Holy Spirit,
20 and teaching them to obey everything I have commanded you. And surely I am with you always, to the very end of the age." (New International Version)

The fight is the LORD's. He has empowered us to fight for what we know we need to do. And that is do what the Bible tells us to do. The world needs what we have on the inside of us.

Seeing how we have dominion here on earth because the LORD God gave it to us, then it seems that we can make things happen.

Still not quite sure about this dominion mandate? Still not sure if we are in control down here?

Why was Jesus here only about thirty years? Why not say forty years? That would be like the time when Jesus fasted and prayed for forty days and forty nights. God sent the rain during the Genesis 7 flood for forty days and forty nights. Moses was gone for forty days and forty nights on the mountain. The Israelites walked in the desert for forty years. After Jezebel threatened Elijah with death after all the prophets of Baal were killed, he left the area on a journey that lasted for forty days.

Now why is this significant? Let's consider the next thought. Why is Jesus coming back to the earth? Here are some thoughts to ponder.

1. To defeat satan and his fallen ones.
2. To defeat the armies that had attacked Israel at the end of the great Tribulation Period. It's believed He will be battling Egypt first. That's when His garment will be stained with their blood.
3. To set up His Kingdom, His thousand year reign!

Could the reason why Jesus is coming back to earth fighting be because we didn't do all we could have for mankind when we were here on earth? What do I mean by that? If we were to love like how God loves us all the time, our light too would shine wherever we go, whatever we do, serving others, catering to their needs. Wherever we go, we can heal people right on the spot, cast out demons, cause the lame to walk, the blind to see, etc. Is it possible today to be able to do that? Can this be done? Can we be as powerful as Peter was?

Acts 5:15; *As a result, people brought the sick into the streets and laid them on beds and mats so that at least Peter's shadow might fall on some oj them as he passed by.* (New International Version)

If we have a dominion mandate, that basically means we control things here on earth. God has granted that to us and has given us the power to do so when we properly exercise it.

1 John 4:4; *But you belong to God, my dear children. You have already won a victory over those people, because the Spirit who lives in you is greater than the spirit who lives in the world.* (New Living Translation)

God told us the powers we now possess. So what does the LORD want us to do?

1. Do the righteous thing.

2. Show mercy towards others.
3. Walk humbly with our God.

   Micah 6:8: *He has showed you, O man, what is good. And what does the LORD require of you? To act justly and to love mercy and to walk humbly with your God.* (New International Version)

   Amos 3:3; *Do two walk together unless they have agreed to do so?* (New International Version)
4. Go to where the people are and preach the gospel.

   Mark 16:15; *Then Jesus said to them, "So wherever you go in the world, tell everyone the Good News.* (GOD'S WORD® Translation)
5. When they get saved, baptize them

   Mark 16:16; *Whoever believes and is baptized will be saved, but whoever does not believe will be condemned.* (New International Version)
6. Cast out demons in Jesus name.

   Mark 16:17; *"These are the miraculous signs that will accompany believers: They will use the power and authority of my name to force demons out of people. They will speak new languages.* (GOD'S WORD® Translation)
7. Lay hands on the sick so they will be healed.

   Mark 16:18 *They will pick up snakes, and if they drink any deadly poison, it will not hurt them. They will place their hands on the sick and cure them."* (GOD'S WORD® Translation)
8. Lame to walk

   Acts 14:8-10;

   8 In Lystra there sat a man crippled in his feet, who was lame from birth and had never walked.

   9 He listened to Paul as he was speaking. Paul looked directly at him, saw that he had faith to be healed

   10 and called out, "Stand up on your feet!" At that, the man jumped up and began to walk. (New International Version)

   Notice what Paul saw in the man. Paul saw the man had the faith to be healed. Ponder that for a while.
9. The blind to see.

   Acts 9:17-18;

   17 Then Ananias went to the house and entered it. Placing his hands on Saul, he said, "Brother Saul, the

Lord—Jesus, who appeared to you on the road as you were coming here—has sent me so that you may see again and be filled with the Holy Spirit."
18 Immediately, something like scales fell from Saul's eyes, and he could see again. He got up and was baptized, (New International Version)
Mark 10:51-52;
51 "What do you want me to do for you?" Jesus asked him. The blind man said, "Rabbi, I want to see."
52"Go," said Jesus, "your faith has healed you." Immediately he received his sight and followed Jesus along the road. (New International Version)

10. The mute to speak
    Matthew 9:33; *And when the demon was driven out, the man who had been mute spoke. The crowd was amazed and said, "Nothing like this has ever been seen in Israel."* (New International Version)
11. The deaf to hear
    Mark 7:37; *People were overwhelmed with amazement. "He has done everything well," they said. "He even makes the deaf hear and the mute speak."* (New International Version)
12. Healing a man suffering from a bad case of diarrhea and fever.
    Acts 28:7-8;
    7 A man named Publius, who was the governor of the island, had property around the area. He welcomed us and treated us kindly, and for three days we were his guests.
    8 His father happened to be sick in bed. He was suffering from fever and dysentery. Paul went to him, prayed, placed his hands on him, and made him well. (New International Version)
13. Raise people from the dead.
    Acts 9:36-41;
    36 In Joppa there was a disciple named Tabitha (which, when translated, is Dorcas), who was always doing good and helping the poor.
    37 About that time she became sick and died, and her body was washed and placed in an upstairs room.

38 Lydda was near Joppa; so when the disciples heard that Peter was in Lydda, they sent two men to him and urged him, "Please come at once!"
39 Peter went with them, and when he arrived he was taken upstairs to the room. All the widows stood around him, crying and showing him the robes and other clothing that Dorcas had made while she was still with them.
40 Peter sent them all out of the room; then he got down on his knees and prayed. Turning toward the dead woman, he said, "Tabitha, get up." She opened her eyes, and seeing Peter she sat up.
41 He took her by the hand and helped her to her feet. Then he called the believers and the widows and presented her to them alive. (New International Version)

Acts 20:9-12;

9 Seated in a window was a young man named Eutychus, who was sinking into a deep sleep as Paul talked on and on. When he was sound asleep, he fell to the ground from the third story and was picked up dead.
10 Paul went down, threw himself on the young man and put his arms around him. "Don't be alarmed," he said. "He's alive!"
11 Then he went upstairs again and broke bread and ate. After talking until daylight, he left.
12 The people took the young man home alive and were greatly comforted. (New International Version)

14. Love one another.

I would think that it would be a very good start to do what the LORD wants us to do. Do you agree? All of that is the most powerful ministry any Christian can possibly have for their life. And we have been empowered to do that in Jesus' name. Do you believe you can perform such miracles?

Which brings me to the solutions of how we can change the world. There are enough Christians in the world today for us to effect such changes in ways that they would be drawn to the LORD our God by emulating what we do for the people.

People today want to see, they want to feel, they want to know that there is something so real so they can believe in it. They are hungering and searching for the love of God. They are lost and are seeking for our Glorious Lord and Savior Jesus Christ.

Hence that is why God wants us to pass the 1 Corinthians 13 test. We can spread the love of the LORD God throughout the four corners of the earth. Then people will repent. They will turn back to God, to His glory and honor.

People refuse to accept the LORD and Jesus' sacrifice on the cross. How sad it is. What is unfortunate is that people will not humble themselves, confess their sin, or feel they don't need God at all. But yet God will grant them what they desire. Unless they change their mind, they will not be with Him for all eternity. And they will be cast into the lake of fire that burns with fire and brimstone.

What is Really at Stake Here?

As the old saying goes, "after everything was said and done…" All these things in our present time will vanish and be gone one day. It's all about the eternal souls of mankind.

Could people in hell be crying out in pain and agony for hundreds if not thousands of years? Here is a scenario that could be happening right now to somebody.

The memories of my past life are a distant memory. It is so hot here. I have trouble breathing. To breathe with ease is a luxury. There is no water to drink to quench my thirst. I long for just a drop of water to cool my tongue.

Luke 16:24; *So he called to him, 'Father Abraham, have pity on me and send Lazarus to dip the tip of his finger in water and cool my tongue, because I am in agony in this fire.'* (New International Version)

There is no rest. Day and night I struggle to find just a moment of comfort. The feelings of worms crawling all over and through my body is horrific. I am in absolute agony. The feeling of these worms chewing on and in my body day and night is more than I can handle.

Mark 9:48; *where "'the worms that eat them do not die, and the fire is not quenched.'* (New International Version)

I hear others scream. They are experiencing the same horrific events I'm trying to endure. The pleasantness, the memories of feeling God's love all over the earth are vanished. I cry out in pain and torment because I can't stand it anymore. It seems to be getting worse.

Matthew 8:12; *But the subjects of the kingdom will be thrown outside, into the darkness, where there will be weeping and gnashing of teeth."* (New International Version)

Matthew 13:42; *They will throw them into the blazing furnace, where there will be weeping and gnashing of teeth.* (New International Version)

How can I stand this anymore? When will I get out of this place? I've been here for so long, I have no idea how long that has been. I can't sit down because it burns continually when I do. If I stand, it burns the bottom of my feet. I feel as though I'm about to die, I'm so dehydrated because I haven't drunk any water for so long.

I cry out to someone, anyone who can hear my voice for help. All I hear are other voices doing the same thing I am doing. The shrill noise of their voices is worse than fingernails raking across a chalkboard.

I can see across a great chasm, a great divide. I see pleasantness, green grass, water running freely from a waterfall over there. There used to be people there. I'm told the people there could speak to us over here. But they are gone now. I try to go over there, but something is blocking me. When can I get out of this place? Welcome to Hell.

This is the place (hell) that people talk about causally, a place where you tell someone to go to, whether in jest or otherwise. People joke around that this place is hell. Or stated there is no hell. You will remember the chance you had before you arrived to accept Jesus Christ as your personal Savior, trusting His shed blood that was spilled for our transgressions. You might have mocked it, got proud and said 'I don't need or want God'.

Psalm 53:1; *For the director of music. According to mahalath. A maskil of David. The fool says in his heart, "There is no God." They are corrupt, and their ways are vile; there is no one who does good.* (New International Version)

The Ten Commandants

There are a few movies made about the Ten Commandants. I have a favorite one too. Instead of basing our beliefs of what happened in the movie, let's see what actually happened, according to the Bible.

There was for the law and the commandants.

Exodus 24:12; *The LORD said to Moses, "Come up to me on the mountain and stay here, and I will give you the tablets of stone with the law and commandments I have written for their instruction."* (New International Version)

The tablets were written by the finger of God!

Exodus 31:18; *When the LORD finished speaking to Moses on Mount Sinai, he gave him the two tablets of the covenant law, the tablets of stone inscribed by the finger of God.* (New International Version)

Now, what isn't generally known is God inscribed on BOTH sides of the tablets.

Exodus 32:15; *Moses turned and went down the mountain with the two tablets of the covenant law in his hands. They were inscribed on both sides, front and back.* (New International Version)

Most people know they were given twice to us. Actually, they were given to us three times. The first time was verbally at Mount Sinai.

Exodus 20:1-20;
1 And God spoke all these words:
2 "I am the LORD your God, who brought you out of Egypt, out of the land of slavery.
3 "You shall have no other gods before me.
4 "You shall not make for yourself an image in the form of anything in heaven above or on the earth beneath or in the waters below.
5 You shall not bow down to them or worship them; for I, the LORD your God, am a jealous God, punishing the children for the sin of the parents to the third and fourth generation of those who hate me,
6 but showing love to a thousand generations of those who love me and keep my commandments.
7 "You shall not misuse the name of the LORD your God, for the LORD will not hold anyone guiltless who misuses his name.
8 "Remember the Sabbath day by keeping it holy.
9 Six days you shall labor and do all your work,
10 but the seventh day is a sabbath to the LORD your God. On it you shall not do any work, neither you, nor your son or daughter, nor your male or female servant, nor your animals, nor any foreigner residing in your towns.
11 For in six days the LORD made the heavens and the earth, the sea, and all that is in them, but he rested on the seventh day. Therefore the LORD blessed the Sabbath day and made it holy.
12 "Honor your father and your mother, so that you may live long in the land the LORD your God is giving you.
13 "You shall not murder.
14 "You shall not commit adultery.
15 "You shall not steal.
16 "You shall not give false testimony against your neighbor.
17 "You shall not covet your neighbor's house. You shall not covet your neighbor's wife, or his male or female servant, his ox or donkey, or anything that belongs to your neighbor."

18 When the people saw the thunder and lightning and heard the trumpet and saw the mountain in smoke, they trembled with fear. They stayed at a distance
19 and said to Moses, "Speak to us yourself and we will listen. But do not have God speak to us or we will die."
20 Moses said to the people, "Do not be afraid. God has come to test you, so that the fear of God will be with you to keep you from sinning." (New International Version)

The Tower of Babel

Most of us Christians know the story about the building of this tower (and city). There are those who believe its location was in Iraq. Some others believe it might be located in Syria. Wherever it was located, God saw what they were doing and decided to change their language so they won't understand each other.
(Source: http://www.answersingenesis.org/articles/arj/v4/n1/where-is-tower-babel)

It is estimated this multi-year construction project began around 2144 B.C. The flood started around 2319 B.C. If we do the math, about one hundred and seventy five years had past when Nimrod and man again rebelled against God. Just one hundred and seventy five years. You would think they would have learned while the remembrance of the flood was still pretty fresh in their memories.

So who is this Nimrod? He is the son of Cush. Cush was the son of Ham. And Ham was the son of Noah. Nimrod went by many names after the many languages were created. Some of them were Gilgamesh, Baal, Adonis, Orion, Apollo, Ra, Osiris, and many others. Keep in mind, Nimrod and many of the descendants of Ham were Nephilim or the descendant of the Nephilim. In Genesis 6, it says they were in the land and also afterwards. That afterwards we believe to be after the flood.

There appears to be a few reasons why it was being built.

1. What is interesting is some believe the tower was built so it would withstand another flood. Then they would continue to live despite the judgment of God. The reality of the situation is this tower if it could be built

that high, would need to rise above Mount Everest, which is 29,035 feet in height or over 5.5 miles high. At that level, there would not be enough oxygen to breathe and live for very long.

2. Yet others believe it was built in revenge against God's judgment on Nimrod's ancestors, the Nephilim. Can you image the folly of that kind of thinking? The vanity of this? Here, the LORD God just judged the earth, and they still didn't learn from that situation.
3. Some scholars speculate that there is some type of gateway or a portal they wanted to use so they would be able to travel through. Where it took them if that is what it did, is unknown at the moment. Maybe it was an opening that would allow us to go back and forth to heaven. There is a lot we do not know or understand about the different dimensions yet. So, could this have been a portal or gateway? Whatever it was, because God is the overall project manager of everything, He didn't approve of it and thus shut it down.

There was evidence all around us of the event called the flood. Yet some men just didn't get the hint that sin caused this to occur upon the earth. It just makes you wonder today doesn't it? There are those who are called by God into the Apostolic, Prophetic, and Seer ministries to convey prophetic words, teach, instruct, inform, warn the people of the outcome of their actions. But do they take heed of it or repent? Many times, nope. The Bible gives evidence of this very same thing. Then sometimes people will just simply ignore what is being told to them and guess what happens? Then they go and blame someone else when the problem lies right within their own life, their own thinking, in what they are doing. Sometimes they attack the messenger either verbally and/or physically. It just shows people sometimes really don't want to hear what God says or what God wants them to do. The problem isn't the knowledge of what happened and how, its people don't want to know or think that there is a God who wants them to do this or that. They don't want to yield to the LORD God of Abraham, Isaac, and Jacob. It's just that simple.

This rebellion against God and building this tower reminds me of a situation that Noah and his three sons were in after the flood. The passage makes it plain that the demonic spirits were creating havoc among them. And this would be just about the right time that Nimrod would have become evil and turned against our God.

Before I get too far into this, I do want to state that it's our choices we make that we are ultimately responsible for when we stand before God.

I realize the next passage of text was included in another area of this book. However, I think it is important enough to read it again. We need to understand what fueled the falling away.

Jubilee 10:1-14;
1 And in the third week of this jubilee the unclean demons began to lead astray the children of
2 the sons of Noah, and to make to err and destroy them. And the sons of Noah came to Noah their father, and they told him concerning the demons which were leading astray and blinding and
3 slaying his sons' sons. And he prayed before the Lord his God, and said: 'God of the spirits of all flesh, who hast shown mercy unto me And hast saved me and my sons from the waters of the flood, And hast not caused me to perish as Thou didst the sons of perdition; For Thy grace has been great towards me, And great has been Thy mercy to my soul; Let Thy grace be lift up upon my sons, And let not wicked spirits rule over them Lest they should destroy them from the earth.
4 But do Thou bless me and my sons, that we may increase and Multiply and replenish the earth.
5 And Thou knowest how Thy Watchers, the fathers of these spirits, acted in my day: and as for these spirits which are living, imprison them and hold them fast in the place of condemnation, and let them not bring destruction on the sons of thy servant, my God; for these are malignant, and
6 created in order to destroy. And let them not rule over the spirits of the living; for Thou alone canst exercise dominion over them. And let them not have power over the sons of the righteous

7 ,8 from henceforth and for evermore.' And the Lord our God bade us to bind all. And the chief of the spirits, Mastema, came and said: 'Lord, Creator, let some of them remain before me, and let them harken to my voice, and do all that I shall say unto them; for if some of them are not left to me, I shall not be able to execute the power of my will on the sons of men; for these are for corruption and leading astray before my judgment, for great is the wickedness of the sons of men.'
9 And He said: Let the tenth part of them remain before him, and let nine parts descend into the
10 place of condemnation.' And one of us He commanded that we should teach Noah all their
11 medicines; for He knew that they would not walk in uprightness, nor strive in righteousness. And we did according to all His words: all the malignant evil ones we bound in the place of condemna-
12 tion and a tenth part of them we left that they might be subject before Satan on the earth. And we explained to Noah all the medicines of their diseases, together with their seductions, how he
13 might heal them with herbs of the earth. And Noah wrote down all things in a book as we instructed him concerning every kind of medicine. Thus the evil spirits were precluded from
14 (hurting) the sons of Noah. And he gave all that he had written to Shem, his eldest son; for he

It's believed the tower of Babel was actually a tall step pyramid. Some believe it was built long before the pyramids in Egypt.

While many people never really thought about how tall this tower could become, there is some information that you might find interesting. Based on the information that is in the Bible, they can calculate the total potential height the tower could end up being.

Genesis 11:1-3;

1 The whole world had one language with a common vocabulary.

2 As people moved toward the east, they found a plain in Shinar [Babylonia] and settled there.
3 They said to one another, "Let's make bricks and bake them thoroughly." They used bricks as stones and tar as mortar. (New International Version)

A study was done as to how tall this tower could rise. What they did was make the brick according to how the Bible described they made it back then. They used the same basic materials which were available to them back in those days too.

I would like to focus on the word "thoroughly". There were a few methods of making bricks back then. The best method would be to bake them "thoroughly". Essentially, the best way to make the strongest and the most enduring brick possible was to bake it in some type of oven. It could be up to seven times stronger than the sun-dried counterpart.

In this study mentioned below, they performed a stress test on the "thoroughly" baked brick to see how much pressure it could handle before it would crumble or break apart. Based on these test results, they calculated the tower could reach as high as two miles into the sky. (Source: History Channel, 2008, Dr. Linn W Hobbs, Professor of Materials Science, Massachusetts Institute of Technology)

To give you some type of reference as to how high that is, they estimate Mount Everest is around 29,035 feet tall. That means the tower could have been more than 1/3 the height of Mount Everest. To further put that into perspective, at just under 10,000 feet, there is just 2/3 of the amount of oxygen that is available at sea level.

(Source: http://www.teameverest03.org/everest_info/index.html)

Genesis 11:4-7;
4 *Then they said, "Let's build a city for ourselves and a tower with its top in the sky. Let's make a name for ourselves so that we won't become scattered all over the face of the earth."*
5 The LORD came down to see the city and the tower that the descendants of Adam were building.
6 The LORD said, "They are one people with one language. This is only the beginning of what they will do! Now nothing they plan to do will be too difficult for them.

7 Let us go down there and mix up their language so that they won't understand each other." (GOD'S WORD® Translation)

Ever wonder why we use the word babble? We might say, "Hey, what are you babbling about?" Why do we say that? Because we don't understand what the other person is saying. This could very well be the reason why. After the languages were changed, they couldn't understand one another.

God thought it important enough to stop this construction project and change all the languages so it wouldn't continue.

This might be hard for us to understand today. We have built tall buildings, skyscrapers that 'touch the sky' so to speak. It's interesting we call them 'skyscrapers'. We fly airplanes that touch the heavens. We send spaceships to distant planets and beyond our asteroid belt. We sent men to the moon multiple times and brought them back. God didn't stop us from exploring the sky and outer space. So what was going on back then? Was something else happening there that we are not understanding?

It's believed that Tower in Babel was a pyramid. Others believe it was a ziggurat.

There is another version of what might have happened at the Tower of Babel.

Talk about a building project. Check this information out!

1. This city was so big, it would take three days to walk around it.
2. They had a plan to attack God. They divided themselves up in three groups.
3. Interestingly enough, right before that, Abram was born. That is the same Abram that later God changed his name to Abraham. It is believed that Abraham was born 1948 years from creation. What is so interesting about that? When did Israel become a nation again? You got it… in 1948 A.D.
   Jasher 8:1-4;
   1 And it was in the night that Abram was born, that all the servants of Terah, and all the wise men of Nimrod, and his conjurors came and ate and drank in the house of Terah, and they rejoiced with him on that night.

> 2 And when all the wise men and conjurors went out from the house of Terah, they lifted up their eyes toward heaven that night to look at the stars, and they saw, and behold one very large star came from the east and ran in the heavens, and he swallowed up the four stars from the four sides of the heavens.
> 3 And all the wise men of the king and his conjurors were astonished at the sight, and the sages understood this matter, and they knew its import.
> 4 And they said to each other, This only betokens the child that has been born to Terah this night, who will grow up and be fruitful, and multiply, and possess all the earth, he and his children for ever, and he and his seed will slay great kings, and inherit their lands.

Have you ever wondered how tall it rose up to the heavens? Look at this passage of text.

Jubilees 10:18-20
18 unto generation, till the day of judgment. And in the three and thirtieth jubilee, in the first year in the second week, Peleg took to himself a wife, whose name was Lomna the daughter of Sina'ar, and she bare him a son in the fourth year of this week, and he called his name Reu; for he said: 'Behold the children of men have become evil through the wicked purpose of building for themselves
19 a city and a tower in the land of Shinar.' For they departed from the land of Ararat eastward to Shinar; for in his days they built the city and the tower, saying, 'Go to, let us ascend thereby into
20 heaven.' And they began to build, and in the fourth week they made brick with fire, and the bricks served them for stone, and the clay with which they cemented them together was asphalt which

It appears they started this project by starting to make brick. It took them almost a month to build the ovens that will bake the molded brick material. It explains below where they got the water from too. Then construction began.

Jubilees 10:21
21 comes out of the sea, and out of the fountains of water in the land of Shinar. And they built it: forty and three years [1645–1688 A.M.] were they building it; its breadth was 203 bricks, and the height (of a brick) was the third of one; its height amounted to 5433 cubits and 2 palms, and (the extent of one wall…)

This project went on for forty three years. There are not very many projects that have lasted that long.

I would like you to note the height of this tower was 5,433 cubits. Now if you remember, there were many different lengths of the measurement of a cubit. Some were around seventeen inches to the Hebrew cubit of just over twenty five inches. Let's be conservative and pick eighteen inches. Let's multiply the 5,433 cubits by eighteen inches, or a foot and a half. You would get about 8,150 feet. A mile is 5,280 feet. If we divide that into the 8,150 feet we get 1.5434… miles. So this tower rose over a mile and a half into the air. Did you catch that? A mile and a half…

Now if we use the Hebrew cubit and just calculate a cubit at two feet, then the tower would have been 10,560 feet tall or around two miles tall. That is absolutely incredible. There is no building today, anywhere in the world that is close to that height.

Now let's put that into perspective. Saudi Arabia is said to be constructing a mile high tower in Jeddah. However, due to the geology of the area, it has been scaled back somewhat. It's somewhat fitting that the proposed tallest building in the world is in the same region as the old Tower of Babel.

As you will read below, they were still building that Tower of Babel when construction was halted.

The passage below also mentions two walls. The measure is called stades. A stade appears to be about 185 meters or about 202 yards. According to the measurements given, one wall was 13 stades. It would make it 2,626 yards long. One mile equals 1,760 yards. That would make that one wall almost 1.49 miles long.

Now the other wall was 30 stades. Multiply 30 times 202 yards and we get 6,060. That would make the other wall 3.443 miles long. Those are two massive walls.

Jubilees 10:22-27
22 was) thirteen stades (and of the other thirty stades). And the Lord our God said unto us: Behold, they are one people, and (this) they begin to do, and now nothing will be withholden from them. Go to, let us go down and confound their language, that they may not understand one another's speech, and they may be dispersed into cities and nations, and one purpose will no longer abide with
23 them till the day of judgment.' And the Lord descended, and we descended with him to see the
24 city and the tower which the children of men had built. And he confounded their language, and they no longer understood one another's speech, and they ceased then to build the city and the
25 tower. For this reason the whole land of Shinar is called Babel, because the Lord did there confound all the language of the children of men, and from thence they were dispersed into their
26 cities, each according to his language and his nation. And the Lord sent a mighty wind against the tower and overthrew it upon the earth, and behold it was between Asshur and Babylon in the
27 land of Shinar, and they called its name 'Overthrow'.

Jasher 9:21-39
21 And all the princes of Nimrod and his great men took counsel together; Phut, Mitzraim, Cush and Canaan with their families, and they said to each other, Come let us build ourselves a city and in it a strong tower, and its top reaching heaven, and we will make ourselves famed, so that we may reign upon the whole world, in order that the evil of our enemies may cease from us, that we may reign mightily over them, and that we may not become scattered over the earth on account of their wars.
22 And they all went before the king, and they told the king these words, and the king agreed with them in this affair, and he did so.

23 And all the families assembled consisting of about six
hundred thousand men, and they went to seek an extensive piece
of ground to build the city and the tower, and they sought in the
whole earth and they found none like one valley at the east of the
land of Shinar, about two days' walk, and they journeyed there
and they dwelt there.
24 And they began to make bricks and burn fires to build the city
and the tower that they had imagined to complete.
25 And the building of the tower was unto them a transgression
and a sin, and they began to build it, and whilst they were
building against the Lord God of heaven, they imagined in their
hearts to war against him and to ascend into heaven.
26 And all these people and all the families divided themselves
in three parts; the first said We will ascend into heaven and fight
against him; the second said, We will ascend to heaven and place
our own gods there and serve them; and the third part said, We
will ascend to heaven and smite him with bows and spears; and
God knew all their works and all their evil thoughts, and he saw
the city and the tower which they were building.
27 And when they were building they built themselves a great
city and a very high and strong tower; and on account of its
height the mortar and bricks did not reach the builders in their
ascent to it, until those who went up had completed a full year,
and after that, they reached to the builders and gave them the
mortar and the bricks; thus was it done daily.
28 And behold these ascended and others descended the whole
day; and if a brick should fall from their hands and get broken,
they would all weep over it, and if a man fell and died, none of
them would look at him.
29 And the Lord knew their thoughts, and it came to pass when
they were building they cast the arrows toward the heavens, and
all the arrows fell upon them filled with blood, and when they
saw them they said to each other, Surely we have slain all those
that are in heaven.
30 For this was from the Lord in order to cause them to err, and
in order; to destroy them from off the face of the ground.
31 And they built the tower and the city, and they did this thing
daily until many days and years were elapsed.

32 And God said to the seventy angels who stood foremost before him, to those who were near to him, saying, Come let us descend and confuse their tongues, that one man shall not understand the language of his neighbor, and they did so unto them.
33 And from that day following, they forgot each man his neighbor's tongue, and they could not understand to speak in one tongue, and when the builder took from the hands of his neighbor lime or stone which he did not order, the builder would cast it away and throw it upon his neighbor, that he would die.
34 And they did so many days, and they killed many of them in this manner.
35 And the Lord smote the three divisions that were there, and he punished them according to their works and designs; those who said, We will ascend to heaven and serve our gods, became like apes and elephants; and those who said, We will smite the heaven with arrows, the Lord killed them, one man through the hand of his neighbor; and the third division of those who said, We will ascend to heaven and fight against him, the Lord scattered them throughout the earth.
36 And those who were left amongst them, when they knew and understood the evil which was coming upon them, they forsook the building, and they also became scattered upon the face of the whole earth.
37 And they ceased building the city and the tower; therefore he called that place Babel, for there the Lord confounded the Language of the whole earth; behold it was at the east of the land of Shinar.
38 And as to the tower which the sons of men built, the earth opened its mouth and swallowed up one third part thereof, and a fire also descended from heaven and burned another third, and the other third is left to this day, and it is of that part which was aloft, and its circumference is three days' walk.
39 And many of the sons of men died in that tower, a people without number.

It’s interesting to learn how Nimrod died. It should give you a slightly different perspective of Esau.

Jasher 27:3-16;
3 And Nimrod was observing Esau all the days, for a jealousy was formed in the heart of Nimrod against Esau all the days.
4 And on a certain day Esau went in the field to hunt, and he found Nimrod walking in the wilderness with his two men.
5 And all his mighty men and his people were with him in the wilderness, but they removed at a distance from him, and they went from him in different directions to hunt, and Esau concealed himself for Nimrod, and he lurked for him in the wilderness.
6 And Nimrod and his men that were with him did not know him, and Nimrod and his men frequently walked about in the field at the cool of the day, and to know where his men were hunting in the field.
7 And Nimrod and two of his men that were with him came to the place where they were, when Esau started suddenly from his lurking place, and drew his sword, and hastened and ran to Nimrod and cut off his head.
8 And Esau fought a desperate fight with the two men that were with Nimrod, and when they called out to him, Esau turned to them and smote them to death with his sword.
9 And all the mighty men of Nimrod, who had left him to go to the wilderness, heard the cry at a distance, and they knew the voices of those two men, and they ran to know the cause of it, when they found their king and the two men that were with him lying dead in the wilderness.
10 And when Esau saw the mighty men of Nimrod coming at a distance, he fled, and thereby escaped; and Esau took the valuable garments of Nimrod, which Nimrod's father had bequeathed to Nimrod, and with which Nimrod prevailed over the whole land, and he ran and concealed them in his house.
11 And Esau took those garments and ran into the city on account of Nimrod's men, and he came unto his father's house wearied and exhausted from fight, and he was ready to die through grief when he approached his brother Jacob and sat before him.
12 And he said unto his brother Jacob, Behold I shall die this day, and wherefore then do I want the birthright? And Jacob

acted wisely with Esau in this matter, and Esau sold his birthright to Jacob, for it was so brought about by the Lord.

The man who gave up his birthright for a bowl of food and was robbed of the blessing from his father Isaac, killed the King of Babylon, Nimrod. Isn't that ironic? Now you can begin to understand why Jacob ran after stealing Esau's blessing. He knew what his brother was capable of doing to him. However, a few scholars think Nimrod was killed by Shem.

Another interesting bit of information about Nimrod was the characterization in Wikipedia. It was thought that the cartoon character of Elmer Fudd was sarcastically made fun of by Bugs Bunny. In that, Nimrod was Elmer and was portrayed as a hunter.
(Source: http://en.wikipedia.org/wiki/Nimrod)

The Obelisk

The history about the obelisk is interesting. Until I started researching this book, I never realized what they were or should I say what they represent. It appears the Bible actually mentions them. Quite a few times too!

It seems to be called a "Pillar" in the Bible. Others feel that "Pillar" could be referring to the great pyramid of Giza. These obelisks are supposed to be the dwelling place of the sun god. (Source: Illustrated Dictionary of Symbols in Eastern and Western Art by James Hall, published by HarperCollins, 1994, page 75.)

The following verses appear to be addressing this obelisk. The different translations call it usually either an image or a pillar. That Hebrew word is "matstsebah" which means something stationed like a column (or memorial stone); by anal, an idol: garrison, (standing) image, pillar.

Exodus 23:24;
You must not worship the gods of these nations or serve them in any way or imitate their evil practices. Instead, you must utterly destroy them and smash their sacred pillars. (New Living Translation)

Exodus 34:13;
Instead, you must break down their pagan altars, smash their sacred pillars, and cut down their Asherah poles. (New Living Translation)

Asherah is believed to be the fertility goddess of Baal. And what is another name of a fertility goddess? That would be Ishtar. And Ishtar is another name for easter. Yep, that same easter as in easter Sunday. And Ishtar is said to be Semiramis, the wife of Nimrod. This verse could mean; cut down those poles that glorify Semiramis who is the wife of Nimrod.

Baal pops up from time to time in the Old Testament. It is one of the names for Nimrod too. Between the temples and monuments of Baal to its priests and worshipers, it has always been a temptation for the people of God. God's people eventually did turn away from their faith in the LORD God. There are those who openly condemn Israel for committing such a hideous sin. Yet, believe it or not, it hasn't changed from thousands of years ago to today. God's people are turning away and worshiping other false gods or in participating in the rituals of false/pagan god.

Leviticus 26:1;
Do not make idols or set up an image or a sacred stone for yourselves, and do not place a carved stone in your land to bow down before it. I am the LORD your God. (New International Version)

Deuteronomy 7:5; *This is what you are to do to them: Break down their altars, smash their sacred stones, cut down their Asherah poles and burn their idols in the fire.* (New International Version)

Deuteronomy 12:3; *Break down their altars, smash their sacred stones and burn their Asherah poles in the fire; cut down the idols of their gods and wipe out their names from those places.* (New International Version)

1 Kings 14:23 *They also set up for themselves high places, sacred stones and Asherah poles on every high hill and under every spreading tree.* (New International Version)

2 Kings 3:2; *He did what was evil in the LORD's sight, but not to the same extent as his father and mother. He at least tore down the sacred pillar of Baal that his father had set up.* (New International Version)

2 Kings 10:26-27;
26 They demolished the sacred stone of Baal and tore down the temple of Baal, and people have used it for a latrine to this day.
27 They brought the sacred stone out of the temple of Baal and burned it. (New International Version)

Latrine comes from the Hebrew word "motsaah", a family descent; also a sewer (marg.; compare tsow'ah) -- draught house; going forth.

2 Chronicles 14:3; *He removed the foreign altars and the high places, smashed the sacred stones and cut down the Asherah poles.* (New International Version)

2 Chronicles 31:1; *When all this had ended, the Israelites who were there went out to the towns of Judah, smashed the sacred stones and cut down the Asherah poles. They destroyed the high places and the altars throughout Judah and Benjamin and in Ephraim and Manasseh. After they had destroyed all of them, the Israelites returned to their own towns and to their own property.* (New International Version)

Isaiah 17:8; *They will not look to the altars, the work of their hands, and they will have no regard for the Asherah poles and the incense altars their fingers have made.* (New International Version)

The Hebrew word for Asherah from Stronge's Exhaustive Concordance 842 is "Asherah" and it means a Phoenician goddess, also an image of the same. This appears to be talking about Ishtar. Here are two more verses for you.

2 Chronicles 34:3; *In the eighth year of his reign, while he was still young, he began to seek the God of his father David. In his* *twelfth year he began to purge Judah and Jerusalem of high places, Asherah poles and idols.* (New International Version)

Isaiah 27:9; *By this, then, will Jacob's guilt be atoned for, and this will be the full fruit of the removal of his sin: When he makes all the altar stones to be like limestone crushed to pieces, no Asherah poles or incense altars will be left standing.* (New International Version)

The words "incense altars" (or in some translations the word is image) in Hebrew from Strong's Exhaustive Concordance can mean "sun-pillar". It can also mean "sun-idol."

Sometimes these were carved in wood which had face-like images on them. Similar to what we call a totem pole.

Deuteronomy 16:21-22;
21 "You shall not plant for yourself an Asherah of any kind of tree beside the altar of the LORD your God, which you shall make for yourself.
22 "You shall not set up for yourself a sacred pillar which the LORD your God hates. (New American Standard Bible)

The word "obelisk" literally means 'Baal's Shaft' or Baal's organ of reproduction. This should be especially shocking when we realize that we have a gigantic obelisk in our nation's capital known as the Washington Monument." Dr. Cathy Burns, Masonic and Occult Symbols Illustrated.
(Source: http://www.jesusisfreedom.net/the-obelisk.html)

It is horrible what these obelisk and pillars mean. Do you get the idea that the LORD God hates these? Then why do we have them on some of the churches? We call them steeples but in Egypt they are called obelisk. The Egyptians and those that worship the sun gods know what those steeples mean and represent. Why are they there? I believe we shouldn't have any symbol of pagan images on ANY of our churches. God hates them… period.

It is challenging to understand that it doesn't matter what it means to us, but it matters what it means to God. Whether you agree with that right now or not. One day you will. When we all stand before God and give a literal account of all that was done, all of a sudden you will remember this and will probably think, "Yes it did matter…"

The Two Bethlehem's in Israel

Most people are not aware there actually were two of them. The one most people are familiar with is the one in Judah. It is slightly west and south of Jerusalem.

Genesis 35:19-20;
19 So Rachel died and was buried on the way to Ephrath (that is, Bethlehem).
20 Over her tomb Jacob set up a pillar, and to this day that pillar marks Rachel's tomb. (New International Version)

Micah 5:2; *"But you, Bethlehem Ephrathah, though you are small among the clans of Judah, out of you will come for me one who will be ruler over Israel, whose origins are from of old, from ancient times."* (New International Version)

David would be born there. Samuel arrives in Bethlehem to find the next king of Israel. The story of Ruth mostly takes place in Bethlehem too.

1 Samuel 16:4-5;
4 Samuel did what the LORD said. When he arrived at Bethlehem, the elders of the town trembled when they met him. They asked, "Do you come in peace?"
5 Samuel replied, "Yes, in peace; I have come to sacrifice to the LORD. Consecrate yourselves and come to the sacrifice with me." Then he consecrated Jesse and his sons and invited them to the sacrifice. (New International Version)

1 Samuel 17:12; *Now David was the son of an Ephrathite named Jesse, who was from Bethlehem in Judah. Jesse had eight sons, and in Saul's time he was very old.* (New International Version)

King Herod would have all the male children aged two years and below to be killed.

Matthew 2:16; *When Herod realized that he had been outwitted by the Magi, he was furious, and he gave orders to kill all the boys in Bethlehem and its vicinity who were two years old and under, in accordance with the time he had learned from the Magi.* (New International Version)

Joseph and Mary would leave Nazareth in Galilee to go to Bethlehem in Judea.

Luke 2:1-4;
1 In those days Caesar Augustus issued a decree that a census should be taken of the entire Roman world.
2 (This was the first census that took place while Quirinius was governor of Syria.)
3 And everyone went to their own town to register.
4 So Joseph also went up from the town of Nazareth in Galilee to Judea, to Bethlehem the town of David, because he belonged to the house and line of David. (New International Version)

The other Bethlehem is located northwest of Nazareth and west of the Sea of Galilee.

Joshua 19:10-15;
10 The third lot came up for Zebulun according to its clans: The boundary of their inheritance went as far as Sarid.
11 Going west it ran to Maralah, touched Dabbesheth, and extended to the ravine near Jokneam.
12 It turned east from Sarid toward the sunrise to the territory of Kisloth Tabor and went on to Daberath and up to Japhia.
13 Then it continued eastward to Gath Hepher and Eth Kazin; it came out at Rimmon and turned toward Neah.
14 There the boundary went around on the north to Hannathon and ended at the Valley of Iphtah El.

15 Included were Kattath, Nahalal, Shimron, Idalah and Bethlehem. There were twelve towns and their villages. (New International Version)

Ezekiel's Wife

What? Ezekiel had a wife? Yes he did! So why am I bringing her up?

Ezekiel had done many things in his life that were, shall I say, out of the ordinary.

One of them was when around 593 B.C., the LORD God commanded him to lie on his left side for three hundred and ninety nine (390) days and mix human dung with his food. Imagine what that conversation was like if he told his wife what he was suppose to do for the LORD. These things were needed to be done because he was commanded to do them. Ezekiel bore the sins of Israel. Then he was commanded to lie on his right side for forty days. This was so Ezekiel can bear the sin of Judah. Don't believe it? Check out the verses below.

Ezekiel 4:4-8;

4 Then lie on your left side and put the sin of the people of Israel upon yourself. You are to bear their sin for the number of days you lie on your side.

5 I have assigned you the same number of days as the years of their sin. So for 390 days you will bear the sin of the people of Israel.

6 "After you have finished this, lie down again, this time on your right side, and bear the sin of the people of Judah. I have assigned you 40 days, a day for each year.

7 Turn your face toward the siege of Jerusalem and with bared arm prophesy against her.

8 I will tie you up with ropes so that you cannot turn from one side to the other until you have finished the days of your siege. (New International Version)

So Ezekiel was separated from his wife for over fifteen months. I often wondered if she visited him. It takes a very special lady to be a prophet's wife for many reasons. It is also long time to be apart from the one you love the most. Yes, loved the most as you will see in the next paragraph.

The second one was a very sad event for Ezekiel.

Ezekiel 24:16-17;

16 "Son oj man, with one blow I'm going to take away from you the person you love the most. But you must not mourn, cry, or let tears run down your face.

17 Groan silently. Don't grieve for the person who dies. Tie on your turban, and put on your sandals. Don't cover your face or eat the food that mourners eat." (GOD'S WORD® Translation)

What is interesting is the traditions of Jewish mourning which is quite extensive and varies depending on who dies and the relationship the mourner has with those who have died. In the case of Ezekiel, he would normally be allowed to do the following;

1. Sit in a low stool or on the floor, symbolizing how low one feels in the grief process.
2. Prayers would be given where they lived for up to seven days.
3. Some people would be able to come by and give their condolences, but would wait to speak out of respect for the mourner until they are addressed. These visits might last between thirty and forty five minutes.
4. They would be allowed to ask questions about the deceased.
5. Humor and laughter is allowed if it was appropriate to the situation.
6. They would be allowed to mourn intensely for a month. Jewish law realizes that such a traumatic loss of a spouse is so great that one may never be completely consoled. Then he is supposed to ease back into a 'normal' schedule.

(Source; http://www.jcjcr.org/kyn_article_view.php?aid=25)

There are other ways, which were probably allowed. But it seems that Ezekiel was not allowed to follow any of those ways or traditions. Would you be able to do this? Would you do as you were commanded by the LORD not to mourn or cry openly?

I remember when I read this passage a long time ago. It touched my heart in so many ways. One of them was somewhat interesting. Here is the LORD God telling Ezekiel that the person you love the most I'm going to take from your life. God was not threatened by the love he had for his beautiful wife. God saw them as one flesh!

Here is another point I will bring up. Notice what Ezekiel did right after God told him what was going to happen to his wife.

Ezekiel 24:18; *So I proclaimed this to the people the next morning, and in the evening my wife died. The next morning I did everything I had been told to do.* (New Living Translation)

Did you catch all that? God had Ezekiel speaking to His people about what is happening to him. Why?

Let's put this into perspective for us in our present time. Let's say you have a spouse or a child that you love more than anyone else. You are told or find out they are going to die that day. They live with you, nearby whether it is five miles or an hour's drive away from you. What's the first thing you want to do? What does your heart want to do? What does your mind start almost screaming for you to do? When you feel that first rush of panic. That sense of shock and horror of hearing the news. You want to go and be by their side. You literally drop everything to go. You go to be with them in their final moments of their life. You would want to speak with them, hold their hand, and have those few precious remaining minutes or hours with them. You want to share your last thoughts you both have with each other. Did Ezekiel get to do that? Nope.

Ezekiel loved his wife so very much. She must have been a very special lady. It's challenging being married to a prophet, a seer, or someone who is the apostolic calling. Of course, that depends on how you want to look at it.

Could it be the way she looked at him that at times melted his heart? How she held his hand? How he felt when she hugged him? When she entered into the room, did his eyes light up and make his heart skip a beat? Was she a trusted confidant? Were her words wise, knowledgeable, and delivered with full understanding? Did he love her more than she did him? Or did they both fully love each other like in 1 Corinthians chapter 13? Were they kind to each other, in honoring preferring one another like it says in Romans 12:10? Maybe it was all of the above.

Here is how the various translations explained how Ezekiel felt about his beloved wife as stated in Ezekiel 24:16.

1. The delight of your eyes. (New International Version)
2. Your dearest treasure. (New Living Translation)
3. The desire of your eyes. (New American Standard Bible)
4. Your most precious treasure. (International Standard Version)
5. The person you love the most. (GOD'S WORD® Translation)
6. The desire of thine eyes. (American Standard Version)

You get the idea; Ezekiel really loved and appreciated his wife. It appeared to be a very deep relationship… truly as it is supposed to be. As seemingly unique of a relationship they had, it's interesting the Bible doesn't give us her name. I did some research to find what her name was. At the time of this writing, I have yet to find out this information.

There is another person who described his wife or someone whom he loved affectionately like Ezekiel in the Bible. And that was Solomon. It's believed he wrote a whole book about the love he felt. It's the Song of Solomon. Yet it just doesn't seem the same thing that Ezekiel had with his wife, what they both shared together.

Would you be able to do what Ezekiel did? If you had to do the things Ezekiel did, would you be able to do this for the LORD God? As close of a relationship Ezekiel had with his dearly beloved wife, his relationship with the LORD God was even closer! The LORD is the potter and Ezekiel was the clay.

So why did Ezekiel preach this event to the people then? I would think this is something personal that you would keep to yourself doesn't it. It actually was a warning and prophetic message to the people of Israel as you will see in the following verses. See the almost uncaring response they give him.

Ezekiel 24:19-24;

19 Then the people asked me, "Won't you tell us what these things have to do with us? Why are you acting like this?"
20 So I said to them, "The word of the LORD came to me:
21 Say to the people of Israel, 'This is what the Sovereign LORD says: I am about to desecrate my sanctuary—the stronghold in which you take pride, the delight of your eyes, the object of your affection. The sons and daughters you left behind will fall by the sword.
22 And you will do as I have done. You will not cover your mustache and beard or eat the customary food of mourners.
23 You will keep your turbans on your heads and your sandals on your feet. You will not mourn or weep but will waste away because of your sins and groan among yourselves.
24 Ezekiel will be a sign to you; you will do just as he has done. When this happens, you will know that I am the Sovereign LORD.' (New International Version)

Wow, wow, wow… So what Ezekiel had gone through lying on his sides for many, many months and the death of his beloved wife was indeed a warning to all of Israel of things to come. It was an example of what they will go through.

The Bible is filled with all sorts of events and circumstances that lead to bigger and greater things. Some have a much deeper meaning than we could ever realize. We just need to seek it out.

Abortion and Birth Control Methods

In my research, I discovered great many things. One of them is killing, the taking of innocent life in the womb of a woman. It's really amazing how people are void of awareness that there is nothing new under the sun.

Enoch 69:12; The fifth is named Kasadya; it is he who revealed to the children of the people the various flagellations of all evil - the flagellation of the souls and the demons, the smashing of the embryo in the womb so that it may be crushed, the flagellation of the soul, snake bites, sunstrokes, the son of the serpent, whose name is Taba'ta.

Flagellations, or flogging, is basically beating or whipping in a methodical way. One example of this is when Jesus was whipped with a cat of nine tails.

Here is one birth control method.

Book of Jasher 2:17-25
17 And Lamech, the son of Methusael, became related to Cainan by marriage, and he took his two daughters for his wives, and Adah conceived and bare a son to Lamech, and she called his name Jabal.
18 And she again conceived and bare a son, and called his name Jubal; and Zillah, her sister, was barren in those days and had no offspring.
19 For in those days the sons of men began to trespass against God, and to transgress the commandments which he had commanded to Adam, to be fruitful and multiply in the earth.
20 And some of the sons of men caused their wives to drink a draught that would render them barren, in order that they might retain their figures and whereby their beautiful appearance might not fade.
21 And when the sons of men caused some of their wives to drink, Zillah drank with them.
22 And the child-bearing women appeared abominable in the sight of their husbands as widows, whilst their husbands lived, for to the barren ones only they were attached.
23 And in the end of days and years, when Zillah became old, the Lord opened her womb.
24 And she conceived and bare a son and she called his name Tubal Cain, saying, After I had withered away have I obtained him from the Almighty God.
25 And she conceived again and bare a daughter, and she called her name Naamah, for she said, After I had withered away have I obtained pleasure and delight.

The Chip Implant, Mark of the Beast

So much has been written about this mark. What it means, what it is supposed to do, and what the consequences are if someone has the mark. There are not too many topics that are covered more extensively than this one.

Revelation 13:15-18;
15 He was then permitted to give life to this statue so that it could speak. Then the statue of the beast commanded that anyone refusing to worship it must die.
16 He required everyone—small and great, rich and poor, free and slave—to be given a mark on the right hand or on the forehead.
17 And no one could buy or sell anything without that mark, which was either the name of the beast or the number representing his name.
18 Wisdom is needed here. Let the one with understanding solve the meaning of the number of the beast, for it is the number of a man. His number is 666. (New Living Translation)

What is so highly debated and discussed in many circles is who this person or being is going to be. He will require many people to take the mark or die. That's if they can find you. Who is this man of sin, the lawless one, or son of perdition? Many people have discussed this with great anticipation, trying to determine who he or it is and where this man or it will come from.

2 Thessalonians 2:3-4;
3 Don't let anyone deceive you in any way, for that day will not come until the rebellion occurs and the man of lawlessness is revealed, the man doomed to destruction.
4 He will oppose and will exalt himself over everything that is called God or is worshiped, so that he sets himself up in God's temple, proclaiming himself to be God. (New International Version)

There are some theories that state he is not alive now. He will be resurrected from the dead by reactivating his DNA. He might be a mighty ruler from days past. Actually more like many centuries past. In Revelation 13, there are two beasts that rise. One will rise from the sea and the other from the land. This thing could capture the minds of the whole world that the beast can raise people from the dead.

Revelation 13:1 + 11;
1 The dragon stood on the shore of the sea. And I saw a beast coming out of the sea. It had ten horns and seven heads, with ten crowns on its horns, and on each head a blasphemous name.

11 Then I saw a second beast, coming out of the earth. It had two horns like a lamb, but it spoke like a dragon. (New International Version)

I find it interesting that the beast seemingly copies the LORD God by requiring His people to be marked on their foreheads too.

Revelation 7:3; *"Wait! Don't harm the land or the sea or the trees until we have placed the seal of God on the foreheads of his servants."* (New Living Translation)

You have those who interpret what that mark means in the following ways;

1. Someone receives a tattoo on either the right hand or forehead. The tattoo is invisible to the naked eye. But when that area is held up to a scanning device such as an infra-red scanner, the mark will be displayed. The mark would have some numerical value like a social security number, but with many more numbers added to it because of the billions of people who might take a number. Without it, people could not buy or sell anything. In today's almost completely cashless society, that would present a problem. Hence, the reason for this mark… so the 'beast' can monitor everyone and everything.
2. There was a time when people didn't get those plastic credit cards because it was thought that perhaps this could lead to receiving the mark.
3. At one point, it was believed that instead of the number six hundred and sixty-six, it could be interrupted as six hundred and sixteen. However, that theory was quickly pushed aside.
(Source; http://en.wikipedia.org/wiki/Number_of_the_Beast)

4. Another one is add all the numbers and include 36, the total would be 666 (e.g. 1+2+3+4…. + 36).
5. Yet still some have thought up the numerical value of a name or the meaning of such names.
6. The mark could be a banner that is worn on the right arm or forehead. Yet another mark could be on the forehead because when some pray in a particular religion, there forehead touches the ground many times a day. That would leave a mark on the forehead.
7. Another theory surfaced in the late 1990's. A new pope would appear and reign a short time. The total will remain at 665. Then a new pope will be voted in. His name will be equal to 666.
   (Source; http://www.666beast.net/)
8. Here is one from November 15, 1914. The title of the Pope in Rome is Vicarius Filii Dei [Latin for "Vicar of the Son of God"]. This is inscribed on his mitre. Take the letters of his title. They represent Latin numerals (printed large) and add them together they come to 666. See the information below.

V	I	C	a	r	I	V	s		F	I	L	I	I		D	E	I
5	1	100			1	5				1	50	1	1		500		1

(Source; http://www.pickle-publishing.com/papers/666.htm

9. It was circulated that the Roman Empire named Nero could come back from the dead because when his name was assigned a numerical value, it also came up as 666.
10. Then there is the bar code that appears on almost everything you buy today. It was widely thought that maybe that would be it too. The Greek root meaning of the word "mark" is palisade, a picket fence, a succession of vertical bars, just like the barcode.
    (Source; http://www.atlanteanconspiracy.com/2009/02/numerology-666-part-1.html)

11. There is the microchip. It is small enough so it can be embedded in your sinus cavity in your forehead or

inside your right hand. What is interesting is this one is still being discussed. There was the version that allowed all your personal information to be placed on a chip so your identity can always be checked out. However, the more advanced type, at the time of this writing, is this chip not only keeps your personal information, but could also transform and rewrite your DNA. It's more of a biochip than anything else. It actually would interweave with your nervous system etc. In some cases, it could allow a person to unnaturally live longer or even die sooner. There is also the theory that this rewriting of the DNA will make those who take it un-redeemable. Can no longer claim salvation through Jesus Christ. This is the one which could create a human/animal hybrid. That is what was done during the days of Noah in Genesis 6.

12. Then there could simply be a mark that will be similar to the one given to Cain.
    Genesis 4:15; *But the LORD said to him, "Not so ; anyone who kills Cain will suffer vengeance seven times over." Then the LORD put a mark on Cain so that no one who found him would kill him.* (New International Version)
13. Then there is the theory that some injection will be given that rewrites a person's DNA. It will change them into a super human. They will be told they can live up to 500 years, without sickness and pain. Yet it will have side effects, the mark it leaves will be visible to everyone because it will appear either on the forehead of the right hand or arm.

It is clear in the Bible that we are **NOT** to take the mark of the beast.

Revelation 18:4; *Then I heard another voice calling from heaven, "Come away from her, my people. Do not take part in her sins, or you will be punished with her.* (New Living Translation)

Gates of Hell

I find it interesting there are published articles on the Internet discussing this topic. Why are they doing this? Is it our outright defiance towards God? Or is God giving people their final warning before the end time judgment begins? I don't believe there are just mere consequences in life. This has been revealed on purpose.

As the article states, they found this 'gate' which suddenly appeared to spew forth poisonous and lethal gases from within the earth. Some have tagged this site as one that can do this forever. It is located in Pergamum, which is a city located in the western part of Turkey. It is south of Istanbul, southeast of Troy, and east of Ephesus.

What I also find interesting is there's a passage in Revelation that talks about this very city. Where satan has his throne and where he lives…

Revelation 2:12-13;
12 "To the angel of the church in Pergamum write: These are the words of him who has the sharp, double-edged sword.
13 I know where you live—where Satan has his throne. Yet you remain true to my name. You did not renounce your faith in me, not even in the days of Antipas, my faithful witness, who was put to death in your city—where Satan lives. (New International Version)

Is There More to Why Cain Murdered Abel

The story between of two brothers is interesting as it is related to us in Genesis. Cain is the older brother of Abel. Cain was the farmer and Abel took care of the flocks he had.

Genesis 4:2; *Later she gave birth to his brother Abel. Now Abel kept flocks, and Cain worked the soil.* (New International Version)

We learned they both made an offering to the LORD God. God accepted Abel's while not accepting Cain's. Then we learn that Cain gets angry.

Genesis 4:3-7;
3 In the course of time Cain brought some of the fruits of the soil as an offering to the LORD.
4 And Abel also brought an offering—fat portions from some of the firstborn of his flock. The LORD looked with favor on Abel and his offering,
5 but on Cain and his offering he did not look with favor. So Cain was very angry, and his face was downcast.
6 Then the LORD said to Cain, "Why are you angry? Why is your face downcast?
7 If you do what is right, will you not be accepted? But if you do not do what is right, sin is crouching at your door; it desires to have you, but you must rule over it." (New International Version)

Then they go into the field, and Cain slays his brother Abel.

Genesis 4:8; *Now Cain said to his brother Abel, "Let's go out to the field." While they were in the field, Cain attacked his brother Abel and killed him.* (New International Version)

God asks Cain where his brother is. Cain's reply to God was, "Am I my brother's keeper"?

Genesis 4:9-10;
9 Then the LORD said to Cain, "Where is your brother Abel?" "I don't know," he replied. "Am I my brother's keeper?"
10 The LORD said, "What have you done? Listen! Your brother's blood cries out to me from the ground. (New International Version)

He is to become a wanderer on the earth. He thinks that when people find out who he is, he will be hunted down and killed. But God says no to that and places a mark on him. If anyone kills him, vengeance will be sevenfold.

Genesis 4:12-15;

12 *When you work the ground, it will no longer yield its crops for you. You will be a restless wanderer on the earth."*
13 Cain said to the LORD, *"My punishment is more than I can bear.*
14 Today you are driving me from the land, and I will be hidden from your presence; I will be a restless wanderer on the earth, and whoever finds me will kill me."
15 But the LORD *said to him, "Not so; anyone who kills Cain will suffer vengeance seven times over." Then the* LORD *put a mark on Cain so that no one who found him would kill him.* (New International Version)

Then God sends Cain away from that area, and he winds up in the land of Nod and builds a city. It's east of Eden.

Genesis 4:16; *So Cain went out from the* LORD*'s presence and lived in the land of Nod, east of Eden.* (New International Version)

This is common knowledge to most Christians. Yet there is some more information that should be considered with this event. According to this ancient text, there was an argument between Cain and Abel. This is quite interesting.

Jasher 1:14-33
14 And the boys grew up and their father gave them a possession in the land; and Cain was a tiller of the ground, and Abel a keeper of sheep.
15 And it was at the expiration of a few years, that they brought an approximating offering to the Lord, and Cain brought from the fruit of the ground, and Abel brought from the firstlings of his flock from the fat thereof, and God turned and inclined to Abel and his offering, and a fire came down from the Lord from heaven and consumed it.
16 And unto Cain and his offering the Lord did not turn, and he did not incline to it, for he had brought from the inferior fruit of the ground before the Lord, and Cain was jealous against his brother Abel on account of this, and he sought a pretext to slay him.
17 And in some time after, Cain and Abel his brother, went one day into the field to do their work; and they were both in the

field, Cain tilling and ploughing his ground, and Abel feeding his flock; and the flock passed that part which Cain had ploughed in the ground, and it sorely grieved Cain on this account.
18 And Cain approached his brother Abel in anger, and he said unto him, What is there between me and thee, that thou comest to dwell and bring thy flock to feed in my land?
19 And Abel answered his brother Cain and said unto him, What is there between me and thee, that thou shalt eat the flesh of my flock and clothe thyself with their wool?
20 And now therefore, put off the wool of my sheep with which thou hast clothed thyself, and recompense me for their fruit and flesh which thou hast eaten, and when thou shalt have done this, I will then go from thy land as thou hast said?
21 And Cain said to his brother Abel, Surely if I slay thee this day, who will require thy blood from me?
22 And Abel answered Cain, saying, Surely God who has made us in the earth, he will avenge my cause, and he will require my blood from thee shouldst thou slay me, for the Lord is the judge and arbiter, and it is he who will requite man according to his evil, and the wicked man according to the wickedness that he may do upon earth.
23 And now, if thou shouldst slay me here, surely God knoweth thy secret views, and will judge thee for the evil which thou didst declare to do unto me this day.
24 And when Cain heard the words which Abel his brother had spoken, behold the anger of Cain was kindled against his brother Abel for declaring this thing.
25 And Cain hastened and rose up, and took the iron part of his ploughing instrument, with which he suddenly smote his brother and he slew him, and Cain spilt the blood of his brother Abel upon the earth, and the blood of Abel streamed upon the earth before the flock.
26 And after this Cain repented having slain his brother, and he was sadly grieved, and he wept over him and it vexed him exceedingly.
27 And Cain rose up and dug a hole in the field, wherein he put his brother's body, and he turned the dust over it.

28 And the Lord knew what Cain had done to his brother, and the Lord appeared to Cain and said unto him, Where is Abel thy brother that was with thee?
29 And Cain dissembled, and said, I do not know, am I my brother's keeper? And the Lord said unto him, What hast thou done? The voice of thy brother's blood crieth unto me from the ground where thou hast slain him.
30 For thou hast slain thy brother and hast dissembled before me, and didst imagine in thy heart that I saw thee not, nor knew all thy actions.
31 But thou didst this thing and didst slay thy brother for naught and because he spoke rightly to thee, and now, therefore, cursed be thou from the ground which opened its mouth to receive thy brother's blood from thy hand, and wherein thou didst bury him.
32 And it shall be when thou shalt till it, it shall no more give thee its strength as in the beginning, for thorns and thistles shall the ground produce, and thou shalt be moving and wandering in the earth until the day of thy death.
33 And at that time Cain went out from the presence of the Lord, from the place where he was, and he went moving and wandering in the land toward the east of Eden, he and all belonging to him.

God is speaking to the serpent in the Garden of Eden.

Genesis 3:15; *And I will put enmity between you and the woman, and between your offspring and hers; he will crush your head, and you will strike his heel."* (New International Version)

Could it be that satan is trying to strike back at the bloodline of the Messiah, Jesus Christ? By creating a rift between the two brothers? If you don't think so, in another part of this book, you will read a passage of text where the sons of Noah (Shem, Ham, and Japheth) came to their father and asked for help with some beings that were creating great havoc in their son's lives. Now did satan tempt Cain? To stir up anger in him because, maybe, Cain found out he is not part of Adam's bloodline? Check it out. Cain is NOT mentioned in the bloodline of Adam.

It could very well have been that Cain did weep and repent of what he had done, according to the text above.

1 John 1:9; *If we confess our sins, he is faithful and just and will forgive us our sins and purify us from all unrighteousness.* (New International Version)

Death Angel or Angel of Death

When people in the Bible see an angel, they are usually very frightened. More than likely they think they are going to die right then. That is probably why we call them by such names.

Usually at one point in our lives, we hear the above term in one way or another. Sometimes the concept would appear in a movie. Regardless of where, the question I ask is, is there really a "death angel." Some might call it a grim reaper. In any case, does the Bible mention there is such an angel? Let's check out the following verses.

Exodus 12:23; *When the LORD goes through the land to strike down the Egyptians, he will see the blood on the top and sides of the doorframe and will pass over that doorway, and he will not permit the destroyer to enter your houses and strike you down.* (New International Version)

1 Chronicles 21:15; *And God sent an angel to destroy Jerusalem. But as the angel was doing so, the LORD saw it and relented concerning the disaster and said to the angel who was destroying the people, "Enough! Withdraw your hand." The angel of the LORD was then standing at the threshing floor of Araunah the Jebusite.* (New International Version)

2 Kings 19:35; *That night the angel of the LORD went out and put to death a hundred and eighty-five thousand in the Assyrian camp. When the people got up the next morning--there were all the dead bodies!* (New International Version)

Proverbs 16:14; *The wrath of a king is as messengers of death: but a wise man will pacify it.* (King James Bible)

Job 33:32; *They are at death's door; the angels oj death wait for them.* (New International Version)

As you can tell, the above verse in Job states there are angels of death. I don't believe it is there only job. It is one of many things they do for the LORD God.

The First Flood

According to the Book of Jasher, there was a flood before the one talked about in Genesis 6. It covered about one-third of the land. This happened during the time that Enosh (means 'mortal' man) lived. Enosh was the son of Seth (means 'appointed').

Jasher 2:3-9;
3 And it was in the days of Enosh that the sons of men continued to rebel and transgress against God, to increase the anger of the Lord against the sons of men.
4 And the sons of men went and they served other gods, and they forgot the Lord who had created them in the earth: and in those days the sons of men made images of brass and iron, wood and stone, and they bowed down and served them.
5 And every man made his god and they bowed down to them, and the sons of men forsook the Lord all the days of Enosh and his children; and the anger of the Lord was kindled on account of their works and abominations which they did in the earth.
6 And the Lord caused the waters of the river Gihon to overwhelm them, and he destroyed and consumed them, and he destroyed the third part of the earth, and notwithstanding this, the sons of men did not turn from their evil ways, and their hands were yet extended to do evil in the sight of the Lord.
7 And in those days there was neither sowing nor reaping in the earth; and there was no food for the sons of men and the famine was very great in those days.
8 And the seed which they sowed in those days in the ground became thorns, thistles and briers; for from the days of Adam was this declaration concerning the earth, of the curse of God,

which he cursed the earth, on account of the sin which Adam sinned before the Lord.
9 And it was when men continued to rebel and transgress against God, and to corrupt their ways, that the earth also became corrupt.

Death of Cain

It appears that Lamech had killed Cain. Keep in mind that this Lamech is of Cain's bloodline, not Seth's.

Jasher 2:26-36;
26 And Lamech was old and advanced in years, and his eyes were dim that he could not see, and Tubal Cain, his son, was leading him and it was one day that Lamech went into the field and Tubal Cain his son was with him, and whilst they were walking in the field, Cain the son of Adam advanced towards them; for Lamech was very old and could not see much, and Tubal Cain his son was very young.
27 And Tubal Cain told his father to draw his bow, and with the arrows he smote Cain, who was yet far off, and he slew him, for he appeared to them to be an animal.
28 And the arrows entered Cain's body although he was distant from them, and he fell to the ground and died.
29 And the Lord requited Cain's evil according to his wickedness, which he had done to his brother Abel, according to the word of the Lord which he had spoken.
30 And it came to pass when Cain had died, that Lamech and Tubal went to see the animal which they had slain, and they saw, and behold Cain their grandfather was fallen dead upon the earth.
31 And Lamech was very much grieved at having done this, and in clapping his hands together he struck his son and caused his death.
32 And the wives of Lamech heard what Lamech had done, and they sought to kill him.

33 And the wives of Lamech hated him from that day, because he slew Cain and Tubal Cain, and the wives of Lamech separated from him, and would not hearken to him in those days.
34 And Lamech came to his wives, and he pressed them to listen to him about this matter.
35 And he said to his wives Adah and Zillah, Hear my voice O wives of Lamech, attend to my words, for now you have imagined and said that I slew a man with my wounds, and a child with my stripes for their having done no violence, but surely know that I am old and grey-headed, and that my eyes are heavy through age, and I did this thing unknowingly.
36 And the wives of Lamech listened to him in this matter, and they returned to him with the advice of their father Adam, but they bore no children to him from that time, knowing that God's anger was increasing in those days against the sons of men, to destroy them with the waters of the flood for their evil doings.

Talk about a family spat or huge argument… Wow… another point here to make is the wives knew the flood of Genesis 7 was coming.

It appears Cain's bloodline ends at the flood in Genesis 6. It's very sad to see what sin does in our lives. It's important to realize this so we can truly understand and love people, just like the LORD our God does with us. That includes when the people don't meet our expectations.

Adam and Eve's Garments God Made for Them

In my research, I came across these entries in an ancient text. I'm not sure what to make of them, but I find it interesting.

Jasher 7:23;
23 And Cush the son of Ham, the son of Noah, took a wife in those days in his old age, and she bare a son, and they called his name Nimrod, saying, At that time the sons of men again began to rebel and transgress against God, and the child grew up, and his father loved him exceedingly, for he was the son of his old age.

24 And the garments of skin which God made for Adam and his wife, when they went out of the garden, were given to Cush.
25 For after the death of Adam and his wife, the garments were given to Enoch, the son of Jared, and when Enoch was taken up to God, he gave them to Methuselah, his son.
26 And at the death of Methuselah, Noah took them and brought them to the ark, and they were with him until he went out of the ark.
27 And in their going out, Ham stole those garments from Noah his father, and he took them and hid them from his brothers.
28 And when Ham begat his first born Cush, he gave him the garments in secret, and they were with Cush many days.
29 And Cush also concealed them from his sons and brothers, and when Cush had begotten Nimrod, he gave him those garments through his love for him, and Nimrod grew up, and when he was twenty years old he put on those garments.
30 And Nimrod became strong when he put on the garments, and God gave him might and strength, and he was a mighty hunter in the earth, yea, he was a mighty hunter in the field, and he hunted the animals and he built altars, and he offered upon them the animals before the Lord.

Abram Lived With Who?

Abram (who later was renamed Abraham) would become the father of all nations. He actually lived with Noah and Shem. Now it makes sense, the faith that Abram had in the LORD God. He received a great education from both of them. As you read below, you will begin to understand how much Abram grew in knowing the LORD God.

Jasher 9:5-19;
5 And when Abram came out from the cave, he went to Noah and his son Shem, and he remained with them to learn the instruction of the Lord and his ways, and no man knew where Abram was, and Abram served Noah and Shem his son for a long time.

6 And Abram was in Noah's house thirty-nine years, and Abram knew the Lord from three years old, and he went in the ways of the Lord until the day of his death, as Noah and his son Shem had taught him; and all the sons of the earth in those days greatly transgressed against the Lord, and they rebelled against him and they served other gods, and they forgot the Lord who had created them in the earth; and the inhabitants of the earth made unto themselves, at that time, every man his god; gods of wood and stone which could neither speak, hear, nor deliver, and the sons of men served them and they became their gods.
7 And the king and all his servants, and Terah with all his household were then the first of those that served gods of wood and stone.
8 And Terah had twelve gods of large size, made of wood and stone, after the twelve months of the year, and he served each one monthly, and every month Terah would bring his meat offering and drink offering to his gods; thus did Terah all the days.
9 And all that generation were wicked in the sight of the Lord, and they thus made every man his god, but they forsook the Lord who had created them.
10 And there was not a man found in those days in the whole earth, who knew the Lord (for they served each man his own God) except Noah and his household, and all those who were under his counsel knew the Lord in those days.
11 And Abram the son of Terah was waxing great in those days in the house of Noah, and no man knew it, and the Lord was with him.
12 And the Lord gave Abram an understanding heart, and he knew all the works of that generation were vain, and that all their gods were vain and were of no avail.
13 And Abram saw the sun shining upon the earth, and Abram said unto himself Surely now this sun that shines upon the earth is God, and him will I serve.
14 And Abram served the sun in that day and he prayed to him, and when evening came the sun set as usual, and Abram said within himself, Surely this cannot be God?

15 And Abram still continued to speak within himself, Who is he who made the heavens and the earth? who created upon earth? where is he?
16 And night darkened over him, and he lifted up his eyes toward the west, north, south, and east, and he saw that the sun had vanished from the earth, and the day became dark.
17 And Abram saw the stars and moon before him, and he said, Surely this is the God who created the whole earth as well as man, and behold these his servants are gods around him: and Abram served the moon and prayed to it all that night.
18 And in the morning when it was light and the sun shone upon the earth as usual, Abram saw all the things that the Lord God had made upon earth.
19 And Abram said unto himself Surely these are not gods that made the earth and all mankind, but these are the servants of God, and Abram remained in the house of Noah and there knew the Lord and his ways' and he served the Lord all the days of his life, and all that generation forgot the Lord, and served other gods of wood and stone, and rebelled all their days.

Abram was brought up in the cave so that he would be hidden from Nimrod who was trying to kill him. Terah was Abram's father and an adviser to Nimrod. So when Nimrod asked Terah for his son, something interesting occurred.

Jasher 8:30-36;
30 And Terah answered the king, saying, I beseech thee my lord and king to let thy servant speak a word before thee, and let the king hear the word of his servant, and Terah said, Let my king give me three days' time till I consider this matter within myself, and consult with my family concerning the words of my king; and he pressed the king greatly to agree to this.
31 And the king hearkened to Terah, and he did so and he gave him three days' time, and Terah went out from the king's presence, and he came home to his family and spoke to them all the words of the king; and the people were greatly afraid.
32 And it was in the third day that the king sent to Terah, saying, Send me thy son for a price as I spoke to thee; and shouldst thou

not do this, I will send and slay all thou hast in thy house, so that thou shalt not even have a dog remaining.
33 And Terah hastened, (as the thing was urgent from the king), and he took a child from one of his servants, which his handmaid had born to him that day, and Terah brought the child to the king and received value for him.
34 And the Lord was with Terah in this matter, that Nimrod might not cause Abram's death, and the king took the child from Terah and with all his might dashed his head to the ground, for he thought it had been Abram; and this was concealed from him from
that day, and it was forgotten by the king, as it was the will of Providence not to suffer Abram's death.
35 And Terah took Abram his son secretly, together with his mother and nurse, and he concealed them in a cave, and he brought them their provisions monthly.
36 And the Lord was with Abram in the cave and he grew up, and Abram was in the cave ten years, and the king and his princes, soothsayers and sages, thought that the king had killed Abram.

Abram Encounters Nimrod

Few people realize that Abram had many challenges in his life, which are not mentioned in the Bible. In the passage below, Abram is brought before Nimrod. What had happened was Abram broke all of his father's idols in his house. Terah, Abram's father, got mad and went to Nimrod concerning this matter. Terah explained all that Abram had done. Then Abram appeared before Nimrod. He starts to give an account of what he had done to idols.

Jasher 11:53-61;
53 And the king said to Abram, What is this that thou hast done to thy father and to his gods? And Abram answered the king in the words that he spoke to his father, and he said, The large god that was with them in the house did to them what thou hast heard.

54 And the king said to Abram, Had they power to speak and eat
and do as thou hast said? And Abram answered the king, saying,
And if there be no power in them why dost thou serve them and
cause the sons of men to err through thy follies?
55 Dost thou imagine that they can deliver thee or do anything
small or great, that thou shouldst serve them? And why wilt thou
not sense the God of the whole universe, who created thee and in
whose power it is to kill and keep alive?
56 0 foolish, simple, and ignorant king, woe unto thee forever.
57 I thought thou wouldst teach thy servants the upright way, but
thou hast not done this, but hast filled the whole earth with thy
sins and the sins of thy people who have followed thy ways.
58 Dost thou not know, or hast thou not heard, that this evil
which thou doest, our ancestors sinned therein in days of old,
and the eternal God brought the waters of the flood upon them
and destroyed latter them all, and also destroyed the whole earth
on their account? And wilt thou and thy people rise up now and
do like unto this work, in order to bring down the anger of the
Lord God of the universe, and to bring evil upon thee and the
whole earth?
59 Now therefore put away this evil deed which thou doest, and
serve the God of the universe, as thy soul is in his hands, and
then it will be well with thee.
60 And if thy wicked heart will not hearken to my words to
cause thee to forsake thy evil ways, and to serve the eternal God,
then wilt thou die in shame in the latter days, thou, thy people
and all who are connected with thee, hearing thy words or
walking in thy evil ways.
61 And when Abram had ceased speaking before the king and
princes, Abram lifted up his eyes to the heavens, and he said,
The Lord seeth all the wicked, and he will judge them.

Abram just finished telling Nimrod to get right with the LORD or else. So Nimrod placed him in prison for ten days. Then he called all the other kings, princes, governors and sages in all the land he had under his control to appear before him. And they came. Nimrod decided to make an example out of Abram for all to see. We will pick up the story from there.

Jasher 12:3-16

3 And the king said to the princes and sages, Have you heard what Abram, the son of Terah, has done to his father? Thus has he done to him, and I ordered him to be brought before me, and thus has he spoken; his heart did not misgive him, neither did he stir in my presence, and behold now he is confined in the prison.

4 And therefore decide what judgment is due to this man who reviled the king; who spoke and did all the things that you heard.

5 And they all answered the king saying, The man who revileth the king should be hanged upon a tree; but having done all the things that he said, and having despised our gods, he must therefore be burned to death, for this is the law in this matter.

6 If it pleaseth the king to do this, let him order his servants to kindle a fire both night and day in thy brick furnace, and then we will cast this man into it. And the king did so, and he commanded his servants that they should prepare a fire for three days and three nights in the king's furnace, that is in Casdim; and the king ordered them to take Abram from prison and bring him out to be burned.

7 And all the king's servants, princes, lords, governors, and judges, and all the inhabitants of the land, about nine hundred thousand men, stood opposite the furnace to see Abram.

8 And all the women and little ones crowded upon the roofs and towers to see what was doing with Abram, and they all stood together at a distance; and there was not a man left that did not come on that day to behold the scene.

9 And when Abram was come, the conjurors of the king and the sages saw Abram, and they cried out to the king, saying, Our sovereign lord, surely this is the man whom we know to have been the child at whose birth the great star swallowed the four stars, which we declared to the king now fifty years since.

10 And behold now his father has also transgressed thy commands, and mocked thee by bringing thee another child, which thou didst kill.

11 And when the king heard their words, he was exceedingly wroth, and he ordered Terah to be brought before him.

12 And the king said, Hast thou heard what the conjurors have spoken? Now tell me truly, how didst thou; and if thou shalt speak truth thou shalt be acquitted.

13 And seeing that the king's anger was so much kindled, Terah said to the king, My lord and king, thou hast heard the truth, and what the sages have spoken is right. And the king said, How couldst thou do this thing, to transgress my orders and to give me a child that thou didst not beget, and to take value for him?
14 And Terah answered the king, Because my tender feelings were excited for my son, at that time, and I took a son of my handmaid, and I brought him to the king.
15 And the king said Who advised thee to this? Tell me, do not hide aught from me, and then thou shalt not die.
16 And Terah was greatly terrified in the king's presence, and he said to the king, It was Haran my eldest son who advised me to this; and Haran was in those days that Abram was born, two and thirty years old.

Terah actually lies to Nimrod, hoping to save himself from being killed. So he offers up his other son instead.

Jasher 12:17-20;
17 But Haran did not advise his father to anything, for Terah said this to the king in order to deliver his soul from the king, for he feared greatly; and the king said to Terah, Haran thy son who advised thee to this shall die through fire with Abram; for the sentence of death is upon him for having rebelled against the king's desire in doing this thing.
18 And Haran at that time felt inclined to follow the ways of Abram, but he kept it within himself.
19 And Haran said in his heart, Behold now the king has seized Abram on account of these things which Abram did, and it shall come to pass, that if Abram prevail over the king I will follow him, but if the king prevail I will go after the king.
20 And when Terah had spoken this to the king concerning Haran his son, the king ordered Haran to be seized with Abram.

So Terah gave up both his sons to Nimrod. Nimrod in turn is going to cast both of them into the fiery furnace that has been burning for three days and three nights. Interesting how the "three days and three nights" appears here.

Jasher 12:21-43
21 And they brought them both, Abram and Haran his brother, to
cast them into the fire; and all the inhabitants of the land and the
king's servants and princes and all the women and little ones
were there, standing that day over them.
22 And the king's servants took Abram and his brother, and they
stripped them of all their clothes excepting their lower garments
which were upon them.
23 And they bound their hands and feet with linen cords, and the
servants of the king lifted them up and cast them both into the
furnace.
24 And the Lord loved Abram and he had compassion over him,
and the Lord came down and delivered Abram from the fire and
he was not burned.
25 But all the cords with which they bound him were burned,
while Abram remained and walked about in the fire.
26 And Haran died when they had cast him into the fire, and he
was burned to ashes, for his heart was not perfect with the Lord;
and those men who cast him into the fire, the flame of the fire
spread over them, and they were burned, and twelve men of
them died.
27 And Abram walked in the midst of the fire three days and
three nights, and all the servants of the king saw him walking in
the fire, and they came and told the king, saying, Behold we
have seen Abram walking about in the midst of the fire, and even
the lower garments which are upon him are not burned, but the
cord with which he was bound is burned.
28 And when the king heard their words his heart fainted and he
would not believe them; so he sent other faithful princes to see
this matter, and they went and saw it and told it to the king; and
the king rose to go and see it, and he saw Abram walking to and
fro in the midst of the fire, and he saw Haran's body burned, and
the king wondered greatly.
29 And the king ordered Abram to be taken out from the fire;
and his servants approached to take him out and they could not,
for the fire was round about and the flame ascending toward
them from the furnace.

30 And the king's servants fled from it, and the king rebuked them, saying, Make haste and bring Abram out of the fire that you shall not die.
31 And the servants of the king again approached to bring Abram out, and the flames came upon them and burned their faces so that eight of them died.
32 And when the king saw that his servants could not approach the fire lest they should be burned, the king called to Abram, O servant of the God who is in heaven, go forth from amidst the fire and come hither before me; and Abram hearkened to the voice of the king, and he went forth from the fire and came and stood before the king.
33 And when Abram came out the king and all his servants saw Abram coming before the king, with his lower garments upon him, for they were not burned, but the cord with which he was bound was burned.
34 And the king said to Abram, How is it that thou wast not burned in the fire?
35 And Abram said to the king, The God of heaven and earth in whom I trust and who has all in his power, he delivered me from the fire into which thou didst cast me.
36 And Haran the brother of Abram was burned to ashes, and they sought for his body, and they found it consumed.
37 And Haran was eighty-two years old when he died in the fire of Casdim. And the king, princes, and inhabitants of the land, seeing that Abram was delivered from the fire, they came and bowed down to Abram.
38 And Abram said to them, Do not bow down to me, but bow down to the God of the world who made you, and serve him, and go in his ways for it is he who delivered me from out of this fire, and it is he who created the souls and spirits of all men, and formed man in his mother's womb, and brought him forth into the world, and it is he who will deliver those who trust in him from all pain.
39 And this thing seemed very wonderful in the eyes of the king and princes, that Abram was saved from the fire and that Haran was burned; and the king gave Abram many presents and he gave him his two head servants from the king's house; the name of one was Oni and the name of the other was Eliezer.

40 And all the kings, princes and servants gave Abram many gifts of silver and gold and pearl, and the king and his princes sent him away, and he went in peace.
41 And Abram went forth from the king in peace, and many of the king's servants followed him, and about three hundred men joined him.
42 And Abram returned on that day and went to his father's house, he and the men that followed him, and Abram served the Lord his God all the days of his life, and he walked in his ways and followed his law.
43 And from that day forward Abram inclined the hearts of the sons of men to serve the Lord.

Parry, J. H.; Lost Books of the Bible (2009-04-14). The Book of Jasher or Sefer ha-Yashar, Translated from the Original Hebrew to English (Kindle Locations 903-910).

When you understand more of what happened to Abram in those younger years, you get to understand how he stepped out on faith later on in life.

Jesus Feeds Thousands of People… Twice

Our Lord Jesus Christ fed some five thousand (5,000) men. When you add the women and children that were probably there, it could be well over ten thousand people.

Matthew 14:15-21;
15 As evening approached, the disciples came to him and said, "This is a remote place, and it's already getting late. Send the crowds away, so they can go to the villages and buy themselves some food."
16 Jesus replied, "They do not need to go away. You give them something to eat."
17 "We have here only five loaves of bread and two fish," they answered.
18 "Bring them here to me," he said.

19 And he directed the people to sit down on the grass. Taking the five loaves and the two fish and looking up to heaven, he gave thanks and broke the loaves. Then he gave them to the disciples, and the disciples gave them to the people.
20 They all ate and were satisfied, and the disciples picked up twelve basketfuls of broken pieces that were left over.
21 The number of those who ate was about five thousand men, besides women and children. (New International Version)

John gives a slightly different account. He mentions a bit more about it. It was clearly a test, not just for Philip, but also for the rest of the disciples. They needed to learn to think and have faith on a much larger scale. Jesus showed them how to do it.

John 6:5-13;
5 When Jesus looked up and saw a great crowd coming toward him, he said to Philip, "Where shall we buy bread for these people to eat?"
6 He asked this only to test him, for he already had in mind what he was going to do.
7 Philip answered him, "It would take more than half a year's wages to buy enough bread for each one to have a bite!"
8 Another of his disciples, Andrew, Simon Peter's brother, spoke up,
9 "Here is a boy with five small barley loaves and two small fish, but how far will they go among so many?"
10 Jesus said, "Have the people sit down." There was plenty of grass in that place, and they sat down (about five thousand men were there).
11 Jesus then took the loaves, gave thanks, and distributed to those who were seated as much as they wanted. He did the same with the fish.
12 When they had all had enough to eat, he said to his disciples, "Gather the pieces that are left over. Let nothing be wasted."
13 So they gathered them and filled twelve baskets with the pieces of the five barley loaves left over by those who had eaten.
(New International Version)

Mark also gives an accounting of this feeding of the five thousand (5,000) men.

Mark 6:35-44;
35 By this time it was late in the day, so his disciples came to him. "This is a remote place," they said, "and it's already very late.
36 Send the people away so that they can go to the surrounding countryside and villages and buy themselves something to eat."
37 But he answered, "You give them something to eat."
They said to him, "That would take more than half a year's wages ! Are we to go and spend that much on bread and give it to them to eat?"
38 "How many loaves do you have?" he asked. "Go and see."
When they found out, they said, "Five—and two fish."
39 Then Jesus directed them to have all the people sit down in groups on the green grass.
40 So they sat down in groups of hundreds and fifties.
41 Taking the five loaves and the two fish and looking up to heaven, he gave thanks and broke the loaves. Then he gave them to his disciples to distribute to the people. He also divided the two fish among them all.
42 They all ate and were satisfied,
43 and the disciples picked up twelve basketfuls of broken pieces of bread and fish.
44 The number of the men who had eaten was five thousand. (New International Version)

What is not widely known is Jesus fed thousands of people, twice. This next time, it was four thousand (4,000) men. When you add the women and children, it could be well over eight thousand people.

The book of Mark, just like the book of Matthew, gives an account of both of these events - the feeding of both the five thousand and the group of four thousand people.

Matthew 15:32-38;
32 Jesus called his disciples to him and said, "I have compassion for these people; they have already been with me

three days and have nothing to eat. I do not want to send them away hungry, or they may collapse on the way."
33 His disciples answered, "Where could we get enough bread in this remote place to feed such a crowd?"
34 "How many loaves do you have?" Jesus asked.
"Seven," they replied, "and a few small fish."
35 He told the crowd to sit down on the ground.
36 Then he took the seven loaves and the fish, and when he had given thanks, he broke them and gave them to the disciples, and they in turn to the people.
37 They all ate and were satisfied. Afterward the disciples picked up seven basketfuls of broken pieces that were left over.
38 The number of those who ate was four thousand men, besides women and children. (New International Version)

Mark 8:1-9;
1 During those days another large crowd gathered. Since they had nothing to eat, Jesus called his disciples to him and said,
2 "I have compassion for these people; they have already been with me three days and have nothing to eat.
3 If I send them home hungry, they will collapse on the way, because some of them have come a long distance."
4 His disciples answered, "But where in this remote place can anyone get enough bread to feed them?"
5 "How many loaves do you have?" Jesus asked. "Seven," they replied.
6 He told the crowd to sit down on the ground. When he had taken the seven loaves and given thanks, he broke them and gave them to his disciples to distribute to the people, and they did so.
7 They had a few small fish as well; he gave thanks for them also and told the disciples to distribute them.
8 The people ate and were satisfied. Afterward the disciples picked up seven basketfuls of broken pieces that were left over.
9 About four thousand were present. After he had sent them away, (New International Version)

Pharmaceutical Drugs in the End Time

The words 'pharmacy' or 'pharmaceutical' come from the Greek word meaning 'pharmakeia'. In Revelation 9:21, the word is 'pharmakon'. Let's see what the Bible says about this topic. It's actually mentioned three times.

Galatians 5:19-21;
19 Now the works of the flesh are evident: sexual immorality, impurity, sensuality,
20 idolatry, sorcery, enmity, strife, jealousy, fits of anger, rivalries, dissensions, divisions,
21 envy, drunkenness, orgies, and things like these. I warn you, as I warned you before, that those who do such things will not inherit the kingdom of God. (English Standard Version)

Revelation 9:21; *nor did they repent of their murders or their sorceries or their sexual immorality or their thefts.* (English Standard Version)

Revelation 18:23; *The light of a lamp will never shine in you again. The happy voices of brides and grooms will never be heard in you again. For your merchants were the greatest in the world, and you deceived the nations with your sorceries.* (New Living Translation)

The words "Sorcery" and "Sorceries" in those verses refer to pharmaceutical drugs. In Galatians, what does it say if you take those things or are involved with them? These are strong words. When you read the above, it makes you go hmmm...

"A pharmaceutical drug, also referred to as a medicine or medication, can be loosely defined as any chemical substance or product comprising such intended for use in the medical diagnosis, cure, treatment, or prevention of disease. The word pharmaceutical comes from the Greek word Pharmakeia. The modern transliteration of Pharmakeia is Pharmacia."
(Source: http://en.wikipedia.org/wiki/Pharmaceutical_drug)

Now these are just some of the different types of ways 'drugs' get into our bodies.

1. You have the ones prescribed by a doctor.

2. Then there are the ones that are over-the-counter.
3. Then there are the ones that make your way into your food that you eat. Did that raise an eyebrow? Good. What happens if you eat meat that is injected with different drugs? Does it get into your system? They do this so the animal can stay alive long enough to take it to the slaughter house.
4. Do you drink milk from a cow that is injected with the bovine growth hormone? That may be another one.
5. Antibiotics that are injected into cattle and chicken.
6. Prescription drugs. Can they enter your home through the water supply? If you get your water from a surface lake, you might be surprised what is in it. Did you know there are so many people taking drugs that when they go to the bathroom, the residual that is left over is eliminated from the body? Then it goes back into that lake and eventually gets reintroduced into your water supply. Do a search in your local area. Better yet, browse the Internet and look at all the reports of pharmaceutical drugs that are present in your tap water.
   (Source; Drugs found in drinking water
   http://usatoday30.usatoday.com/news/nation/2008-03-10-drugs-tap-water_N.htm
   Cancer drugs found in tap water
   http://www.telegraph.co.uk/earth/earthnews/3321519/Cancer-drugs-found-in-tap-water.html)

   If you receive water from your municipality, you will need to ask the hard questions and convince them to release the water test reports with this information. Keep in mind about on average of only 1% of all the water you use in your house is used for drinking and cooking purposes.

The very purpose of this book is so you can better understand the tactics satan uses against us. It is also so you can help others as well.

2 Corinthians 2:10; *in order that Satan might not outwit us. For we are not unaware oj his schemes.* (New International Version)

So is it ok to be taking drugs?

1 Corinthians 6:12; *"All things are lawful for me," but not all things are helpful. "All things are lawful for me," but I will not be enslaved by anything.* (English Standard Version)

1 Corinthians 10:23; *You say, "I am allowed to do anything"--but not everything is good for you. You say, "I am allowed to do anything"--but not everything is beneficial.* (New Living Translation)

1 Corinthians 10:32; *Do not cause anyone to stumble, whether Jews, Greeks or the church of God.* (New International Version)

1 Corinthians 6:19-20;
19 *Do you not know that your bodies are temples of the Holy Spirit, who is in you, whom you have received from God? You are not your own;*
20 you were bought at a price. Therefore honor God with your bodies. (New International Version)

1 Corinthians 15:34; *Become sober-minded as you ought, and stop sinning; for some have no knowledge of God. I speak this to your shame.* (New American Standard Bible)

Titus 2:12; *Teaching us that, denying ungodliness and worldly lusts, we should live soberly, righteously, and godly, in this present world;* (King James Cambridge)

Taking various forms of drugs dates back to the times of pre-flood days of Genesis 6. Then the fallen angels taught man the cutting of roots, etc.
(Source: http://www.pharmacy.wsu.edu/history/A%20History%20of%20Pharmacy%20in%20Pictures.pdf, & http://www.saching.com/Article/History-of-Pharmacy/1454)

The Rx Symbol

The 'Rx' symbol means prescription today. It's a Latin word for 'recipe'; meaning 'receive' or maybe 'take'. Yet others feel it means 'Take thou'.

This next part was taken from the webpage, 'The Open Scroll'. Rx is not, as is frequently supposed, an abbreviation of a

Latin word meaning recipe or compound, but is an invocation to Jupiter, a prayer for his aid to make the treatment effective... sometimes in old medical manuscripts all the R's occurring in the text were crossed." (Devils, Drugs, and Doctors (1931)) (Sources; http://www.straightdope.com/columns/read/1641/what-does-the-pharmacists-symbol-rx-mean, http://en.wikipedia.org/wiki/Rx, http://www.theopenscroll.com/pharmakeia.htm)

Some feel this symbol means it is actually the 'Eye of Horus'. Who is Horus? He is supposed to be an ancient Egyptian god who is usually drawn with the head of a falcon and the body of a man. He was supposed to be a Pharaoh around 25th century B.C. That is right before the time of the flood of Genesis 7. That happened in 2319 B.C. Here, we go back to Genesis 6 again! See how things are pointing back to that time period, the fallen angels, and the Nephilim?

The eye that is in the center of the triangle on the back of our money is claimed to be the all seeing eye. That is usually linked to the "Illuminati". However, it's believed the 'Eye of Horus' actually ends up being linked to 'satan' with the all seeing eye. The fact is satan doesn't see all or everything. Only the LORD God sees everything.

Nuclear War, The Woman in the Basket

What does the Bible say about nuclear war? Is there going to be a nuclear war? Will there be more than one of them?

Zechariah 5:1-11;

1 I looked again, and there before me was a flying scroll.
2 He asked me, "What do you see?" I answered, "I see a flying scroll, twenty cubits long and ten cubits wide."
3 And he said to me, "This is the curse that is going out over the whole land; for according to what it says on one side, every thief will be banished, and according to what it says on the other, everyone who swears falsely will be banished.
4 The LORD Almighty declares, 'I will send it out, and it will enter the house of the thief and the house of anyone who swears falsely by my name. It will remain in that house and destroy it completely, both its timbers and its stones.'

5 Then the angel who was speaking to me came forward and said to me, "Look up and see what is appearing."
6 " I asked, "What is it?" He replied, "It is a basket." And he added, "This is the iniquity of the people throughout the land."
7 Then the cover of lead was raised, and there in the basket sat a woman!
8 He said, "This is wickedness," and he pushed her back into the basket and pushed its lead cover down on it.
9 Then I looked up--and there before me were two women, with the wind in their wings! They had wings like those of a stork, and they lifted up the basket between heaven and earth.
10 "Where are they taking the basket?" I asked the angel who was speaking to me.
11 He replied, "To the country of Babylonia to build a house for it. When the house is ready, the basket will be set there in its place." (New International Version)

Can a flying scroll be the description for a missile? The dimensions given above can be very close to what a missile size is today. Let's check it out!

The word scroll in the Hebrew is called "məgillah". A "məgillah" rolls up into a single scroll where most of the Old Testament books roll up into two scrolls. It's been said the book of Esther is rolled up into a "məgillah", single roll.

Now it says this flying scroll can be twenty cubits long by ten cubits wide. If you remember, a cubit is between seventeen and twenty five inches. That would make the length of twenty cubits just under thirty feet to a bit over forty feet. Now that word "wide" in Hebrew might be better translated into breadth or circumference. If that is the case, then the ten cubits in circumference would be around up to five and a half feet wide.

Thus translated from the Hebrew, here is what those verses read like now. *I looked again, and there before me was a flying* "məgillah" (missile). *He asked me, "What do you see?" I answered, "I see a flying* "məgillah" (missile), *thirty feet long and about five and a half feet wide." And he said to me. "This is the curse that is going out over the whole land;* It is starting to make more sense now, isn't it?

Notice the *"curse that is going out over the whole land."* The world's nuclear missiles are a curse, and they will be going out over all of the land. The worse thing that people fear WILL happen. A total exchange of nuclear weapons will be launched. The question is will it go out over all the earth. Sooner or later… it will.

The Hebrew word that was used for basket is probably better translated as an "ephah" Strongs H374, a container or a cylinder.

Now I'm told that Uranium-235 actually turns into lead as it comes into contact with some type of radioactive material that causes it to decay. This is important for the next passage.

The next Hebrew word for women is "isshah" (Strong's Concordance H802). It can also mean wife. Now "isshah" (Strong's Concordance is H801 and maybe H800) can also mean fire offering.

Here is the next passage. Let's plug in a few different English words so it makes better sense. *I asked, "What is it?" He replied, "It is a 'cylinder'." And he added, "This is the iniquity of the people throughout the land." Then the cover of Uranium-235 was raised, and there in the cylinder sat a fire offering! He said, "This is wickedness," and he pushed fire offering back into the cylinder and pushed its Uranium-235 cover down on it.* Now isn't that wild? As you can tell the cylinder had to be pushed back into the container. It could be spring loaded. Now look at the following verses! What the angel is showing him is the mechanism of either a nuclear or thermonuclear missile.

Then I looked up--and there before me were two fire offerings, with the wind in their wings! They had wings like those of a stork, and they lifted up the cylinder between heaven and earth. "Where are they taking the cylinder?" I asked the angel who was speaking to me. He replied, "To the country of Babylonia to build a structure for it. When the structure is ready, the cylinder will be set there in its place." There is a possibility some type of aircraft lifted up this container or the entire missile and took it to Babylon. It appears they are also building some type of structure, mobile launching platform, or an underground silo to house this missile. Because it states it is transporting the cylinder, I'm wondering if the missile is left behind and the nuclear material is being moved to another location. It might be used to make smaller devices or possibly what is called a 'dirty bomb.'

Before 1945 when the first nuclear weapons were set off, this prophetic passages was hidden from us. And now look at what happened! It begins to make sense.

Zechariah 14:12; *This is the plague with which the LORD will strike all the nations that fought against Jerusalem: Their flesh will rot while they are still standing on their feet, their eyes will rot in their sockets, and their tongues will rot in their mouths.* (New International Version)

Can that be describing the results of a nuclear detonation? It could be a thermonuclear device too.

Isaiah 24:6; *That is why a curse devours the earth, and its people are punished for their guilt. That is why those who live on the earth are burned up, and only a few people are left.* (GOD'S WORD® Translation)

Is this the result of an all-out nuclear exchange where almost everyone dies as a result of this war?

Keep in mind when Zechariah gave those measurements listed previously, it appears he didn't have a yard stick, so-to-speak, to measure it. He was just looking at it. It's been said a cubit, at the time of Solomon, is

20.62 inches. That would make that missile 34.35 inches long. The diameter would be about 5 feet. The measurements given in Zechariah 5 appear to be about the same measurements of a nuclear tipped missile. The Scud missile, shown here, was manufactured by the U.S.S.R. back in those days. Today the former U.S.S.R. is called Russia.

Some translations mention the word diameter. The word is a Greek measurement and shouldn't be used in this context because the word breadth thereof talks about a different way of measurement. Probably a line cast about is better fits this context. To get the breadth of anything is to take a string and wrap it around the object you want to find the breadth thereof. Once one end of the string meets the other end, you would measure that length. That would be how you would find the measurement of breadth.

Isaiah 17:1; *A prophecy against Damascus: "See, Damascus will no longer be a city but will become a heap of ruins.* (New International Standard)

This is interesting because a thermonuclear blast can level the city of Damascus to when someone sees it; it will be like it's not recognizable as a city.

When the atomic weapons were dropped on Japan, everyone within a half mile of the blast zone was charred instantly. The remains of people were stuck to the streets, bridges, and sidewalks. Birds caught fire while in flight and so many building were gone, simply disappeared.

Nuclear weapons today are much more powerful. "Little Boy" and "Fat Man", as these bombs were called back in the 1940's, are a fraction of what the thermonuclear weapons can do today. They are measured in megatons which means today's weapons are over 1,000 times more powerful than the ones dropped on Hiroshima and Nagasaki in 1945.
(Source: http://www.lamblion.com/articles/articles_tribulation5.php)

Malachi 4:1; *The LORD of Heaven's Armies says, "The day of judgment is coming, burning like a furnace. On that day the arrogant and the wicked will be burned up like straw. They will be consumed--roots, branches, and all.* (New Living Translation)

Joel 2:30-31;

30 I will show wonders in the heavens and on the earth, blood and fire and billows of smoke.

31 The sun will be turned to darkness and the moon to blood before the coming of the great and dreadful day of the LORD. (New International Version)

Matthew 24:29; *"Immediately after the anguish of those days, the sun will be darkened, the moon will give no light, the stars will fall from the sky, and the powers in the heavens will be shaken.* (New Living Translation)

The above can be the result of a nuclear winter. The detonations will spew up smoke and debris up into the air. That will block out the sun, the moon, and the stars…

2 Peter 3:10-12;
10 But the day of the Lord will come like a thief. The heavens will disappear with a roar; the elements will be destroyed by fire, and the earth and everything done in it will be laid bare.
11 Since everything will be destroyed in this way, what kind of people ought you to be? You ought to live holy and godly lives
12 as you look forward to the day of God and speed its coming. That day will bring about the destruction of the heavens by fire, and the elements will melt in the heat. (New International Standard)

Revelation 8:7; *The first angel sounded his trumpet, and there came hail and fire mixed with blood, and it was hurled down on the earth. A third of the earth was burned up, a third of the trees were burned up, and all the green grass was burned up.* (New International Version)

Revelation 8:11; *the name of the star is Wormwood. A third of the waters turned bitter, and many people died from the waters that had become bitter.* (New International Version)

Could the above verse be describing the after-effects of a thermonuclear detonation and contamination of the water supply?

Revelation 9:17-18;

17 The horses and riders I saw in my vision looked like this: Their breastplates were fiery red, dark blue, and yellow as sulfur. The heads of the horses resembled the heads of lions, and out of their mouths came fire, smoke and sulfur.
18 A third of mankind was killed by the three plagues of fire, smoke and sulfur that came out of their mouths. (New International Version)

The above were an interesting set of verses. Could this be describing the fighter jets and their pilots?

Matthew 24:21-22;
21 For then there will be great distress, unequaled from the beginning of the world until now--and never to be equaled again.
22 "If those days had not been cut short, no one would survive, but for the sake of the elect those days will be shortened. (New International Version)

Whatever is going to happen in the Great Tribulation period, it will be a time like none other in the past or in the future. It will be so bad as to be almost unimaginable, the sheer shear calamity that it will bring about on the earth. It will be so awful, so terrible, and so gruesome that the LORD God will shorten the days during that time. If He doesn't, none of the elect (God's people) will be left alive. I'm thinking the only way that could be possible is there will be an all-out nuclear war. That could very well mean all the nations on the planet will be releasing their nuclear weapons in an all-out attack.

Ezekiel 39:9-16;
9 'Then those who live in the towns of Israel will go out and use the weapons for fuel and burn them up—the small and large shields, the bows and arrows, the war clubs and spears. For seven years they will use them for fuel.
10 They will not need to gather wood from the fields or cut it from the forests, because they will use the weapons for fuel. And they will plunder those who plundered them and loot those who looted them, declares the Sovereign LORD. "
11 'On that day I will give Gog a burial place in Israel, in the valley of those who travel east of the Sea. It will block the way of

travelers, because Gog and all his hordes will be buried there. So it will be called the Valley of Hamon Gog. "
12 'For seven months the Israelites will be burying them in order to cleanse the land.
13 All the people of the land will bury them, and the day I display my glory will be a memorable day for them, declares the Sovereign LORD.
14 People will be continually employed in cleansing the land. They will spread out across the land and, along with others, they will bury any bodies that are lying on the ground. "'After the seven months they will carry out a more detailed search.
15 As they go through the land, anyone who sees a human bone will leave a marker beside it until the gravediggers bury it in the Valley of Hamon Gog,
16 near a town called Hamonah. And so they will cleanse the land.' (New International Version)

People will be continually cleaning up from this war. It will take them seven months to bury all the bodies that are lying on the ground. They will have a special burial site for them. It is believed to be east of the Dead Sea. Then after that is completed, a more detailed search will be conducted. When someone comes across a bone or a body part, they will leave a marker so those specialists in handling contaminated nuclear waste material can come by and pick it up. With all the radioactivity around from the battle, Surely they need chemical suits to protect them from the harmful effects of the radiation that would still be on the battlefield. But then Jesus our Messiah might take away those harmful effects and neutralize them.

This is one area where the Bible talks about the consequences of these nuclear detonations.

Jeremiah 50:9; *I am going to stir up an alliance of strong nations from the north and bring it against Babylon. Those nations will take up positions against Babylon. Babylon will be captured from the north. Its enemy's arrows will be like skilled soldiers who don't come back empty-handed.* (GOD'S WORD ® Translation)

The above is an interesting passage. Could the word "arrows" refer to missiles? It says it won't return empty handed, meaning it will hit its target almost every time.

The word "arrows" comes from the Hebrew word "chets." It's Strongs #2670. It means; archer, arrow, dart, shaft, staff, wound. From chatsats; properly, a piercer, i.e. An arrow; by implication, a wound; figuratively, (of God) thunder-bolt; (by interchange for ets) the shaft of a spear, archer, arrow, dart, shaft, staff, wound.

The missiles of today are guided by various means. They can be called laser guided, precision guided, or smart bombs. They can also be self-guided or someone guiding the missiles to its target. Then there are heat missiles. They track and strike targets which give off heat. Then other missiles are programmed where to strike their targets.

These verses below are very interesting.

Jeremiah 50:13; *Because of the LORD's anger she will not be inhabited but will be completely desolate. All who pass Babylon will be appalled; they will scoff because of all her wounds.* (New International Version)

Jeremiah 50:26; *Come against her from afar. Break open her granaries; pile her up like heaps of grain. Completely destroy her and leave her no remnant.* (New International Version)

Jeremiah 50:39-40;
39 "So desert creatures and hyenas will live there, and there the owl will dwell. It will never again be inhabited or lived in from generation to generation.
40 As I overthrew Sodom and Gomorrah along with their neighboring towns," declares the LORD, "so no one will live there; no people will dwell in it. (New International Version)

Jeremiah 51:26; *No rock will be taken from you for a cornerstone, nor any stone for a foundation, for you will be desolate forever,"* (New International Version)

Jeremiah 51:29; *The earth quakes and trembles because the LORD's intentions against Babylon stand: to make the land of Babylon an uninhabited desolation.* (New International Version)

Jeremiah 51:37; *Babylon will be a heap of ruins, a haunt of jackals, an object of horror and scorn, a place where no one lives.* (New International Version)

The coming desolation is going to be so severe in Babylon that it will be uninhabitable. People will not be able to live there.

Nuclear War, The Destruction of Saudi Arabia

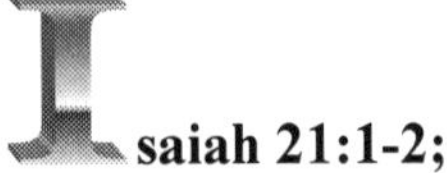**saiah 21:1-2;**

1 This is the divine revelation about the desert by the sea. Like a storm sweeping through the Negev, an invader will come from the desert, from a terrifying land.
2 I was shown a harsh vision. The traitor betrays. The destroyer destroys. Go to war, Elam! Surround them, Media! I will put an end to all the groaning. (GOD'S WORD ® Translation)

Isaiah 21:9; *Look, here comes a man in a chariot with a team of horses. And he gives back the answer: 'Babylon has fallen, has fallen! All the images of its gods lie shattered on the ground!'"* (New International Version)

Isaiah 34:8-13;

8 For the LORD has a day of vengeance, a year of retribution, to uphold Zion's cause.
9 Edom's streams will be turned into pitch, her dust into burning sulfur; her land will become blazing pitch!
10 It will not be quenched night or day; its smoke will rise forever. From generation to generation it will lie desolate; no one will ever pass through it again.
11 The desert owl and screech owl will possess it; the great owl and the raven will nest there. God will stretch out over Edom the measuring line of chaos and the plumb line of desolation.

12 Her nobles will have nothing there to be called a kingdom, all her princes will vanish away.
13 Thorns will overrun her citadels, nettles and brambles her strongholds. She will become a haunt for jackals, a home for owls. (New International Version)

Elam is believed to be Iran and Edom (Babylon) is Saudi Arabia. Is is conjectured that Iran is likely to attack Saudi Arabia with thermonuclear weapons during the Tribulation Period.

Revelation 14:8; *Then another angel followed him through the sky, shouting, "Babylon is fallen—that great city is fallen—because she made all the nations of the world drink the wine of her passionate immorality."* (New International Version)

Revelation 18:2; *With a mighty voice he shouted: "'Fallen! Fallen is Babylon the Great!' She has become a dwelling for demons and a haunt for every impure spirit, a haunt for every unclean bird, a haunt for every unclean and detestable animal.* (New International Version)

Revelation 18:8-14;
8 Therefore in one day her plagues will overtake her: death, mourning and famine. She will be consumed by fire, for mighty is the Lord God who judges her.
9 "When the kings of the earth who committed adultery with her and shared her luxury see the smoke of her burning, they will weep and mourn over her.
10 Terrified at her torment, they will stand far off and cry: "'Woe! Woe to you, great city, you mighty city of Babylon! In one hour your doom has come!'
11 "The merchants of the earth will weep and mourn over her because no one buys their cargoes anymore—
12 cargoes of gold, silver, precious stones and pearls; fine linen, purple, silk and scarlet cloth; every sort of citron wood, and articles of every kind made of ivory, costly wood, bronze, iron and marble;
13 cargoes of cinnamon and spice, of incense, myrrh and frankincense, of wine and olive oil, of fine flour and wheat;

cattle and sheep; horses and carriages; and human beings sold as slaves.
14 "They will say, 'The fruit you longed for is gone from you. All your luxury and splendor have vanished, never to be recovered.' (New International Version)

There is much discussion on whether the LORD God will do these Himself, through His angels. Can He do it Himself? Of course! He is God. After all, He did have one angel destroy 185,000 soldiers at night time once.

Isaiah 37:36; *Then the angel of the LORD went out and put to death a hundred and eighty-five thousand in the Assyrian camp. When the people got up the next morning - there were all the dead bodies!* (New International Version)

But then there are those who believe that God might just remove the restrainer from us down here on earth and let man do what he wants to do. And that is to destroy each other. If you really look at the plagues, some of them do exactly that very thing. Men killing each other for one reason or another. Why? Because they hate, rather than love one another.

2 Thessalonians 2:7; *For the mystery of lawlessness is already at work. Only he who now restrains it will do so until he is out of the way.* (English Standard Version)

There actually is another part of the Bible which talks about nuclear material and war.

Acts 2:17-21;
17 "'And in the last days it shall be, God declares, that I will pour out my Spirit on all flesh, and your sons and your daughters shall prophesy, and your young men shall see visions, and your old men shall dream dreams;
18 even on my male servants and female servants in those days I will pour out my Spirit, and they shall prophesy.
19 And I will show wonders in the heavens above and signs on the earth below, blood, and fire, and vapor of smoke;

20 the sun shall be turned to darkness and the moon to blood, before the day of the Lord comes, the great and magnificent day. 21 And it shall come to pass that everyone who calls upon the name of the Lord shall be saved.' (English Standard Version)

The word "vapor" in verse 19 can be translated as cloud, clouds, or a plume. It would be a plume of smoke that is rising up and spreading out. If you have ever seen a mushroom grow, it has a stem that rises up and expands at the top. That would be a good visual picture of what we call today a mushroom cloud caused by a nuclear detention. This concept is something to ponder.

Electronic Devices

The Bible actually talks about the various devices that will appear in the end time. Well, actually, it indirectly refers to them. Let's read the next passage.

Matthew 24:15-18;
15 "So when you see standing in the holy place 'the abomination that causes desolation,' spoken of through the prophet Daniel—let the reader understand
16 then let those who are in Judea flee to the mountains.
17 Let no one on the housetop go down to take anything out of the house.
18 Let no one in the field go back to get their cloak. (New International Version)

Did you take note of the word "see" in the above passage? It appears 'the abomination that causes desolation' will be seen by people around the world. It is a possibility the world might pause for this event. It might be a mandatory event that will appear on everyone's device that has the capability of receiving the broadcast. How is that going to be done? Through the television and the Internet.

Due to the abilities of the modern day wireless phone and these small tablet computers (with wireless technology), streaming video will be able to appear on these devices wherever they are located. People in the fields, on rooftops, at the mall, wherever, they are, can see the video/telecast simultaneously. Look what else will be televised to the whole world.

Revelation 11:7-12;
7 Now when they have finished their testimony, the beast that comes up from the Abyss will attack them, and overpower and kill them.
8 Their bodies will lie in the public square of the great city—which is figuratively called Sodom and Egypt—where also their Lord was crucified.
9 For three and a half days some from every people, tribe, language and nation will gaze on their bodies and refuse them burial.
10 The inhabitants of the earth will gloat over them and will celebrate by sending each other gifts, because these two prophets had tormented those who live on the earth.
11 But after the three and a half days the breath of life from God entered them, and they stood on their feet, and terror struck those who saw them.
12 Then they heard a loud voice from heaven saying to them, "Come up here." And they went up to heaven in a cloud, while their enemies looked on. (New International Version)

Apparently, the world will see these two witnesses through television and the internet. They will be lying in the streets for all to see. The world will celebrate their deaths. They will think it is a glorious victory. While the whole world watches as they lie in the street dead, the whole world will witness and see them being resurrected up and being taken up into the heavens. All of them will see it live and later on video.

Traditions of Men

Mark 7:8; *"Neglecting the commandment of God, you hold to the tradition of men."* (New American Standard Bible)

Colossians 2:8; *See to it that no one takes you captive by philosophy and empty deceit, according to human tradition, according to the elemental spirits of the world, and not according to Christ.* (English Standard Version)

We are going to be discussing the different traditions we have in the United States of America. Some of these same traditions are also observed in other parts of the world.

Let me ask you this question. Why do you need to read the following information? Could it be you have been observing and participating in rituals and festivities which are totally against the LORD God and His commands? What if they are an abomination to Him? What if they are detestable to the King of the Universe?

Origins of christmas, valentine's Day, lent, and easter

These same holidays are the ones which come every year. Many people in the world celebrate that day as the birth day of the Messiah Jesus Christ, the Son of the Most High God. However, Jesus was not born on that day. It appears He wasn't born in December at all. So why does the world actually celebrate on that day? Isn't the world at enmity with God? If that is the case, why is the world celebrating His birthday on that day?

James 4:4; *You adulterers! Don't you realize that friendship with the world makes you an enemy of God? I say it again: If you want to be a friend of the world, you make yourself an enemy of God.* (New Living Translation)

Actually, it's a false religion. There is reason to believe it was started by Cush, who was a son of Ham and the grandson of Noah. This false religion did not grow much under Cush. It was Nimrod, the son of Cush, who promoted it. As a result, it spread because of Nimrod's influence with the nations of the earth. And yes this is the same Nimrod from the Tower of Babel in the Book of Genesis.

Nimrod's wife, Semiramis, supposedly told the people of Babylon when Nimrod died, he became a sun god. She also claimed an evergreen tree sprang up immediately overnight from a dead tree stump which was near to where Nimrod was buried. Supposedly every year she would visit this tree and leave presents under it on December 25th. It appears Nimrod is probably one of the first anti-Christ's according to some Bible scholars.

Semiramis claimed she became pregnant by the rays of the sun. This was several months after his death. Seeing how Nimrod became a sun god after his death, Semiramis laid claim that this baby was Nimrod reincarnated. When Semiramis gave birth to a son, he was named Tammuz. And guess when Tammuz was born? Yep, on December 25th also. Tammuz was claimed to be a false Christ also.

Now Tammuz died while out hunting when he was 40. As a result, women mourned for forty days, in the hope of bringing him back to life, which is where the forty days of Lent started. Now do you understand what "Ash Wednesday" is all about? For those of you who observe it, now you know why you are asked to give up something for during that time period? No matter what the spin the church puts on it, no matter how they present it to you, that is where it all originated, back to Nimrod's day.
(Source: http://www.cai.org/bible-studies/christmas)

There is another theory which states the reason why people give up something for lent. They give it up so Tammuz can enjoy in the afterlife.

What is interesting is Tammuz is actually mentioned in the Bible. Women are at a statue of Tammuz, mourning his death. Keep in mind, they are doing this in the LORD God's temple.

Ezekiel 8:14-15;
14 Then he brought me to the entrance of the north gate of the house of the LORD, and I saw women sitting there, mourning the god Tammuz.
15 He said to me, "Do you see this, son of man? You will see things that are even more detestable than this." (New International Version)

As you can see, the LORD God thinks this type of practice is just plain not acceptable at all. And He is about to show Ezekiel something, which is more detestable.

Ezekiel 8:16-17;
16 He then brought me into the inner court of the house of the LORD, and there at the entrance to the temple, between the portico and the altar, were about twenty-five men. With their backs toward the temple of the LORD and their faces toward the east, they were bowing down to the sun in the east.
17 He said to me, "Have you seen this, son of man? Is it a trivial matter for the people of Judah to do the detestable things they are doing here? Must they also fill the land with violence and continually arouse my anger? Look at them putting the branch to their nose! (New International Version)

The putting of the branch through to nose is some type of pagan ritual. This could be a ritual dating back to the death of Nimrod, when the evergreen tree sprung up overnight at the time of his death. What could they accomplish by putting the branch into their nose? More spiritual growth or enlightenment? I don't know.

It was claimed Tammuz rose up on a day that is called Ishtar (pronounced" eas-tar or easter). Ishtar is the pagan goddess of fertility. Actually, Ishtar is linked all the way back to Semiramis. Ishtar, translated into English means easter.
(Source; http://www.bibleplus.org/prophecy/rev/23_babylon.htm)

So when you say Happy easter, you are acknowledging a pagan goddess who was given the status of goddess on that day. That means you are participating in this pagan festival. Is the LORD God pleased with that?

There are actually more traditions that accompany the easter season. I will briefly touch on these here.

1. Sunrise service. It seems that this service on easter has some significant meaning. It is believed that the priests of Ishtar would impregnate some young virgins on the altar during this sunrise service. Then they would take the babies who were about three months old from the previous years' sunrise service and sacrifice them. They would drain the blood from those sacrificed babies and would dip Ishtar's eggs into the blood of the babies just murdered. Some churches or organizations to this very day still color eggs in red at this time of year. They

don't know why they always color them red. They just do it. Do you still want to color those eggs and participate in that egg hunt?

2. Semiramis, the wife of Nimrod, supposedly died, went to heaven and was rebirthed. Because of her 'supposed purity' she was sent back to earth… in an egg. The egg opened up over the Euphrates River. She turned a bird into an egg-laying rabbit. That could very well be why the bunny and the egg laying "tradition" came into being. She was then turned into a sex goddess. It has been said that the playboy bunny has it origins dating back to her.
3. The easter ham came into being because supposedly Tammuz was killed by a… wild boar. A wild boar is another name for a wild pig. So when you eat that ham, you are part of the tradition of remembering a pagan god named Tammuz.

No doubt some people might be in a state of disbelief or culture shock. Quite frankly, I understand why. I was too.

Wishing someone a happy easter is paying tribute to a pagan god. As a blood-bought Christian, should you be doing that? Let's check what the Bible says about that. The "Ten Commandants" will do for starters.

Exodus 20:3-4;
3 "You shall have no other gods before me."
4 You shall not make for yourself an image in the form of anything in heaven above or on the earth beneath or in the waters below. (New International Version)

The question is do you want to honor a man like Nimod and his son? Do you want to participate in the holiday of the goddess of fertility?

While some religions break down christmas into "Christ's Mass", the word christmas or Christ's mass is not mentioned in the Bible. Yes, these are traditions that have been around for our life time at least. Here is what the Bible says about it.

Colossians 2:8; *Be careful not to let anyone rob you [of this faith] through a shallow and misleading philosophy. Such a person follows human traditions and the world's way of doing things rather than following Christ.* (GOD'S WORD® Translation)

Are you sure you are not being deceived? Are you sure you are not being lied to blatantly about this pagan sun god worship?

The Bible states Israel was into pagan sun god worship along with worshipping demons (the disembodied spirits of the Nephilim). It has been like that for most of its history.

Deuteronomy 32:17; *They sacrificed to demons that were no gods, to gods they had never known, to new gods that had come recently, whom your fathers had never dreaded.* (English Standard Version)

Psalm 106:37; *They sacrificed their sons and their daughters to the demons;* (English Standard Version)

What that Psalm says is strange to us today. We can't begin to think who would do such a thing today. Yet, it was done long ago.

The Hebrew word for "to the demons" is Strong's #7700, which does mean demons. The demons are disembodied spirits of the Nephilim as I have mentioned elsewhere in this book. That same word also applies to the verse in Deuteronomy 32:17, which I mention above.

Look at the word "new" in the Deuteronomy 32:17. It means new, new thing, new things or something new according to Strong's #2318. It is saying these gods were not known before by their fathers. This takes you all the way back to Genesis 6. Then who appeared in their recent memory? The Nephilim.

Let's look at the word "recently" in that same verse. The Hebrew word is qarob. It is Strong's #7138. It can mean any of the following depending on the usage within the sentence; about, close, close relative, closer, draws near, hand, kinsmen, lately, near, nearby, nearest, neighbors, ones near, related, relative, relatives, short, shortly, soon, who are near, who is near. Now let's look at that verse from a possible different prospective. We will now plug in some of these English words. They sacrificed to the Nephilim that were not gods, to gods they had never known, to new gods that had come through kinsman or relatives, whom your fathers had never dreaded. It does add a different perspective doesn't it? The Nephilim came from the union of the fallen angels and women. Something to think about. These same gods are the ones behind the holidays we are talking about here.

Let's talk about the giving of gifts on the 25th day of the twelfth month of the year.

It's really amazing what people will do around the holidays towards the end of the year. They shop online, they drive to stores, they go to malls to buy gifts so they can give them to others. Is this a good thing? I mean we are supposed to give to others. Yet what is "christmas" all about? Hmmm… Oh yes, to celebrate the Lord Jesus Christ's birthday. So what do you give to Him? The God who made you, the God who loves you more than anyone else, the God who shed His blood so you can be redeemed by trusting in Jesus for your salvation. So what did you give to Him that He would want on the celebration of His birthday?

Some people will think, I'm giving to others because Jesus isn't here. OK, I can understand that. So basically you are bringing to his birthday - gifts for others. I wonder how you would feel if at the celebration of your birthday, people brought gifts for others, and nothing for you. How would that make you feel?

Let's see what the Bible says about this practice.

Matthew 2:10-11;
10 When they saw the star, they were overjoyed.
11 On coming to the house, they saw the child with his mother Mary, and they bowed down and worshiped him. Then they opened their treasures and presented him with gifts of gold, frankincense and myrrh. (New International Version)

Notice if you would please, who they presented the gifts of gold, frankincense and myrrh to… They presented them to Jesus. No one else was given gifts from these wise men.

Oh, you need some gift ideas to give to Jesus? Here are some for you. When you know someone, you try to give them something that they would like or even need in some cases. What do you give to someone who has everything? Who can bring anything to life by just thinking and saying it? They can be challenging to buy for, for many reasons.

Ahhh… here are some gift ideas.

1. Give to the poor

   Matthew 6:2-3;

   2 "Thus, when you give to the needy, sound no trumpet before you, as the hypocrites do in the synagogues and in the streets, that they may be praised by others. Truly, I say to you, they have received their reward.

   3 But when you give to the needy, do not let your left hand know what your right hand is doing, (English Standard Version)

   Matthew 19:21-22;

   21 Jesus said to him, "If you wish to be complete, go and sell your possessions and give to the poor, and you will have treasure in heaven; and come, follow Me."

   22 But when the young man heard this statement, he went away grieving; for he was one who owned much property. (New American Standard Bible)

   Mark 10:21-22;

   21 Jesus looked at him and loved him. "One thing you lack," he said. "Go, sell everything you have and give to the poor, and you will have treasure in heaven. Then come, follow me."

   22 At this the man's face fell. He went away sad, because he had great wealth. (New International Version)

   Luke 11:40-41;

   40 Fools! Didn't God make the inside as well as the outside?

   41 So clean the inside by giving gifts to the poor, and you will be clean all over. (New Living Translation)

   Luke 12:33;

   33 Sell your possessions and give to the poor. Provide purses for yourselves that will not wear out, a treasure in heaven that will never fail, where no thief comes near and no moth destroys. (New International Version)

Luke 14:13-14;
13 But when you give a banquet, invite the poor, the crippled, the lame, the blind,
14 and you will be blessed. Although they cannot repay you, you will be repaid at the resurrection of the righteous." (New International Version)
Luke 18:22; *When Jesus heard this, he said to him, "You still lack one thing. Sell everything you have and give to the poor, and you will have treasure in heaven. Then come, follow me."* (New International Version)
Luke 19:8-9;
8 But Zacchaeus stood up and said to the Lord, "Look, Lord! Here and now I give half of my possessions to the poor, and if I have cheated anybody out of anything, I will pay back four times the amount."
9 Jesus said to him, "Today salvation has come to this house, because this man, too, is a son of Abraham. (New International Version)

2. **Loving the LORD Your God and Everyone Else.**
   Matthew 22:36-40;
   36 *"Teacher, which is the greatest commandment in the Law?"*
   37 Jesus replied: "'Love the Lord your God with all your heart and with all your soul and with all your mind.'
   38 This is the first and greatest commandment.
   39 And the second is like it: 'Love your neighbor as yourself.'
   40 All the Law and the Prophets hang on these two commandments." (New International Version)
   Mark 12:30; *Love the Lord your God with all your heart and with all your soul and with all your mind and with all your strength.'* (New International Version)
   Luke 10:27; *He answered, "'Love the Lord your God with all your heart and with all your soul and with all your strength and with all your mind'; and, 'Love your neighbor as yourself.'"* (New International Version)
   Basically, the LORD really wants us to love Him and love each other, each and every day. I'm going to touch on something else this passage talks about with a

question. How can you love anyone else when they love God with all their heart, their soul and mind? We have to change our paradigm of what love is and is not. I could write another whole series of books on this topic alone. This fulfills what the law says and what the Prophets have preached for thousands of years.

John 14:15; *"If you love me, keep my commands.* (New International Version)

John 13:34-35;

34 "A new command I give you: Love one another. As I have loved you, so you must love one another.

35 By this everyone will know that you are my disciples, if you love one another." (New International Version)

John 15:12; *My command is this: Love each other as I have loved you.* (New International Version)

John 15:17; *This is my command: Love each other.* (New International Version)

Love is about giving to others. Giving the gift of loving another person far outweighs receiving it. Most people will never see it or understand it. But you continue to love people anyway. Why? That's what our Heavenly Father does all the time! More on this later. If you would give Him those two gifts I mentioned above, I believe Jesus would be pleased with it!

Below you will find other traditions people follow today. Yet there are others I did not include.

Traditions of Men

santa

Let's look at something else that is very much a tradition; santa. Rearrange the letters, you can spell the word satan. It's apparent that satan is right in your face about this holiday. satan is the accuser of the brethren.

Revelation 12:10; *Then I heard a loud voice shouting across the heavens, "It has come at last--salvation and power and the Kingdom of our God, and the authority of his Christ. For the accuser of our brothers and sisters has been thrown down to* *earth--the one who accuses them before our God day and night.* (New Living Translation)

It's been thought santa claus came from saint Nicholas (saint Nick), a Roman Catholic bishop from the fifth century. In reality, it is not the same person with a name change. Nicholas is said to have given gifts to the poor in secret on the eve of his birthday, the 6th day of the twelfth month. Over time, this tradition of men moved the date to 25th.

There are many stories about Nicholas. Slowly the name starts to change to saint Nick to santa and then santa claus. Then mrs. santa claus appears in a wonderfully presented setting, which captures the hearts of so many people. Now you hear mostly of santa and hardly anything about saint Nick.

Some believe this dates back to the Norse legends.

There is another possibility of the origins of saint Nick. Bible mentions a sect in the Book of Revelation.

Revelation 2:6; *But you have this in your favor: You hate the practices of the Nicolaitans, which I also hate.* (New International Version)

Revelation 2:15; *Likewise, you also have those who hold to the teaching of the Nicolaitans.* (New International Version)

Now the question is who are the "Nicolaitans"? They are followers of Nicolas. They were a group that claimed to be Christians, but were very sexually immoral and wicked. They led other Christians astray with their false teachings and doctrine along with eating meat that was sacrificed to idols. Paul actually talks about this situation in 1 Corinthians and the Book of Acts. These Nicolaitans were rejected by the early church. So, they went to another country and set up a church there. And where is that church? In Rome.

Here is what Gill's Exposition says about their doctrine. "These impure heretics sprung up in the time of the apostolic church, but their doctrines were not received, and their deeds were hated, see Revelation 2:6. This seems to design the doctrines of the church of Rome, which in this period took place; which forbid marriage to the priests, and recommended celibacy

and virginity to others also; which were the source of all uncleanness and abominable lusts; for which pardons and indulgences were given, and, in process of time, brothel houses were set up, and licensed and encouraged by authority,"
(Source: http://biblehub.com/revelation/2-15.htm)

These Nicolaitans has infiltrated many churches with their false doctrine and teachings. They are similar to what the Pharisees did. They added to and took away from the laws of the LORD.

While there are other stories about the emergence of santa, the bottom line is God is not pleased with the image we have created of santa… or should it read… satan…

Traditions of Men

santa Down the Chimney

There is another ancient belief that santa enters the house through the chimney could come from an old Norse legend. The Norse believed that the goddess Hertha appeared in the fireplace and brought good luck to the home.

Traditions of Men

The christmas Tree

Jeremiah 10:3-4;
3 *Their ways are futile and foolish. They cut down a tree, and a craftsman carves an idol.*
4 *They decorate it with gold and silver and then fasten it securely with hammer and nails so it won't fall over.* (New Living Translation)

I would say those verses are very, VERY clear. Jeremiah describes the tradition of the tree (usually evergreen), chopping it down, decorating it with ornaments and garland, and right on down to securing it in a tree stand.

There are some who believe idols were created from these trees. Faces and symbols were carved on them. Maybe both possibilities are true.

While that did happen, so were these trees used in pagan sun god worship. It dates all the way back to Nimrod. It's believed people left presents under an evergreen tree after his death. His wife Semiramis continued the practice, and it became part of the traditions of men. It's believed he also died on the 25th day of the twelfth month.

Where does it say in the Bible we are to bring trees into our homes and decorate them? Yet the pagan's did. The LORD God tells us not to learn the ways of the heathen.

Deuteronomy 18:9; *"When you enter the land the LORD your God is giving you, be very careful not to imitate the detestable customs oj the nations living there.* (New Living Translation)

Traditions of Men

The Eight Pointed Star

In the Sumerian culture, the eight pointed star represented Ishtar, who was also known as the goddess "The Lightbringer." In the circle of the star is the symbol of the sun god.
(Source: http://www.moroccoboard.com/features/92-sarah-tricha/821-origins-and-meanings-of-the-eight-point-star)

That is the same Ishtar who was Nimrod's wife.

Traditions of Men

Mistletoe

During a Festival of the Winter Solstice, the pagan custom of kissing under the mistletoe was practiced. It was to celebrate the ending of the sun and the beginning of a new sun. The actual mistletoe is like a parasite to a tree that it might attach itself. Holly berries are thought to be sacred to the sun god.

It was also thought that some Celtic people believed the plant had mystical powers to ward off evil spirits. Romans supposedly fornicated under the mistletoe. That is the reason where the tradition probably started, having people kiss under the mistletoe.

Traditions of Men

Yule Log

This too goes right along with the sun god worship. The Chaldeans called Yule day as the "day of the infant". They are referring to Tammuz, who was the son of the god, Nimrod. This is pure paganism. There is believed to be yet another custom that it was dedicated to the fertility goddess Ishtar (easter) because she gave birth to Tammuz. Animals and slaves were sacrificed each night for something like twelve days. The queen of heaven mentioned in the Bible is believed to be Ishtar also.

Jeremiah 7:18; *The children gather wood, the fathers light the fire, and the women knead the dough and make cakes to offer to the Queen of Heaven. They pour out drink offerings to other gods to arouse my anger.* (New International Version)

Jeremiah 44:17-19;
17 We will certainly do everything we said we would: We will burn incense to the Queen of Heaven and will pour out drink offerings to her just as we and our ancestors, our kings and our officials did in the towns of Judah and in the streets of Jerusalem. At that time we had plenty of food and were well off and suffered no harm.
18 But ever since we stopped burning incense to the Queen of Heaven and pouring out drink offerings to her, we have had nothing and have been perishing by sword and famine."
19 The women added, "When we burned incense to the Queen of Heaven and poured out drink offerings to her, did not our husbands know that we were making cakes impressed with her image and pouring out drink offerings to her?" (New International Version)

Jeremiah 44:25; *This is what the LORD Almighty, the God of Israel, says: You and your wives have done what you said you would do when you promised, 'We will certainly carry out the vows we made to burn incense and pour out drink offerings to the Queen of Heaven.'* (New International Version)

Traditions of Men

christmas Celebration Banned

Centuries ago, some people apparently knew more about the above than we do today. In 1651 the Massachusetts General Court passed the following bill;

"For preventing disorders arising in several places within this jurisdiction, by reason of some still observing such festivals, as were superstitiously kept in other countries, to the great dishonor of God and offense to others: It is therefore ordered by this Court and the authority thereof, that whosoever shall be found observing any such day as Christmas or the like, either by forbearing labour, feasting, or any other way upon any such account as aforesaid, every such person so offending, shall pay five shillings as a fine to the country."

Businesses remained open on that day and conducted transactions as usual.

In England, the ban was lifted in 1660. It did not become a holiday until 1856. Yet schools remained open on that day until 1870.

(Source; http://www.livescience.com/32891-why-was-christmas-banned-in-america-.html)

In the United States, christmas was proclaimed a holiday in 1870. Before the civil war, the north was against christmas and the south had been for it. Alabama was the first state to legalize it in 1836. Louisiana and Arkansas followed in 1838. Notice these first three states were from the south? It just shows the south was for it. It is believed the last state to legalize it was Oklahoma in 1890.

Charles Spurgeon, one of the greatest preachers of the faith and pastor who is still quoted today in many Christian circles, had this to say in a sermon on December 24, 1871 about christmas;

We have no superstitious regard for times and seasons. Certainly we do not believe in the present ecclesiastical arrangement called Christmas. First, because **we do not believe in the mass at all, but abhor it**, whether it be sung in Latin or in English. Secondly, because **we find no Scriptural warrant whatever for observing any day as the birthday**

of the Savior; and consequently, its observance is a superstition, because not of divine authority. 'Superstition' has fixed most positively the day of our Savior's birth, although there is no possibility of discovering when it occurred....
(Source: http://www.davidbenariel.org/cog/c-h-spurgeon-christmas-roman-catholicism.htm)

Leviticus 18:30; *Keep my requirements and do not follow any of the detestable customs that were practiced before you came and do not defile yourselves with them. I am the LORD your God.'"* (New International Bible)

Here is a verse that tells you not to try and turn these holidays into one that worship the LORD God. Some people believe, "God knows my heart, and I'm worshiping Him in my own way." Someone else might think, "That's not what it means to me." Here is a verse for you to ponder.

Deuteronomy 12:3-4;
3 Break down their altars, smash their sacred stones and burn their Asherah poles in the fire; cut down the idols of their gods and wipe out their names from those places.
4 You must not worship the LORD your God in their way. (New International Version)

In other words, do NOT try to Christianize anything that is of another god or goddess.

Deuteronomy 12:8 & 29-32;
8"You shall not do at all what we are doing here today, every man doing whatever is right in his own eyes; (New American Standard Bible)

29 The LORD your God will cut off before you the nations you are about to invade and dispossess. But when you have driven them out and settled in their land,
30 and after they have been destroyed before you, be careful not to be ensnared by inquiring about their gods, saying, "How do these nations serve their gods? We will do the same."
31 You must not worship the LORD your God in their way, because in worshiping their gods, they do all kinds of detestable

things the LORD hates. They even burn their sons and daughters in the fire as sacrifices to their gods.
32 See that you do all I command you; do not add to it or take away from it. (New International Version)

A final note on this topic. Why did it take over two hundred years for christmas to be legalized and celebrated in our country? Did they realize that it is a pagan holiday that should not be celebrated by Christians?

Does this mean you shouldn't get together with people on those pagan holidays to eat at their home or at a restaurant? I'm saying avoid saying the phrase "happy easter" or "merry christmas". And don't participate in Lent either. Don't get involved in the gift exchanges. You can give gifts to people anytime you wish. If you participated in them in the past, it could be a little awkward at first, but after a while you will get the hang of it.

But look at the bigger picture with this. Do you want to take away the glory the LORD God (who loves you enough to die in public humility for your sins on a rugged cross) deserves to have and give it to a pagan god? Would you rather have the LORD God upset at you and be in harmony with your friends, relatives, or family? Or would you rather be in harmony with your Creator, the LORD God, and possibly feel slightly out of balance, so-to-speak, with your family?

Matthew 10:34-39;
34 "Do not suppose that I have come to bring peace to the earth. I did not come to bring peace, but a sword.
35 For I have come to turn "'a man against his father, a daughter against her mother, a daughter-in-law against her mother-in-law—
36 a man's enemies will be the members of his own household.'
37 "Anyone who loves their father or mother more than me is not worthy of me; anyone who loves their son or daughter more than me is not worthy of me.
38 Whoever does not take up their cross and follow me is not worthy of me.

39 Whoever finds their life will lose it, and whoever loses their life for my sake will find it. (New International Version)

When you know the truth, the truth will set you free. This is all part of the deception that satan has over all of us. We need to come out of it so we can live and dwell as the LORD God had intended us to live! The choice is always yours. And when you stand before God, at that Great White Throne Judgment, you will see the grand "sea of faces" who ever lived (except for the beast and the false prophet who are already in the Lake of Fire which burns with fire and brimstone), you will understand the vastness, the gravity of the situation. You will look back and see the results of the choices you made in your life.

Revelation 20:11-15;
11 Then I saw a great white throne and him who was seated on it. The earth and the heavens fled from his presence, and there was no place for them.
12 And I saw the dead, great and small, standing before the throne, and books were opened. Another book was opened, which is the book of life. The dead were judged according to what they had done as recorded in the books.
13 The sea gave up the dead that were in it, and death and Hades gave up the dead that were in them, and each person was judged according to what they had done.
14 Then death and Hades were thrown into the lake of fire. The lake of fire is the second death.
15 Anyone whose name was not found written in the book of life was thrown into the lake of fire. (New International Version)

Traditions of Men

valentine's Day

You will find it interesting to note that valentine's day also dates back to Nimrod. Supposedly Tummuz marries his mother Semiramis, who would be Nimrod's wife.

Is there anything wrong with some of the symbols of this holiday?

1. Red rose was supposed to be the flower of Venus, the Roman goddess of strong feelings. Venus is the goddess of love.
2. Dove are symbols of loyalty. They mate for life. They also share the care of their children.
3. Cupid, in Roman myth, is the son of Venus. Cupid is the god of desire. The arrows of Cupid are to enhance romantic love.
4. It is quite interesting how sometimes Roman parents named their children after the famous man who was first called valentine thousands of years ago. That famous man was Lupercus, the hunter. But who was Lupercus? god of shepherds. He was called "Pan". Now the Semites called "Pan" "Baul" or "Baal". Baal is mentioned many times in the Word of God. Yet those were merely another name for Nimrod, "the mighty hunter"

   Genesis 10:9; *Since he was the greatest hunter in the world, his name became proverbial. People would say, "This man is like Nimrod, the greatest hunter in the world."* (New Living Translation).

   It appears Nimrod was a hero, a mighty man, and an original valentine to many. Yet another of one of Nimrod's many names was "*Sanctuc*" or "s*anta*".

With all that said, what are your choices? We always have them don't we? Do we stop participating in these pagan rituals or continue with the "Traditions of Men"?

The Israelites had their pagan gods they turned to thousands of years ago. They turned to them time and time again. God would send prophets to tell them about their sinful ways, to turn back to the LORD God. Yet they did not. They even mocked and killed those prophets whom they thought didn't deliver a message that was positive and upbeat. God is NOT concerned as to whether or not He needs to deliver a message that is "positive". He has already done that over and over again.

John 7:7; *The world cannot hate you, but it hates me because I say that what everyone does is evil.* (GOD'S WORD® Translation)

The LORD God is telling you right now you should not be doing these things. But when His people are entertaining ways that are an abomination to Him, then He will tell you to straighten up, or judgment is coming. Here is what the Bible says about these things.

Romans 2:4-5;
4 Or do you show contempt for the riches of his kindness, forbearance and patience, not realizing that God's kindness is intended to lead you to repentance?
5 But because of your stubbornness and your unrepentant heart, you are storing up wrath against yourself for the day of God's wrath, when his righteous judgment will be revealed. (New International Version)

Judges 2:13; *because they forsook him and served Baal and the Ashtoreths.* (New International Version)

1 Samuel 7:4; *So the Israelites put away their Baals and Ashtoreths, and served the LORD only.* (New International Version)

Romans 11:3-4;
3 "Lord, they have killed your prophets and torn down your altars; I am the only one left, and they are trying to kill me"?
4 And what was God's answer to him? "I have reserved for myself seven thousand who have not bowed the knee to Baal." (New International Version)

Ashtoreth listed above is believed to be an obelisk. The obelisk date back to the time of Nimrod too.

A common comment people have after reading this material or discussing it is this; "Well, that's not why I celebrate valentine's day. That's not what it means to me. I focus on Jesus during this time period. And God knows my heart too…"

I can appreciate those thoughts and intensity. Yet we need to understand that it's not about what we intend to do. It is all about how God wants us to worship Him. How pure our intentions are doesn't really matter. It's NOT about how we want to worship Him, but how HE WANTS US TO WORSHIP HIM!

Remember, His ways are higher than our ways. The LORD God made the rules. We MUST follow them!

Putting It All Together

Present Times and During Genesis 6

With all the information that is contained in this book, there is far more I didn't put into it. Maybe there we be a 'Missing Knowledge, What if' 2. In any case, let's put it all together with comparing Genesis 6 (Days of Noah) to the end-times we are living in today.

Abortion

Present day

Estimations from various sources state there are up to 1.4 million babies are aborted each year using various methods.

Time before the flood

Estimations are unknown. However, it was done.
Enoch 69:12; The fifth is named Kasadya; it is he who revealed to the children of the people the various flagellations of all evil - the flagellation of the souls and the demons, the smashing of the embryo in the womb so that it may be crushed, the flagellation of the soul, snake bites, sunstrokes, the son of the serpent, whose name is Taba'ta.

Birth Control

Present

There are so many of them in our society, they usually break them down into three to five different categories.

Time before the flood

Book of Jasher 2:19-22.
19 For in those days the sons of men began to trespass against God, and to transgress the commandments which he had commanded to Adam, to be fruitful and multiply in the earth.

20 And some of the sons of men caused their wives to drink a draught that would render them barren, in order that they might retain their figures and whereby their beautiful appearance might not fade.
21 And when the sons of men caused some of their wives to drink, Zillah drank with them.
22 And the child-bearing women appeared abominable in the sight of their husbands as widows, whilst their husbands lived, for to the barren ones only they were attached.

Genetically Engineered/Altered People and Animals

Present

Remains have been found of a being with the body of an alligator and the head of a man. The website below also includes dogs that glows red, modified pigs, fish, and mice. There is far, far more evidence in other websites as well.
(Source; http://www.smashinglists.com/10-mutant-and-genetically-modified-organisms/2/)

Ligers are a cross between a male lion and a female tigress. (Source: http://en.wikipedia.org/wiki/Lion) I think it is interesting that the Sphinx is a body of a lion and the head of a man. Why would anybody want to do such a thing? See the connection yet?

Time before (and after) the flood

Satyrs in ancient myth were half man / half horse. People tend to write off this as untrue. I believe there will be the revelation of genetically altering of humans coming up either right before or at the start of the Tribulation Period.

1 Chronicles 11:22: *Benaiah the son of Jehoiada, the son of a valiant man of Kabzeel, who had done many acts; he slew two lionlike men of Moab: also he went down and slew a lion in a pit in a snowy day.* (King James Bible, Cambridge Edition)

Book of Jasher, 4:18; And their judges and rulers went to the daughters of men and took their wives by force from their husbands according to their choice, and the sons of men in those days took from the cattle of the earth, the beasts of the field and the fowls of the air, and taught the mixture of animals of one species with the other, in order therewith to provoke the LORD; and God saw the whole earth and it was corrupt, for all flesh had corrupted its ways upon earth, all men and all animals.

Genetically Engineered/Altered Food

Present

Today, with the presence of GM (genetically modified) & GMO (genetically modified organism) in our food today, I really don't need to include it here. And we wonder why we are sick, lethargic, have brain fog, you name it. The list can go on and on.

Time after the flood

The Israelite spies cut a single cluster of grapes. It was so large, it took two men to carry it back on a pole.

Number 13:23; *When they came to the valley of Eshcol, they cut down a branch with a single cluster of grapes so large that it took two of them to carry it on a pole between them! They also brought back samples of the pomegranates and figs.* (New Living Translation)

At the time of this writing, I have not found a type of grape that was as large as what they brought back to the Israelite camp. Image genetically altering grapes so they could become that huge. If they could combine the species to make a totally different group of animals, why not do the same thing to the food? These giants had to have their stomachs filled up when they became hungry. Remember, bigger being, bigger stomach.

Lawlessness

Present

Matthew 24:12; *And because lawlessness will be increased, the love of many will grow cold.* (English Standard Version)

With Christians allowing our country's government to take God out of the schools, government and add to that watering down God's Word in churches and not teaching ALL of God's

Word (ALL OF WHAT'S IN THE BIBLE and not PICKING OUT what you understand or are not sure what to think `concerning some principle or the other), it's no wonder why violence, crime, hatred, and un-forgiveness are increasing in our society. If we ignore the laws God has given us, then people think they can do what they want. It's survival of the fittest. They are not concerned about being right or wrong. Their truth becomes foggy. It changes on a whim. Everyone does that which is right in their own eyes. When men are deceived into thinking and believing they know what is right, they think up or manufacture some thoughts that they ultimately believe is best for them, then you get all of the above mentioned in this paragraph and so much more. Remember what Pilot said when Jesus was brought to him?

John 18:37-38;
37 "You are a king, then!" said Pilate. Jesus answered, "You say that I am a king. In fact, the reason I was born and came into the world is to testify to the truth. Everyone on the side of truth listens to me."
38 "What is truth?" retorted Pilate. With this he went out again to the Jews gathered there and said, "I find no basis for a charge against him. (New International Version)

Look what Jesus said in the verse below. He said the following to get them to wake up to what they believed.

John 8:43; *Why can't you understand what I am saying? It's because you can't even hear me! For you are the children of your father the devil, and you love to do the evil things he does. He was a murderer from the beginning. He has always hated the truth, because there is no truth in him. When he lies, it is consistent with his character; for he is a liar and the father of lies.* (New Living Translation)

2 Timothy 3:1-7;
1 But mark this: There will be terrible times in the last days.
2 People will be lovers of themselves, lovers of money, boastful, proud, abusive, disobedient to their parents, ungrateful, unholy,

3 without love, unforgiving, slanderous, without self-control, brutal, not lovers of the good,
4 treacherous, rash, conceited, lovers of pleasure rather than lovers of God—
5 having a form of godliness but denying its power. Have nothing to do with such people.
6 They are the kind who worm their way into homes and gain control over gullible women, who are loaded down with sins and are swayed by all kinds of evil desires,
7 always learning but never able to come to a knowledge of the truth. (New International Version)

Time before the flood

Genesis 6:5; *The LORD saw how great the wickedness of the human race had become on the earth, and that every inclination of the thoughts of the human heart was only evil all the time. The LORD regretted that he had made human beings on the earth, and his heart was deeply troubled.* (New International Version)

This next passage of text was about the time period after Noah was born.

Jasher 4:16; And all the sons of men departed from the ways of the Lord in those days as they multiplied upon the face of the earth with sons and daughters, and they taught one another their evil practices and they continued sinning against the Lord. And every man made unto himself a god, and they robbed and plundered every man his neighbor as well as his relative, and they corrupted the earth, and the earth was filled with violence.

Book of Jubilees 5:1-3;
1 And it came to pass when the children of men began to multiply on the face of the earth and daughters were born unto them, that the angels of God saw them on a certain year of this jubilee, that they were beautiful to look upon; and they took themselves wives of all whom they
2 chose, and they bare unto them sons and they were giants. And lawlessness increased on the earth and all flesh corrupted its way, alike men and cattle and beasts and birds and everything

that walks on the earth –all of them corrupted their ways and their orders, and they began to devour each other, and lawlessness increased on the earth and every imagination of the thoughts of all men
3 (was) thus evil continually. And God looked upon the earth, and behold it was corrupt, and all flesh had corrupted its orders, and all that were upon the earth had wrought all manner of evil.

Cannibalism

Present

There are more and more of this happening in the world today. It's increasing in number. With the advent of Zombies appearing in movies and television shows; it just fuels it even more.

Time before the flood

Enoch 7:3-5;
3 These giants consumed the produce of all the people until the people detested feeding them.
4 So the giants turned against the people in order to eat them.
5 And they began to sin against birds, wild beasts, reptiles, and fish. And their flesh was devoured the one by the other, and they drank blood.

Because God's people turn away from Him, the unthinkable (evil) act of cannibalism can and did happen.

Leviticus 26:28-29;
28 then in my anger I will be hostile toward you, and I myself will punish you for your sins seven times over.
29 You will eat the flesh of your sons and the flesh of your daughters. (New International Version)

It is believed this happened when Jerusalem was besieged by Nebuchadnezzar's army around October 10, 589 B.C.

Deuteronomy 28:53-55
53 *Because of the suffering your enemy will inflict on you during the siege, you will eat the fruit of the womb, the flesh of the sons and daughters the* LORD *your God has given you.*
54 Even the most gentle and sensitive man among you will have no compassion on his own brother or the wife he loves or his surviving children,
55 and he will not give to one of them any of the flesh of his children that he is eating. It will be all he has left because of the suffering your enemy will inflict on you during the siege of all your cities. (New International Version)

DNA Manipulation

Present

As you have read here, with all the DNA testing which is done all the time today for many reasons, you can begin to see why they are really doing it. They want to ultimately corrupt the seed (DNA) of man so somehow / someway man will turn away from the LORD God and follow those angels and demons into the Lake of Fire that burns with fire and brimstone. There are those that believe there will be some sort of change in man's DNA. What the Bible says is people will not be able to sell or purchase anything without the Mark of the Beast. There are many possibilities as to how this can happen.

1. An injection of some type through medicine from the pharmaceutical companies which is presented as;
    a. A cure for some plagues.
    b. So everyone could live for five hundred years.
    c. A person will not age and will have great health.
2. A chip implant that will monitor and rewrite a person's DNA to conform to an image of the seed of satan.
3. Some type infra-red scanning device that will place a bar-code image on your right hand and forehead.
4. Human / Animal hybrids grown in UK Labs. I hope you are shocked to know that there are at least one hundred and fifty human / animal hybrid embryos in labs.

(Source; http://www.dailymail.co.uk/sciencetech/article-2017818/Embryos-involving-genes-animals-mixed-humans-produced-secretively-past-years.html#axzz2K4ZAdIQK)

Time before the flood

Book of Jasher, 4:17-18;
17 And every man made unto himself a god, and they robbed and plundered every man his neighbor as well as his relative, and they corrupted the earth, and the earth was filled with violence.
18 And their judges and rulers went to the daughters of men and took their wives by force from their husbands according to their choice, and the sons of men in those days took from the cattle of the earth, the beasts of the field and the fowls of the air, and taught the mixture of animals of one species with the other, in order therewith to provoke the LORD; and God saw the whole earth and it was corrupt, for all flesh had corrupted its ways upon earth, all men and all animals.

Gog and MaGog

Before I move on, I found an interesting festival that is held in England called the Lord Mayor Show. In this parade, they display these huge wicker giants that are supposed to be, according to folklore, be guardians of the city of London. What I found interesting is what they named them. They are called Gog and the other MaGog. The Bible states the LORD God is against Gog (which we believe are people) in the land of MaGog (which is the area or region). Now sometimes instead of them being called Gog and MaGog, they are referred to as Gog MaGog and Corineus. Now to make it more interesting, these two mythical characters are linked to the giants after the flood. Now if that isn't wild enough, here are some other items of interest.

1. There is an area called Gog MaGog Downs about three miles south of Cambridge in England.
2. There are supposed to be three hidden chalk carvings which were found in the Gog MaGog Hills. As a result of their 'discovery', Gog and his consort, MaGog is represented by the sun and moon. Sounds like some of their origins are in ancient Greek mythology.

3. It is believed according to ancient Irish mythology and the book "The Book of Invasions", Gog and MaGog ancestry dates back to Japheth, one of Noah's sons.
4. There are two ancient oak trees which are named Gog and MaGog.
5. President George W. Bush apparently had a conversation with the then French President Jacques Chirac. In the conversation, President Bust stated Biblical prophecies are being fulfilled in the Middle East. Gog and MaGog are modern-day Iraq. It is important that we stop them.
(Sources; http://www.lordmayorsshow.org/history/gog-and-magog.html, http://en.wikipedia.org/wiki/Gog_and_Magog,) (Source; http://www.cleveland.com/opinion/index.ssf/2009/08/agog_over_bushs_comments_on_go.html)

What to Look for and Observe

There are many things that have been discussed here in these pages. There are far more things that are happening which simply could not be written about because there is so much of it. With that said, let's look at what to watch for so we will be prepared.

By being prepared, we will not be deceived.

Matthew 24:3-5;
3 As Jesus was sitting on the Mount of Olives, the disciples came to him privately. "Tell us," they said, "when will this happen, and what will be the sign of your coming and of the end of the age?"
4 Jesus answered: "Watch out that no one deceives you.
5 For many will come in my name, claiming, 'I am the Messiah,' and will deceive many. (New Living Translation)

Matthew 24:24-25;
24 For false messiahs and false prophets will appear and perform great signs and wonders to deceive, if possible, even the elect.
25 See, I have told you ahead of time. (New Living Translation)

1 Timothy 4:1; *The Spirit says clearly that in later times some believers will desert the Christian faith. They will follow spirits* *that deceive, and they will believe the teachings of demons.* (GOD'S WORD® Translation)

Galatians 1:8; *But even if we or an angel from heaven should preach a gospel other than the one we preached to you, let them be under God's curse!* (New International Version)

2 Corinthians 11:13-15;
13 For such people are false apostles, deceitful workers, masquerading as apostles of Christ.
14 And no wonder, for Satan himself masquerades as an angel of light.
15 It is not surprising, then, if his servants also masquerade as servants of righteousness. Their end will be what their actions deserve. (English Standard Version)

The coming great deception will be so powerful, and it will fool many people. If you do not know what to look for and be on watch for these things, you to can be deceived.

2 Corinthians 11:3-4;
3 However, I'm afraid that as the snake deceived Eve by its tricks, so your minds may somehow be lured away from your sincere and pure devotion to Christ.
4 When someone comes to you telling about another Jesus whom we didn't tell you about, you're willing to put up with it. When you receive a spirit that is different from the Spirit you received earlier, you're also willing to put up with that. When someone tells you good news that is different from the Good News you already accepted, you're willing to put up with that too. (GOD'S WORD® Translation)

Could it be these shape-shifting demonic angels will appear in the sky masquerading as some alien life form? What is coming will be like nothing we have ever seen before. Be aware of what will be happening, it will seem real enough that Christians will be fooled into believing the lie.

Here is one possible scenario.

A space ship appears in the sky. They announce to all they come in peace.

"Thousands of years ago, we were the ones that made Adam and placed him in what you call 'The garden of Eden'. Yes, there was a place like that many years ago. We made Eve also. We helped you in your development as a race. Then some other beings appeared on your planet and corrupted all life. We were forced to destroy what these other beings had done to your world. We worked to save your race so you can start over again without interference from other life forms outside of your planet."

"Many have come and stated they are the messiah, but they were not. We kept close watch on the activity on your earth and determined it is finally time for us to reveal ourselves to you."

"We come in peace and wish to assist you before those other beings come and try to destroy you again. We will partner with you and your leaders. We want to restore peace on your planet. Let us help you to pick a few global leaders of your own kind who have the vision and leadership skills to bring you to your next state of existence. We can help you produce a greater presence, a much higher calling so you can fulfill your life for all those you love."

"We have seen this before. We have helped other people and their civilizations on other planets. We seeded them also. Our people can teach you what to look for and how to handle those who are overly religious zealots that sow discord and havoc among you."

"There are those who state someone or something came and died for you. Use your common sense. How can someone else die for another person? They say they are the true and living god. These gods bring down upon earth all types of diseases, plagues, earthquakes, floods, fires, and all other types of judgments. Death and destruction lurk everywhere."

"Sometimes they appear from the heavens just as we have come from the heavens. We believe that in the near future, there will be another attack that will be launched upon the earth that will attack you and your civilization. This god will want to sit on the throne of the world, rule and reign over you and your land. This god will come in great force. But we believe this god will be defeated if we work together. But we must in one accord. If we can do this, we can gather all of the world's military might into one location to combat and defeat this enemy who wants to rule over you and change your way of life."

"We have a system that works. We can help you with setting it up. If you wish for us to assist you, then we will provide support upon your invitation. We will join your civilization."

This could happen or something similar to it. Who knows but the LORD God. You need to be aware of what could possibly take place right before your very eyes.

Keep in mind, whatever you see, whatever seems real, whatever appears to solve a problem, check it against what the Word of God says. The Bible tells us the following;

Revelation 17:17; *God has made them do what he wants them to do. So they will give their kingdom to the beast until God's words are carried out.* (GOD'S WORD® Translation)

2 Thessalonians 2:7-12;
7 For the secret power of lawlessness is already at work; but the one who now holds it back will continue to do so till he is taken out of the way.
8 And then the lawless one will be revealed, whom the Lord Jesus will overthrow with the breath of his mouth and destroy by the splendor of his coming.
9 The coming of the lawless one will be in accordance with how Satan works. He will use all sorts of displays of power through signs and wonders that serve the lie,
10 and all the ways that wickedness deceives those who are perishing. They perish because they refused to love the truth and so be saved.
11 For this reason God sends them a powerful delusion so that they will believe the lie
12 and so that all will be condemned who have not believed the truth but have delighted in wickedness. (New International Version)

The coming events will be a delusion and will be extremely powerful. According to the Bible, here is a possible sequence of what will happen as best as I can understand it from the Word of God.

1. Peace will disappear from the earth and people will start to slaughter each other.
2. There could be a man-made famine.
3. Prices will go sky high. Many goods we need could become scarce and in short supply.
4. Wild animals that never bothered man will turn and attack humanity.
5. Then twenty five percent of the population of the earth will either be killed in wars or die because of famines and plagues.
6. At the time of this writing, there are about seven billion people on the planet. That means about 1.75 billion people will die leaving 5.25 billion people left.
7. There will be huge earthquakes.
8. The sun will turn black, and the full moon will turn to red as the color of blood. Part of this might be caused by the result of thermonuclear war. Debris will rise and darken the sky.
9. The stars will fall from the sky. Then the sky will vanish like a shade that is rolled up.
10. The mountains could be leveled. Islands will be moved.
11. The leaders of the earth like presidents, kings, generals, the rich, the powerful and others will hide themselves in caves and rocks in the mountains. They will cry out and attempt to hide from the LORD because the frightening day of His wrath has arrived.
12. Then there will be silence in heaven for about a half hour.
13. An angel will throw an incense burner that was just used to offer incense on the gold altar in front of the throne. When that angel throws it to the earth, thunder, noise, lightning, and an earthquake will take place upon this planet.
14. First trumpet. Hail and fire mixed with blood will be thrown upon the earth. One third of the earth burned up along with one third of the trees, and all the green grass will be burned up.
15. Second trumpet. A huge mountain will be thrown into the sea. One third of the sea turned to blood, one third

of the creatures in the sea will die, and one third of the ships will be destroyed.

16. Third trumpet. A huge flaming star will fall from the sky, turning one third of the rivers and springs into wormwood. Many will die because of it. These are wild and terrifying events that will take place. The thing is, the judgments will continue.
17. Forth trumpet. A third part of the sun, the moon, and the stars will be struck that will cause them to turn black and not give off any light during the day or at night.
18. Fifth trumpet. The bottomless pit will be opened up, and smoke will come out like smoke from a large furnace. It will darken the sun and the air. It will be difficult to see and breathe. Locusts will come out and will sting the people like scorpions, the people who do not have the Seal of God on their foreheads. They look like horses prepared for battle. People will not die from the stings, though they will seek it intently. These locusts will torture them for five months. Apollyon (satan) will rule them.
19. Sixth trumpet. The four captive angels held under the Euphrates river will be released along with two hundred million (200,000,000) soldiers. Their horses will have heads like lions and tails like snakes that will hurt people. They will kill one third of the people of the earth by fire, smoke, and sulfur. From the above total, another 1.75 billion people will die. That is a lot of coffins. Yet, you would think after all that has happened so far, people would realize that God is judging the people on this planet. Again, they did not repent and turn away from their sin. They continued their wicked lifestyle.
20. The two witnesses will remain for 1,260 days. When they actually appear, is unknown at this time. I believe these are both Enoch and Elijah. Why? Because they never died. The Bible says it's appointed unto men once to die, then after this the judgment.

    If anyone tries to hurt them, fire will come out of their mouths and burn them up. They have the authority to keep it from raining during this time they are speaking what God has revealed to them. They can turn water into blood, create any plague they wish; as often as they wish. As a result, they will be hated.

21. The beast will conquer and kill them. They will lie in the streets for three and a half days. They will not bury them, and the people of the world will gloat over their deaths. They will actually celebrate their deaths because the witnesses tormented them. At the end of the three and a half days, God raises them up, and a voice came down from heaven saying; "Come up here". Then they left in a cloud.
22. A woman appears. She is clothed with the sun and has the moon under her feet. She has a crown of twelve stars on her head and will give birth to a son. Next, a fiery red serpent (dragon) with seven heads, ten horns and seven crowns on its head appears. It will sweep away one third of the stars and throw them at the earth.
23. Michael and his heavenly angels throw out satan and his follower angels out of heaven permanently. Now the devil's fierce anger will be released upon the earth.
24. The devil goes after the woman who gave birth to the son. But she escapes to her hiding place. The devil pours out a river of water trying to flush her away from her hiding place. But the earth opens up and swallows the water. The devil leaves and starts the attack on God's people who follow God's commands.

I will stop here. Some of the events I wrote about can be unclear. It would take another book to explain all these events.

One Person Can Make a Difference

Keep in mind, one person can make a difference in the case are overwhelming odds that were against them. The Bible talks about these types of situations many times. When there are overwhelming odds against someone or the nation of Israel, that's when the LORD God shines the most because He can demonstrate His awesome power and might. Then the love He has for us shines through, for the whole world to see, because He is glorified. He is our Deliverer!

The reason why I've supplied you with this much information is so you can survive what is coming up and that you are not deceived. It is not about just surviving, it's about serving others because we will be needed during these times. With that said, I want to explain to you the differences between what I call the hierarchy of the religious leaders within Israel back some two thousand years ago.

There are basically four different groups that I'm going to focus on. You have the Scribe, Pharisees, Sadducees, and the Sanhedrin. So let's quickly look at each one and understand what their primary purpose was during the time Jesus walked on the earth and afterwards. Keep in mind this is a quick overview of them. However, just like any job, their roles changed and expanded as time went on.

1. **Scribe**. These were the ones whose main focus was on the details of the law. They studied and knew them. They made copies of the law and different manuscripts too. Some might call them 'Lawyers' so to speak. Yet they taught the law also. Some have described them as government officials or possibly even government bureaucrats. The New Testament in some translations actually used the phrase; "Teachers of the Law".
   Mark 7:1; *The Pharisees and some of the teachers of the law who had come from Jerusalem gathered around Jesus.* (New International Version)
   They were present at the trail of Jesus too.
   Matthew 26:57; *Then those who had seized Jesus led him to Caiaphas the high priest, where the scribes and the elders had gathered.* (English Standard Version)
   Keep in mind Ezra, who was a very powerful religious leader in the Old Testament, was a priest and a scribe too.
   Ezra 7:6; *this Ezra came up from Babylon. He was a teacher well versed in the Law of Moses, which the LORD, the God of Israel, had given. The king had*

granted him everything he asked, for the hand oj the LORD his God was on him. (New International Version)

2. **Pharisees**. This group was primarily the ones that believed pretty much almost all of the Old Testament books plus a few other ones. They were somewhat rigid. They were from the working class. Not from the elitist or ruling class. They believed in a general resurrection. Paul the Apostle was a Pharisee.
   Philippians 3:5; *circumcised on the eighth day, oj the people oj Israel, oj the tribe oj Benjamin, a Hebrew of Hebrews; in regard to the law, a Pharisee;* (New International Version)
   The seven 'woes' in Matthew chapter 23 were primarily pointed to the Pharisees. Yet it appears they tried to warn Jesus about those who were trying to kill Him.
   Luke 13:31; *At that time some Pharisees came to Jesus and said to him, "Leave this place and go somewhere else. Herod wants to kill you."* (New International Version)
3. **Sadducees**. They were similar to the Pharisees in a few ways. However, they basically only believed in the first five books of the Bible. They also believed there was no general resurrection of the body. They were mostly from the elitist or ruling class. The Pharisees and the Sadducees did not get along either.
4. **Sanhedrin**. These were basically the judges, the law of the land. They might be like the Supreme Court in the United States. This group was the ones that held the trail, if you would call it a trial, and condemned Jesus to death.
   Matthew 26:57-64;
   57 Those who had arrested Jesus took him to Caiaphas the high priest, where the teachers of the law and the elders had assembled.
   58 But Peter followed him at a distance, right up to the courtyard of the high priest. He entered and sat down with the guards to see the outcome.
   59 The chief priests and the whole Sanhedrin were looking for false evidence against Jesus so that they could put him to death.

60 But they did not find any, though many false witnesses came forward. Finally two came forward
61 and declared, "This fellow said, 'I am able to destroy the temple of God and rebuild it in three days.'"
62 Then the high priest stood up and said to Jesus, "Are you not going to answer? What is this testimony that these men are bringing against you?"
63 But Jesus remained silent. The high priest said to him, "I charge you under oath by the living God: Tell us if you are the Messiah, the Son of God."
64 "You have said so," Jesus replied. "But I say to all of you: From now on you will see the Son of Man sitting at the right hand of the Mighty One and coming on the clouds of heaven." (New International Version)

I mention these groups so when you read or hear about them in the Bible, you will see how the Lord Jesus Christ spoke to each group a little bit differently. It was subtle when He did it, but nevertheless, it's there. That's why sometimes when Jesus would instruct us as to what to do and what not to do, he would use either the Sadducees or the Pharisee as examples of what NOT to do.

Let's look at some of those leaders who made a difference in the Bible.

1. **Moses.** Here is one man God had called out in a unique way to lead the Israelites, who were in severe bondage, out of Egypt to freedom. He would lead them out of that country with all the spoils they could bring with them. With the LORD God leading the way, he would lead them through the Red Sea on dry ground, and the Egyptian army would drown because they came after His people. He would lead them through the desert for forty years because they would not conquer the Promised Land the LORD God said was theirs to take. He would hear their grievances and settle matters for them. He would lead them up to the river Jordan so they can go in and possess the land flowing with milk and honey. There were times when he stood in the gap and

asked the LORD God to not destroy Israel because they were a rebellious and stiffed-necked people.

2. **Elijah.** Here is a prophet who told Ahad, in 1st Kings Chapter 18, to gather all the children of Israel to meet him on Mount Carmel to offer sacrifices. In a duel between the false prophets of Baal against the true and Living LORD God of Israel. When the false prophets of Baal made a fool of themselves, Elijah rained down fire from heaven to consume the sacrifice Elijah offered to Him.
3. **Gideon.** He was a man who really didn't think too highly of himself. But the LORD God called him into service to defeat Midianites who were oppressing the nation of Israel. Hence why he put out the fleece of wool on the floor and asked that it should be wet with dew and nothing around it would be wet in the morning. Then asked for the exact opposite the next morning. When that happened, he realized the LORD God was with him. He and only three hundred men went and defeated the Midianites. What is so unique about the Midianites? They were descendants of the Nephilim. They were giants.

   What is also interesting is some of the leaders of the oppressors, the Midianites were King Zebah and King Zalmunna, of Midian. They were Islamic. Look at the verse below.

   Judges 8:21; *Zebah and Zalmunna said, "Get up and do it yourself! It's a man's job!" So Gideon got up and killed them. Then he took the half-moon ornaments that were on their camels' necks.* (GOD'S WORD ® Translation)

   The half-moon ornaments Gideon took off the camels' neck is the symbol of Islam. This took place right around 1194 B.C. This goes to show you how long Islam has been around… for thousands of years.

   Around ninety-two years later, Samson will reign as a judge in Israel. Keep in mind Saul was born during Samson's reign. (Source; Reese Chronological Bible)
4. **David.** God called him to be the next King of Israel. This happened while he was tending his father's sheep in

the field. A man after God's own heart. He was probably a teenager during that time. Can you image being told by the Prophet Samuel that you are to be the next King of Israel? He was one of the few righteous rulers. Most of Israel's kings were involved in pagan sun god worship. King David suggests in 1 Chronicles Chapter 17 he wants to build a temple for the LORD to dwell in. But the LORD will tell him that his son, Solomon will build it. When the armies of Israel would not come against Goliath (a Nephilim descendent), he defeated the uncircumcised Philistine.

5. **Solomon.** He became known as the greatest King of the world until the Lord Jesus Christ graced us with His presence. He was given that right after he had made a thousand burnt offerings to the LORD.

   2 Chronicles 1:6; *There in front of the Tabernacle, Solomon went up to the bronze altar in the LORD's presence and sacrificed 1,000 burnt offerings on it.* (New Living Translation)

   He settled a dispute between two mothers who both claimed the same baby was theirs by offering to cut it in half. There were many of these wise rulings. However, those who were closest to him, including his half brother, plotted to gain Solomon's throne because they determined he might be too weak to lead Israel.

   One of the few verses of the LORD mentioning He loved someone was when He said he loved Solomon right at the beginning of his life.

   2 Samuel 12:24-25;

   24 Then David comforted Bathsheba, his wife, and slept with her. She became pregnant and gave birth to a son, and David named him Solomon. The LORD loved the child

   25 and sent word through Nathan the prophet that they should name him Jedidiah (which means "beloved of the LORD"), as the LORD had commanded. (New Living Translation)

   Yet, with all the wisdom and knowledge he received from the LORD, he reintroduced pagan sun god worship back into Israel. Actually, he provided altars to other

> gods to be established throughout the land too. Israel would never totally get rid of this paganism and sun god worship until they were carried away to Babylon.

We as human beings live in our own little world. Oh yes. We are not alone in the environment outside of us, which we share with other people. But really, when you think about it, we create our own little world. We have our likes and dislikes. We have the things we do and don't do. We have our own thinking processes. We want to build and maintain our own little life within us… our own Utopia if I may. We welcome everything that enhances that and makes us feel good. We tend to push away from or resist anything that can change that, even if it for our good in the long run. Sometimes we need to change our paradigm.

I remember years ago, some of my mentors gave me some valuable advice that I use to this very day. I am getting better at following it one hundred percent of the time. I strive to get closer and closer to that goal. And that is to be in a teachable state as much as possible. To listen and consider other people's ideas even if they differ from mine. While I understood what that meant back then, over the years I came to appreciate this Biblical concept more and more.

Some people think they are teachable and want to have, be, and do the best they can in life. However, in order to accomplish this, we need to have a particular mindset. After all, we don't know what we don't know. The actual test of learning is to be better than we were yesterday.

How do you respond when someone offers correction to what you say, questions your belief, or says no to you? Do you respond in a positive attitude or do you get upset or maybe even angry? Do you lash out at them with angry words or just harbor that anger in your heart? Be honest with yourself. If you get upset or angry, then that needs to be corrected.

How teachable are you? What does this have to do with this book? If you are not teachable, the information, the evidence being presented to you in this book could not be accepted. Here is what the Bible says about teachability.

Proverbs 1:23; *Turn to me when I warn you. I will generously pour out my spirit for you. I will make my words known to you.* (GOD'S WORD® Translation)

Proverbs 9:8; *Do not rebuke a mocker or he will hate you; rebuke a wise man and he will love you.* (New International Version)

Proverbs 13:1; *A wise child accepts a parent's discipline; a mocker refuses to listen to correction.* (New Living Translation)

Proverbs 15:31; *The ear that listens to a life-giving warning will be at home among wise people.* (GOD'S WORD® Translation)

Proverbs 17:10; *A reprimand impresses a person who has understanding more than a hundred lashes impress a fool.* (GOD'S WORD® Translation)

Proverbs 18:13; *Spouting off before listening to the facts is both shameful and foolish.* (New Living Translation)

Proverbs 19:25; *Strike a mocker, and a gullible person may learn a lesson. Warn an understanding person, and he will gain more knowledge.* (GOD'S WORD® Translation)

Proverbs 25:12; *To one who listens, valid criticism is like a gold earring or other gold jewelry.* (New Living Translation)

Proverbs 29:20; *There is more hope for a fool than for someone who speaks without thinking.* (New Living Translation)

Ecclesiastes 7.5; *Better to be criticized by a wise person than to be praised by a fool.* (New Living Translation)

Leviticus 19:17; *Do not nurse hatred in your heart for any of your relatives. Confront people directly so you will not be held guilty for their sin.* (New Living Translation)

The reason why I spent time on this subject is that what you have read and are about to read could very well challenge what you think, what you think you know, and what you think you believe. I've listed all these verses above so you can see and understand how important it is to remain in a teachable state.

Solutions

Congratulations! If you are reading this and understanding what all this could mean, then the following verses apply to you.

Matthew 16:13-17;
13 Now when Jesus came into the district of Caesarea Philippi, he asked his disciples, "Who do people say that the Son of Man is?"
14 And they said, "Some say John the Baptist, others say Elijah, and others Jeremiah or one of the prophets."
15 He said to them, "But who do you say that I am?"
16 Simon Peter replied, "You are the Christ, the Son of the living God."
17 And Jesus answered him, "Blessed are you, Simon Bar-Jonah! For flesh and blood has not revealed this to you, but my Father who is in heaven. (English Standard Version)

1 Corinthians 2:14; *But people who aren't spiritual can't receive these truths from God's Spirit. It all sounds foolish to them and they can't understand it, for only those who are spiritual can understand what the Spirit means.* (New Living Translation)

1 Corinthians 12:1; *Now about spiritual gifts, brothers, I do not want you to be ignorant.* (New International Version)

The LORD our God does not want us to be ignorant. This phrase or something almost exactly like it appears many times in the Bible. Here are some of those verses; 1 Thessalonians 4:13, Romans 1:13, 1 Corinthians 10:1, Romans 11:25, and 2 Corinthians 1:8 for starters. Also remember the following verse.

Isaiah 45:7; *I make light and create darkness. I make blessings and create disasters. I, the LORD, do all these things.* (GOD'S WORD® Translation)

Actually the whole forty-fifth chapter of Isaiah discusses our very life and our creation.

All this seems overwhelming, doesn't it? Do you feel you might not be able to combat this? This situation is bigger than you can possibly even image, let alone have to combat it?

Do we sit around, do nothing and hope for the best? Or are there things for us to start doing now? Here are some thoughts to consider.

1. Turn away from our pagan sun god worship. Stop participating in their festivities and holidays. Obedience is the key to having the LORD God change His mind before passing final judgment on America.
   Isaiah 1:10-20;
   10 Hear the word of the LORD, you rulers of Sodom; listen to the instruction of our God, you people of Gomorrah!
   11 "The multitude of your sacrifices— what are they to me?" says the LORD. "I have more than enough of burnt offerings, of rams and the fat of fattened animals; I have no pleasure in the blood of bulls and lambs and goats.
   12 When you come to appear before me, who has asked this of you, this trampling of my courts?
   13 Stop bringing meaningless offerings! Your incense is detestable to me. New Moons, Sabbaths and convocations— I cannot bear your worthless assemblies.
   14 Your New Moon feasts and your appointed festivals I hate with all my being. They have become a burden to me; I am weary of bearing them.
   15 When you spread out your hands in prayer, I hide my eyes from you; even when you offer many prayers, I am not listening. Your hands are full of blood!
   16 Wash and make yourselves clean. Take your evil deeds out of my sight; stop doing wrong.

17 Learn to do right; seek justice. Defend the oppressed. Take up the cause of the fatherless; plead the case of the widow.
18 "Come now, let us settle the matter," says the LORD. "Though your sins are like scarlet, they shall be as white as snow; though they are red as crimson, they shall be like wool.
19 If you are willing and obedient, you will eat the good things of the land;
20 but if you resist and rebel, you will be devoured by the sword." (New International Version)

2. Cry out to the LORD God.
   Jeremiah 16:10-12 & 17-21;
   10 "When you tell the people all these things, they will ask you, 'Why does the LORD threaten us with all these disasters? What have we done wrong? How have we sinned against the LORD our God?'
   11 Then say to them, 'It's because your ancestors abandoned me, declares the LORD. They followed other gods, served them, worshiped them, and abandoned me. They didn't obey my teachings.
   12 You have done worse than your ancestors. All of you are following your own stubborn, evil ways that keep you from obeying me.
   17 I see everything that they do. They can't hide anything from me. Their wickedness can't be hidden; I can see it.
   18 First, I will have them pay twice as much for their wickedness and their sin, because they have polluted my land. They have filled my property with the lifeless statues of their detestable and disgusting idols."
   19 The LORD is my strength and my fortress, my refuge in times of trouble. Nations come to you from the most distant parts of the world and say, "Our ancestors have inherited lies, worthless and unprofitable gods."
   20 "People can't make gods for themselves. They aren't really gods.
   21 That is what I will teach them. This time I will make my power and my strength known to them. Then they will

know that my name is the LORD." (GOD'S WORD ® Translation)

Zechariah 8:20-23;

20 This is what the LORD of Armies says: People and citizens from many cities are going to come.
21 The citizens of one city will come to another city, saying, "Let's make a habit of going to ask the LORD for a blessing and to seek the LORD of Armies. I'm also going."
22 Many people and powerful nations will come to seek the LORD of Armies in Jerusalem and to ask the LORD for a blessing.
23 This is what the LORD of Armies says: In those days ten people from every language found among the nations will take hold of the clothes of a Jew. They will say, "Let us go with you because we have heard that God is with you." (GOD'S WORD ® Translation)

All the lies we have inherited from our forefathers will be acknowledged. Forsake them and turn back to the LORD.

3. Forsake other god's. If we love the LORD God, we keep His commandments. Avoid mentioning and participating in the pagan holidays. I'm referring to one of them on the 25th day of the 12th month of each year and those take place either in the 3rd or 4th month of each and every year among others.
4. We are to worship the LORD God His way. Not the way we want to worship Him. Don't try and justify it with excuses of traditions from our parents, etc. etc. The LORD wants to be worshipped the way He wants to be worshipped. There are too many deceptions all around us which keeps us from seeing and understanding why His ways are higher than our ways!

   Mark 7:8; *You have let go of the commands of God and are holding on to human traditions."* (New International Version)

   Colossians 2:8; *Don't let anyone capture you with empty philosophies and high-sounding nonsense that come from human thinking and from the spiritual powers of this world, rather than from Christ.* (New Living Translation)

Galations 1:14; *I was advancing in Judaism beyond many of my own age among my people and was extremely zealous for the traditions of my fathers.* (New International Version)

The apostle Paul realized many traditions of being a Pharisee were contrary to the Word of God. As a result, he forsook those traditions.

Love

This is an interesting thought, isn't it? Why this topic? Why is this a solution?

Have you ever wondered why the LORD is so patient, so kind, when you have trusted His Son Jesus as the Lord and Savior of your life?

He is quick to forgive and move forward. Have you wondered why He is this way? Actually, in a sense, it's simple.

The God of the Heavens and the Earth wants a very personal relationship with each and every one of you. That's why He has placed inside of every believer in His Son, Jesus, the precious Holy Spirit. He wants to be so close to you that He places Himself right next to your heart.

Before I get into this topic in depth, I want to share with you something I had never seen before in my entire life until recently.

There is this lady I know who is an absolute saint of the LORD our God. She loves Him with all her precious heart, soul, and her strength.

She sings praises to Him throughout the day. Almost every time when I saw her, she would literally glow the love of Jesus. She radiates this beautiful encompassing light, a presence, an essence that I've never seen before. That radiance is so powerful that it reminds me of a huge spotlight that can be seen for miles away. When she would walk into a room, people would sense the love flowing out of her and would be drawn to her. And most of the time, they had no idea why. When she would speak, people would listen intently. When she would really turn on the loving part of her being, it would literally be a wonderful sight to behold. It was as if a touch or a beautiful and wonderful taste of heaven would come down and engulf the people's who were near. My guess is that is probably how Jesus was when He was on earth.

The verses below are what are sometimes called "The Love Chapter". We as Christians know of it. We have read it. We have heard it taught or preached about in a church service. But do we really understand its words? Do we believe it enough to put it into practice? We desire to be more like Jesus in all things. We sing about it, we talk about it, we wish it in our hearts at times. So the question is what are you willing to do? Are you willing to change what you are doing to put into practice the concepts here? To be more like Him who was hanged on a tree (the cross) in a public display of shame for our sins? Let's look at these verses. Then you will see why following the teachings of this precious chapter will change your life and the lives of all those around you and the ones you will come in contact with in the future.

1 Corinthians 13:1-13;

1 1 may speak in the languages oj humans and oj angels. But ij I don't have love, 1 am a loud gong or a clashing cymbal.

2 1 may have the gift to speak what God has revealed, and 1 may understand all mysteries and have all knowledge. 1 may even have enough faith to move mountains. But ij 1 don't have love, I am nothing.

3 1 may even give away all that 1 have and give up my body to be burned. But ij 1 don't have love, none oj these things will help me.

4 Love is patient. Love is kind. Love isn't jealous. It doesn't sing its own praises. It isn't arrogant.

5 It isn't rude. It doesn't think about itself. It isn't irritable. It doesn't keep track of wrongs.

6 It isn't happy when injustice is done, but it is happy with the truth.

7 Love never stops being patient, never stops believing, never stops hoping, never gives up.

8 Love never comes to an end. There is the gift of speaking what God has revealed, but it will no longer be used. There is the gift of speaking in other languages, but it will stop by itself. There is the gift of knowledge, but it will no longer be used.

9 Our knowledge is incomplete and our ability to speak what God has revealed is incomplete.
10 But when what is complete comes, then what is incomplete will no longer be used.
11 When I was a child, I spoke like a child, thought like a child, and reasoned like a child. When I became an adult, I no longer used childish ways.
12 Now we see a blurred image in a mirror. Then we will see very clearly. Now my knowledge is incomplete. Then I will have complete knowledge as God has complete knowledge of me.
13 So these three things remain: faith, hope, and love. But the best one of these is love. (GOD'S WORD® Translation)

I honestly challenge you to read the Bible's 'Love' chapter every day for a month. Really, I honestly challenge you to read it that many times. Why? Because if you do, you will see things so much differently than what you have seen before.

Before we start that discussion, let's see some of the last commandments Jesus gave to us. Actually, He gave us a new one.

John 13:34-35;
34 "A new command I give you: Love one another. As I have loved you, so you must love one another.
35 By this all men will know that you are my disciples, if you love one another." (New International Version)

John 15:12; *My command is this: Love each other as I have loved you.* (New International Version)

John 15:17; *This is my command: Love each other.* (New International Version)

These passages appear to be pretty clear to me. These next verses seem to hone in or clarify what we specifically need to do.

Ephesians 4:31-32;
31 Get rid of your bitterness, hot tempers, anger, loud quarreling, cursing, and hatred.
32 Be kind to each other, sympathetic, forgiving each other as God has forgiven you through Christ. (GOD'S WORD® Translation)

Mark 11:25; *But when you are praying, first forgive anyone you are holding a grudge against, so that your Father in heaven will forgive your sins, too."* (New Living Translation)

Galatians 6:7; *Don't be misled--you cannot mock the justice of God. You will always harvest what you plant.* (New Living Translation)

If you sow love, what will you get in return? Love. If you sow patience, then you will receive patience.

If you truly want to be loved, then learn God's love chapter and understand that it isn't about what you are receiving; it's purely what you are giving. That's what love does each and every day.

Some people might say; "I did that for a while. I gave myself to my spouse. Yet he/she seemingly didn't appreciate it. After a while, I felt empty on the inside. So I stopped doing it."

That is usually the classic response. I'm sorry that you were not loved during that time. Believe it or not, sometimes that's how the LORD our God feels. Dwell on that thought for a while. He gives to us and gives, and gives, then gives so much more. And do you think the people of His creation would say, "Thank You" and "I love you" every once in a while? Most people do not. There are some who love Him, praise, and thank Him for all that He does for them and others too. Try to see that it's not what you are getting back that is the reward. Hopefully you will see more clearly what this means when you are done reading this.

It's the giving of your love, of your kindness, of your forgiveness, of your understanding, of your beautiful self, of all your work, of all your prayers, of all your support that is the reward. Maybe you are shaking your head and wondering what the author is talking about?

Let's get into the verses in 1st Corinthians chapter 13. Each number below represents the verse.

1. *I may speak in the languages of humans and of angels. But if I don't have love, I am a loud gong or a clashing cymbal.*
   Let's say you give such eloquent speeches and communicate so well that other people hang on your

every word or you move them to sit back and relax four or five minutes later. You move them to tears with a story and a few minutes later you get them laughing and having a good time. If you can do all that, but if you don't love the people you are talking with, it's like them hearing the words, but it doesn't reach into their heart… just like a gong or a clashing cymbal.

2. *I may have the gift to speak what God has revealed, and I may understand all mysteries and have all knowledge. I may even have enough faith to move mountains. But if I don't have love, I am nothing.*
   Let's say you can accurately tell someone (prophesy) what's going to happen in their life next week, next month, or next year. You can answer any question they put to you, and explain it so they can understand it. If you have the faith, you can change a group or a nation for Jesus. But if you don't love the people you are helping, it means nothing.
3. *I may even give away all that I have and give up my body to be burned. But if I don't have love, none of these things will help me.*
   If you were to cash in all your savings that you have, sell your bonds, liquidate your 401K and pension, sell your house and your car, along with everything else and give it to the poor but if you don't love people, it won't help you. If you do not deny your faith, when they come to threaten you with death for what you believe. Even if they hang you or start to burn you alive at the stake. After all of that, if you still don't love people, it's not going to help you.
4. *Love is patient.*
   Being patient is one of the greatest things we can do for others. Sometimes people might try and try and try to do this or that with the greatest meaning and best of intentions because they are trying to do the right thing. And yet they haven't reached it yet. So what are we suppose to do? Get frustrated because someone continues to do the same thing over and over again? Nope. Be patient as our heavenly Father in patient. It's

really amazing how many people openly admit they are not patient people. They don't want to make allowances for people who are not living up to their expectation… as they see it. Yet they fall short of the mark. They might even ask the LORD to be patient with them as they learn to do things better. How about the law of sowing and reaping? Could it be a little Mark 11:25 is needed? If you want to be forgiven, how about forgiving others first? Then your Heavenly Father will forgive you of what you did or are doing wrong!

5. *Love is kind.*

   Kindness is also something you give to others! It can sometimes have the greatest impact when it's done at the right time and with the right tone in our voice.

   Proverbs 15:1; *A gentle answer turns away wrath, but a harsh word stirs up anger.* (New International Version)

   We have gotten so intertwined in texting and emailing each other today. As a result, we are losing the art of communicating face to face. A kind word can help someone through the day. It can lift up another one's day. A gentle word with a smile be the difference between life and death to someone who is very severely depressed, to the point of thinking about committing suicide. When a loved one, a spouse, a child, parent, grandparent, etc. is not doing what you need them to do, what do you do? Do we complain and get upset over it? Or do we offer to help them in a loving manner? How about asking the question; 'How can I help you?' Be compassionate also. As you read your Bible, you will notice that many times the LORD had compassion on people, on the crowds that came to Him.

6. *Love isn't jealous.*

   Jealousy (some versions use the word envy) is something that can be very destructive. It means we want something we don't have or can't have in your life. Notice I said the word 'wants'. Now it's fine to want something, but when it internally drives us to think 'why do they get to have that and not me', then that can be devastating. Gaining things for ones self is fine, but once we get it, most of the time it doesn't have the same value as when we were seeking and wanting it. If we are envious or jealous of people, then we do not love them properly. Loving is giving to others like the LORD gives to us all the time. You want them to have the things they wish along with being the best they possibly can be in their life. So instead of being jealous or envious of others, be happy for them. Be joyous that they were blessed enough to get to have it, even if they don't appear to appreciate what they have in their possession or life.

7. *It doesn't sing its own praises.*
   By not singing your own praises allows you to lift up other people. It's all right to receive the positive comments from other people. But it's more important that people feel appreciated. Sometimes, you might be the only person that can lift them up with kind words. It is so incredible how much of an impact a person can have by being uplifting to others. At the base of that mindset is a servant's heart. In the end, it's not about how good you are, it's about how good you are when you are serving and helping others. Remember, Jesus came down from heaven to serve others.
   Matthew 20:27-28;
   27 and whoever wants to be first must be your slave—
   28 just as the Son of Man did not come to be served, but to serve, and to give his life as a ransom for many." (New International Version)
8. *It isn't arrogant*
   Arrogant is someone who really thinks they are better, more important, and/or superior to most everyone else. They walk differently; talk down to people if they talk to others at all. It's the exact opposite of humility. Everyone is equal at the foot of the cross. Those who are arrogant will sooner or later be brought down.
   Matthew 19:30; *But many who are the greatest now will be least important then, and those who seem least important now will be the greatest then.* (New Living Translation)
   Notice the word "seem"…

9. *It isn't rude.*
   Rude are people who have a mindset that they are superior. They act like they are always right and possibly not apologize for something they said or did to another person when it was incorrect or not the best thing to do. They basically have no boundaries as to what they won't say. In the Greek, the word is "aschémoneó". It means to act improperly, unseemly, behave unbecomingly (or even dishonorably). They, for the most part, don't care if what they say hurts another person. Strangely enough, they usually are the ones who are really hurting deep on the inside. If you can get through all the barriers they put up so they can try to protect themselves from other people hurting them, you will usually find a great person on the inside.
10. *It doesn't think about itself.*
   I hope you are noticing the progression of what love is and is not.
   For those of you who had dated, did you notice how you wanted to do things for them as the relationship grew over time? It's the same thing, if not more so for a spouse. It seems like you couldn't do enough for them at times. You really wanted them to have the very best in their life. And they received it and enjoyed it very much. You enhanced their life. And remember when they returned it to you? Remember that time. You felt you were ready to conqueror the world, together! The very essence of love is not the receiving it, but the giving of it to someone else. We all want to be loved.
   This is the mindset the LORD has towards us all the time. Why? Because He wants us to have the best in our lives. So many married couples in the Bible speak towards this concept. They gave to each other without regarding themselves. You see this concept with Ezekiel and his wife, David and Bathsheba, Jacob and Rachel, in the story of Esther and the King in many aspects.
   When Jacob saw Rachel, it was love at first sight. He knew right away when he cast his eyes on her that he

had to marry her. There was no question about it. The Bible states he REALLY loved her. It was proven because he worked for her dad for seven years in exchange for her hand in marriage. But it seemed like those years were just like days to him. He was tricked though, and had to work another seven years before he could marry her. Ezekiel loved his wife as much as Jacob loved Rachel.

Ezekiel 24:16; *"Son of man, with one blow I'm going to take away from you the person you love the most. But you must not mourn, cry, or let tears run down your face.* (GOD'S WORD® Translation).

What a relationship Ezekiel had with his wife. David and Bathsheba got off to a rocky start. There was an adulterous relationship, cover-up of it, and the murder of Uriah, Bathsheba's husband at that time. But as time went on, I personally believe that David captured Bathsheba's heart, and as a result, she gave herself to him. That doesn't always happen in marriages. You would think that a relationship, which started off like that, would be almost impossible to keep together. But God's grace is always abundant in all levels for us. The bottom line is, God can heal any relationship. And let's remember, Bathsheba is mentioned in the genealogy of Jesus our Messiah! I think David needed Bathsheba in ways that enhanced his life. It made him a better King of Israel. The right woman will do that for a man too.

Then there is that touching moment between Rachel and Jacob.

Genesis 29:10-11;

10 Jacob saw Rachel, daughter of his uncle Laban, with his uncle Laban's sheep. He came forward and rolled the stone off the opening of the well and watered his uncle Laban's sheep.

11 Then Jacob kissed Rachel and sobbed loudly. (GOD'S WORD® Translation)

Genesis 29:17-18;

17 Leah had attractive eyes, but Rachel had a beautiful figure and beautiful features.

18 Jacob loved Rachel. So he offered, "I'll work seven years in return for your younger daughter Rachel." (GOD'S WORD® Translation)

Genesis 29:20; *So Jacob served seven years to get Rachel, but they seemed like only a few days to him because oj his love for her.* (GOD'S WORD® Translation)

Despite Jacob being tricked into marrying Leah, Jacob loved Rachel so much he worked another seven years to get her hand in marriage. I'm sure Jacob would agree that good things come to those who are patient. It's interesting that Jacob did not hide the love he had for Rachel. Eventually, Rachel died giving birth to her second son, Benjamin, with Joseph being the first. Though the Bible doesn't say it, I would imagine Rachel was the person Jacob, now called Israel, loved the most. Yet, it was through Leah that gave birth to most of the sons who would become the twelve tribes of Israel.

The world teaches us it's that relationships are fifty-fifty, sixty-forty, or a twenty five–seventy five percent giving at different times in the marriage. Please tell me where in the Bible God says this is the correct way to have a relationship, with anyone. I don't think it is in it. This is the same worldly trash that comes from the father of ALL lies… satan…

You give to others so they can have the best. If you want to be like Jesus, give your best to others. That's what He did all the time while on this earth. So if you really truly want to be like our Lord Jesus, learn to love people unconditionally all the time, no matter what they say or do to you. There is a certain satisfaction that a person receives when this concept is practiced.

11. *It isn't irritable.*

Irritable is like being annoyed, testy or sensitive to what was said or done to them. We need to drop the expectations of what we think people should be in their lives. When we truly understand their struggles, and their shortcomings, then we choose to support them when they are less than what they should be in their lives.

12. *It doesn't keep track of wrongs.*
    I believe this is one of the biggest ways/proof of loving someone else. When someone doesn't keep track of how many times they were wronged by one person or more for that matter, that could very well mean they are forgiving it, they let it go, and are moving forward with it. They more than likely have thrown it behind their back like God does when He doesn't keep track of all the times we have sinned against Him. How many times should we be forgiving other people?
    Matthew 18:21-22;
    21 Then Peter came to Jesus and asked him, "Lord, how often do I have to forgive a believer who wrongs me? Seven times?"
    22 Jesus answered him, "I tell you, not just seven times, but seventy times seven. (GOD'S WORD® Translation)
    Isaiah 38:17; *Surely it was for my benefit that I suffered such anguish. In your love you kept me from the pit of destruction; you have put all my sins behind your back.* (New International Version)
    Now granted, sometimes the situation needs to be discussed. Not that finger pointing can take place, which puts the other person on the defensive, or to seek revenge, but so both parties (and more if the need arises) can understand what happened so they can minimize or keep it from happening again. It's about restoring the relationship to its former state which both have enjoyed. By not keeping track of what people have wrongly done to us allows the relationship to resume and possibly become stronger. Forgiveness and letting go of past hurts gives new life to everyone involved.
13. *It isn't happy when injustice is done, but it is happy with the truth.*
    This is pretty much self-explanatory.
14. *Love never stops being patient*
    'Never stops being patient' is a fitting end to this part of defining what love is. No matter who says it is hopeless, it can't or won't work, love always seeks out a way so it can happen. That is your ultimate positivity. There is a

way to make it work. Find that way. There really isn't a timetable as to how long it might take to bring it about or make it happen. If we can embrace the concept of patience, and grasp hold of how to use it correctly, it's one of the greatest tools we have to bring into or make happen in our life. Always, always, always remember how much God is patient with you.

Romans 2:4; *Or do you show contempt for the riches of his kindness, forbearance and patience, not realizing that God's kindness is intended to lead you to repentance?* (New International Version)

And then there are these verses;

Colossians 3:12-13;

12 Since God chose you to be the holy people he loves, you must clothe yourselves with tenderhearted mercy, kindness, humility, gentleness, and patience.

13 Make allowance for each other's faults, and forgive anyone who offends you. Remember, the Lord forgave you, so you must forgive others. (New Living Translation)

If we are not patient with other people, how can we support, inspire, and strengthen them? Remember, God first loved us. So we should first love others too!

15. *Never stops believing*

    'Never stops believing' is interesting. Unless you are patient, believing can almost become a struggle. The people with the vision, with the dream they have and want to make manifest in their lives almost always comes down to just believing. Jesus mentioned so many times about our belief system. In my opinion, believing is the realization that it can happen, which is different from faith. Faith knows it will happen. When you believe in someone, you realize they can achieve what they set out to do. Sometimes you know when someone can be bigger and better than they thought is possible. That too is believing. The LORD God believes in us. He knows if we will succeed in our purpose. He made us a particular way to accomplish the mission, the reason why we were created. He holds on to hope that we will turn to Him. Then we can find what we are looking for and in turn fulfill our destiny.

16. *Never stops hoping*
    Never stops hoping is next in line. Again, if we are patient and believe, then the hope can bring manifestation from our Most High God.
17. *Never gives up*
    When it seems like there is no way something can be saved or worked out, you never give up. You cut the word 'quit' out of your dictionary. There is no reason to quit, or to give up. That's when we will hold on to the promises that are ours to have and claim so we will never give up.
18. *Love never comes to an end. There is the gift of speaking what God has revealed, but it will no longer be used. There is the gift oj speaking in other languages, but it will stop by itself. There is the gift of knowledge, but it will no longer be used.*
    There is no reason for love to come to an end. You don't want it to end. If it does stop or come to an end, it's because you made it end. You stopped loving. You love, you give love to others because you want them to have it. Someday, those who love God and accept Jesus Christ as their personal Savior will hear the voice of God clearly. So the gift of speaking what God has said everyone will possess. We will be able to speak other languages, so we don't need someone else acting as an interpreter. Someday when we are in heaven, the gift of knowledge which someone had on earth will no longer be needed.
19. *Our knowledge is incomplete and our ability to speak what God has revealed is incomplete.*
    We don't have complete knowledge right now. That is why we need other Christians. Their gifting and calling in that area will reveal to us the bigger picture. So the question is why didn't God give everyone those gifts? Isn't that a reasonable question to ask? So that we learn to rely on each other. So we learn to work with others for the greater purpose.

20. *But when what is complete comes, then what is incomplete will no longer be used.*
    Once we all have full knowledge, the other gifting some others had will no longer be necessary.
21. *When I was a child, I spoke like a child, thought like a child, and reasoned like a child. When I became an adult, I no longer used childish ways.*
    When we get to heaven, we will be completely mature adults. Yet how many people never get out of the childish stage… so to speak. There are those that want what they want, when they want it, and how they want it. It's always about what they want, and when they don't get it, they get mad, get upset, etc. Then it usually affects others around them. Sometimes they stop talking to them, giving them the silent treatment, so they get their way.
22. *Now we see a blurred image in a mirror. Then we will see very clearly. Now my knowledge is incomplete. Then I will have complete knowledge as God has complete knowledge of me.*
    I was always fascinated with the first part of this verse. It has always stood out to me probably since the first time I read it. While we see through a blurred image now, someday we will see everything clearly. I always compared this blurred image to the soap placed on the inside part of the windows in a business establishment when getting ready to open up. You really can't see clearly what is going on inside the store, but sometimes you see these blurry images as people are working on the inside as furniture or material is brought in for display. One of the wisest things anyone can say is; "I don't know…" A wise person will always know this. But somehow, some way they know what to look for so they can find the answer. Or find the 'what.'
23. *So these three things remain: faith, hope, and love. But the best one of these is love.*
    Strip away all the gifting eloquent speech, the prophetic words from a prophet or a seer, selling all that you have, and becoming a martyr, etc. So what remains? Faith,

> hope, and love. The greatest of these three is love. Love is the reason we do all the right things for ourselves, in servitude to others, and to our most Gracious and Holy God. We are reminded in Hebrews that, without faith, it is impossible to please God. So what is greater than faith? Love.

Love can change someone's heart for the better. Love can make a positive and lasting impact. Love can reach their heart like nothing else can do. The heart will pick it up the sincerity in the voice. What they do with it after those moments is another matter.

If we truly understand what love does when we give it, it changes someone else's life, but it gives them the opportunity to offer that same unique, special, action that it is in and of itself is its own reward.

Every great once in a while, I get to see a couple who truly love each other. They are secure in that love. They can say what they want to the other, and it will be taken with respect and kindness by the other. There is an overall, what seems like a, calmness they have with each other. They know everything about the other and love each other anyway. Sometimes they have words and disagree with the other. Sometimes it gets a bit heated when both get a little intense about what they believe. But those emotions settle down, and they go back to loving each other, or better put, giving of the one to the other. Why? Because that is what they want to do. They love how it feels when there is harmony and don't like the vacuum or distance when the disagreement takes place or when an expectation isn't met.

Jesus loves us. He is the Ultimate Example of how we are supposed to do it! If we fall short, are we going to hide behind excuses as to why we can't love others like He continues to do? If we are not cutting it or doing our best all the time to achieve that accomplishment, then we need to change what we are doing.

Here is the 1st Corinthians 13 love test. Here are a couple of questions for you to answer honestly. Remember if you can't be honest with yourself, how are you going to relate to others?

Luke 6:31; *Do to others as you would have them do to you.* (New International Version)

Matthew 7:12; *"Do to others whatever you would like them to do to you. This is the essence of all that is taught in the law and the prophets.* (New Living Translation)

James 1:26; *If a person thinks that he is religious but can't control his tongue, he is fooling himself. That person's religion is worthless.* (GOD'S WORD® Translation)

Philippians 4:8-9;
8 Finally, brothers and sisters, keep your thoughts on whatever is right or deserves praise: things that are true, honorable, fair, pure, acceptable, or commendable.
9 Practice what you've learned and received from me, what you heard and saw me do. Then the God who gives this peace will be with you. (GOD'S WORD® Translation)

Let's look at the following questions.

The Love Test

1. How do you respond when someone you love does not do what you ask them to do over and over again? Do you get mad, angry, upset, hold in your anger, or get bitter over it on the inside?
   Ephesians 4:31-32;
   31 Get rid oj your bitterness, hot tempers, anger, loud quarreling, cursing, and hatred.
   32 Be kind to each other, sympathetic, forgiving each other as God has forgiven you through Christ. (GOD'S WORD® Translation)
2. When someone, for whatever reason, says something that really hurts you, how do you react? Do you instantly lash back at them? Do you wait for the opportunity to get back at them?
   Colossians 3:13; *Put up with each other, and forgive each other ij anyone has a complaint. Forgive as the Lord forgave you.* (GOD'S WORD® Translation)
3. How long do you stay angry when someone hurts you? Minutes, hours, days, weeks, etc? If you don't forgive

them almost instantly, how can you ask our Father in heaven to forgive you when you sin against Him?
Ephesians 4:26; *Be angry without sinning. Don't go to bed angry.* (GOD'S WORD® Translation)
Mark 11:25; *Whenever you pray, forgive anything you have against anyone. Then your Father in heaven will forgive your failures."* (GOD'S WORD® Translation)

4. When a rift or a split happens, what do you do on your part? Do you wait for them to come to you to apologize?
   Matthew 5:23-24;
   23 *"So if you are offering your gift at the altar and remember there that another believer has something against you,*
   24 *leave your gift at the altar. First go away and make peace with that person. Then come back and offer your gift.* (GOD'S WORD® Translation)
5. When you get angry or upset at someone for whatever reason, do you blame them for the most part?
   James 1:19-20;
   19 *Remember this, my dear brothers and sisters: Everyone should be quick to listen, slow to speak, and should not get angry easily.*
   20 *An angry person doesn't do what God approves of.* (GOD'S WORD® Translation)
6. How about when someone doesn't meet your expectations?
   Romans 3:23-24;
   23 *for all have sinned and fall short of the glory of God,*
   24 *and all are justified freely by his grace through the redemption that came by Christ Jesus.* (New International Version)
7. When there is a division between you and someone else, do you take the time to communicate with them so you can reconcile the differences so the relationship can be restored? So you both can go back to the way it was before it happened?
   Acts 7:26; *The next day Moses came upon two Israelites who were fighting. He tried to reconcile them*

by saying, 'Men, you are brothers; why do you want to hurt each other?' (New International Version)

Isaiah 1:18; *"Come now, let's settle this," says the LORD. "Though your sins are like scarlet, I will make them as white as snow. Though they are red like crimson, I will make them as white as wool.* (New Living Translation)

8. When you distance yourself from another believer, did you consider whether you think you were right or not? Have you considered the possibility you did not look at the situation correctly?

   Matthew 7:4-5;

   4 *How can you say to another believer, 'Let me take the piece of sawdust out of your eye,' when you have a beam in your own eye?*

   5 *You hypocrite! First remove the beam from your own eye. Then you will see clearly to remove the piece of sawdust from another believer's eye.* (GOD'S WORD® Translation)

We can be so quick to judge someone, yet not see what we are dealing with in our own lives.

What is the greatest commandment? Hopefully when you are done reading this part of the book, you will see your life differently and help others in ways that will have a great impact on them along with yourself.

Matthew 22:36-40;

36 "Teacher, which commandment is the greatest in Moses' Teachings?"

37 Jesus answered him, "'Love the Lord your God with all your heart, with all your soul, and with all your mind.'

38 This is the greatest and most important commandment.

39 The second is like it: 'Love your neighbor as you love yourself.'

40 All of Moses' Teachings and the Prophets depend on these two commandments." (GOD'S WORD ® Translation)

If we really ponder the passage above, it appears to be one of the most important ones in the whole Bible.

Hate or Prejudice

There are very good reasons why we are to let go of anger and negative emotions as quickly as possible. Positive or negative emotions you hold on to on the inside of your being have an impact on your health.

Proverbs 17:22; *A cheerful heart is good medicine, but a crushed spirit dries up the bones.* (New International Version)

Proverbs 17:22; *A joyful heart is good medicine, but depression drains one's strength.* (GOD'S WORD® Translation)

I gave two different versions of the same text because I thought they both give an explanation of how our emotions affect our body, our organs, and our health. Here is some information that tells us the effect emotions have on the various organs in the body. This information has been around for many hundreds, if not thousands of years. But first, here is the legal stuff in the next paragraph.

The information in this book is for educational purposes only and is in no way to be taken to be or substituted for the provision or practice of medical, nursing or professional healthcare advice, help, diagnosis, services or treatment. The information should not be considered complete and should not be used in place of a visit, call, consultation or advice of your physician or other health care provider. Should you have any health care-related questions, please call or see your physician or health care provider.

The information below is graciously provided by David Osborn MH L. Ac. I want to thank Mr. Osborn for allowing me to use the material at the website listed below;

http://www.greekmedicine.net/hygiene/Emotions_and_Organs.html

This information will give you some insight into how we think and feel can adversely affect our health. By understanding these things, you can start to relate why the Bible tells us to think a certain way or act in this manner.

1. Heart
   It is very sensitive to emotional states. Noble, expansive, uplifting emotions like courage, valor, honesty, forthrightness, altruism and compassion strengthen the heart. Whereas ignoble, constrictive, base emotions like cowardice, timidity, guilt, remorse, deceit and duplicity weaken them. Love and the emotional will to live are also very relevant to the heart; according to Greek Medicine, you CAN die of a broken heart.
   (Authors note; Our thinking plays a big part in this process.)
2. Lungs
   The lungs need a feeling of psychic space within which to function; the phrase, "breathing room" is a common expression. The feeling of being smothered, invalidated, or denied one's psychic space can constrict the lungs and cause respiratory problems like dyspnea and asthma. Conversely, a feeling of dignity and pride puffs up the chest, and allows the lungs to expand and function properly. Negative emotions that sap the will to live are also injurious to the lungs, especially grief and bereavement; many chronic respiratory diseases and conditions develop after a major loss or bereavement.
3. Throat
   The throat is also the upper end of the digestive tract. Acute emotional tensions and anxieties can agitate the liver, causing it to rise and get bottlenecked in the throat. One then feels like one's choking on something, or has something lodged in the throat, a condition called globus hystericus.
4. Liver Gallbladder
   Bile is produced by the liver and stored in the gallbladder, which makes these two organs vulnerable to negative emotions like anger, irritability, frustration, resentment, jealousy and envy. These negative emotions are stored in these organs, and can slowly eat away at them if allowed to fester. Anger and rage can

explode upwards from the liver into the head, causing a lot of havoc in their wake: headaches, migraines; red, sore, bloodshot eyes; and muscular tension in the neck and shoulders. Nervous and emotional tension and stress, as well as melancholic emotions like pensiveness and worry, will affect the liver, which in turn causes nervous, colicky, melancholic disturbances of the digestive functions. This excess melancholy often accumulates under the lower ribs, giving a stuffy, distended, congested feeling in the whole chest and diaphragm area.

5. Stomach
   Choleric emotions like anger, hate, rage and frustration stored here lead to gastritis, ulcers and other stomach conditions. Many of us hold a lot of emotions like anger and resentment in our gut. Melancholic emotional stress and tension, as well as pensiveness, worry and anxiety, will affect the stomach, causing distension, bloating, colic, gas and stomachache. And so, we must always try to be of good cheer when we eat.
6. Spleen
   The spleen is the storage receptacle for black bile. And so, it is adversely affected by negative emotions like pensiveness, anxiety, worry and depression, which affects the digestive system. This could produce colic, gas, distension and bloating throughout the entire abdominal area.
7. Intestines and Bowels
   The intestines are often the effect of emotionally induced digestive disorders that arise in the upper digestive organs - the liver, gallbladder, stomach and spleen. The upper small intestine, or duodenum, being very close to these upper digestive organs, is the part most affected.
8. Colon
   Black bile is essential to proper colon function. The colon is very vulnerable to emotions - especially chronic or deeply held worry, anxiety and nervous or

emotional stress and tension. Security issues and deep insecurities will also impact negatively on the colon since its functioning is intimately connected to our emotional security. These emotional disturbances usually produce disorders like constipation, irritable bowel syndrome, or spastic colon, but if the aggravation is severe, even colitis and more severe degenerative diseases may result.

9. Kidneys
   Fright, fear and shock are most injurious to the kidneys.
10. Adrenal glands
    The adrenal glands, sitting right on top of the kidneys, are injured and drained energetically by excessive stress. The adrenal medulla and its fight-or-flight adrenaline response are excessively provoked by acute stress and emotional outbursts of anger and the like in those whose lives have become an overdramatized emotional roller coaster. Chronic stress aggravates the functioning of the adreno-cortical hormones like cortisol, which can lead to weight gain, especially in the lower body and midriff, as well as rising blood sugar if the stress is constant and unresolved. Since the adrenal glands provide the energetic support for healthy urinary function, the health, vitality and functioning of the kidneys will also be drained, and adversely affected by weakened or challenged adrenals.
11. Brain
    The brain comes last in our discussion of the emotional life of the organs because it's often the effect of humoral and metabolic imbalances arising elsewhere in the body, which send subtle vapors up to the brain to influence its functioning. Choleric vapors agitate, irritate and inflame, provoking anger, rage, envy, jealousy, or irritability. Warm, moist sanguine vapors, can stir up feelings of wellbeing, pleasure, sensuality or even lust. Melancholic vapors provoke feelings of prudence, caution, pensiveness, worry and withdrawal. Cold, wet phlegmatic vapors will dull or fog up the

> brain, producing mental lethargy and dullness. It will cloud objective thinking with excessive sentiment and subjectivity. However, the brain is not all effect; it can also be cause, since the kinds of thoughts that it habitually thinks can have a profound impact on the heart.

Again, for more information, see their website at;

http://www.greekmedicine.net/hygiene/Emotions_and_Organs.html

When this discussion comes up about emotions and how we look at ourselves and others, I usually ask the following question. 'When you are angry, do you like the feeling it gives you? Do you feel enhanced because of it?' Usually when I ask these questions and maybe expound upon it a bit more, it usually makes someone stop and think about the questions.

Romans 2:21-23;
21 As you teach others, are you failing to teach yourself? As you preach against stealing, are you stealing?
22 As you tell others not to commit adultery, are you committing adultery? As you treat idols with disgust, are you robbing temples?
23 As you brag about the laws in Moses' Teachings, are you dishonoring God by ignoring Moses' Teachings? (GOD'S WORD® Translation)

Love

Level 1

Love Level 101? That's what I call the first level. This is simply how I break it down.

It's the ability to love yourself and your immediate family. It's the ability to give that love to your loved ones because you want them to have the very best you can give them. You want to contribute in such a positive manner to these people in your life, so they can and will be enhanced because you are simply with them. You speak life into them. They feel appreciated just because of what you say and do for and maybe with them. You might make them feel like they have never been treated better in their life. That is the way it should be done.

You are not quick with the tongue to lash out because someone doesn't take out the garbage. You are patient when a son or daughter doesn't do their homework. Instead of lecturing them or giving them "The LOOK", you calmly talk with them asking is there anything you can do to help them. When someone you are close to doesn't live up to "YOUR" expectations you have for them, maybe it's time that you back off your expectations for them and allow the LORD God to influence them. Remember the old saying, you can be right and be alone too.

You are kind when a family member gives you a few choice words because they don't like this or care for that. And it ends up that you are the one they take it out on. You don't respond with negativity, but in love because maybe that person is hurting on the inside. You see through their pain. Sometimes you might need to give them some distance unless you want to ask the question; "What's the matter? Is there anything I can do for you? Even if it's just for me to sit here and listen to you so you can get it off your chest."

If you love someone, you look at the best in them, in what they are and are becoming. You encourage and elevate them so they can see what they can become. You speak life into them no matter what they say or do to you. You give them the best you can from you because you think and truly believe they deserve the best you can give them.

You know everything about your mate, your parents, and your children. Yet you love them anyway. You see their shortcomings and their faults. But you also see an opportunity to be of help when they ask or when you see the need arises. When they need encouragement, you support them. Sometimes it's just a touch on the shoulder. Then other times it's a warm hug. Other times it's sitting over a cup of tea and talking together. Sometimes it's not talking at all. Sometimes moments of silence speak more than words ever could.

This is just the beginning of learning to love. Yes, just the beginning. Learning to love this way is something anyone can do.

We are in the me, me, me, now, now, now, I, I, I times today. More and more people are looking to get out of a relationship that is good for them, not what they can give to the relationship. It used to be the other way around. Then we wonder why people are sad, unhappy, unfulfilled, lonely, and taking prescription drugs because of depression and anxiety, etc.

Matthew 24:12; *Because of the increase of wickedness, the love of most will grow cold,* (New International Version)

I hear some people say things like, "I no longer love my spouse." This is exceptionally sad for many reasons. But let's look a little bit more closely at the wording there. "I no longer love…" That is a declaration. Our words have power. That person chooses not to love that other person anymore for whatever reason or reasons. There are many reasons why people separate or divorce. There could be physical abuse involved. But to consciously determine that one doesn't love the other is even sadder. Is that Biblical love?

The above really breaks my heart. Not having someone in your life anymore is one thing. But not love them, to me it seems like there is a much deeper issue going on there.

Matthew 25:37-40;
37 "Then the righteous will answer him, 'Lord, when did we see you hungry and feed you, or thirsty and give you something to drink?
38 When did we see you a stranger and invite you in, or needing clothes and clothe you?
39 When did we see you sick or in prison and go to visit you?'
40 The King will reply, 'Truly I tell you, whatever you did for one of the least of these brothers and sisters of mine, you did for me.' (New International Version)

God's people need to turn back to the LORD. Allow Him to fill you, teach you, and engulf you in what love truly is. We can't rely on television programs to give us that information. We cannot allow secular movies to show us what love is and how we are suppose to love others. Do we really want to miss the lesson the LORD our God wants us to learn?

So many people want to be used in a great way for God's purpose. They really long for it. They ask, plead, and beg for God to use them in a great way. But in the asking, they miss the whole point. One of the greatest attributes of God is His love. But most of us don't see it because we are blinded and deceived as to what love really is and how we are to give it.

What a man or woman of God need to convey to others is love from the Most High God. If we are not patient, kind, thoughtful, not seeking our own gain, etc. the power of God cannot flow through us properly.

I remember how a great prophet of God, John Paul Jackson, made a comment about evil. He gets asked from time to time if God made evil. And to a point, I can understand why a person would ask that type of question. So the question is did God make evil? John Paul Jackson's answer was no. God did not create evil. Just like darkness is the absence of light, sin (evil) is the absence of God. Now I have a slightly different take on it. Evil is the absence of the love of God. God is love. When you take away patience, kindness, understanding, forgiveness, helpfulness, and love, you are removing the very attributes of what God is and what He gives to us. Then the vacuum is created. This brings us to our next topic.

Love Less

That is an interesting title isn't it? That is actually a definition of a word we'll be looking at here.

We all like to feel we are getting closer and closer to the LORD God. We like to think we are making progress in our Christian life, our walk, and our work for Him. Yet we know we have some things to work on so we can grow and have our lives pleasing to Him. That is ALWAYS the correct attitude to have in our daily life. Let's look at some Scriptures here.

1 John 4:20-21;
20 Whoever claims to love God yet hates a brother or sister is a liar. For whoever does not love their brother and sister, whom they have seen, cannot love God, whom they have not seen.
21 And he has given us this command: Anyone who loves God must also love their brother and sister. (New Living Translation)

1 John 3:15; *Anyone who hates another brother or sister is really a murderer at heart. And you know that murderers don't have eternal life within them.* (New Living Translation)

Matthew 24:10; *At that time many will turn away from the faith and will betray and hate each other,* (New Living Translation)

These are some pretty intense verses. That word "hates" or "hate" is a very interesting word. I always thought that "hate" is an extreme word. I thought it was something like really passionate in that it might well bring out intense emotions. But I learned something here that is interesting. "Hates" is the Greek word "miseó" Strongs Concordance 3404. It means properly, to detest (on a *comparative* basis); hence, *denounce*; to *love someone or something less* than someone (something) else, i.e. to renounce one choice in favor of another, or to "love less"…

This might be hard to accept at the first reading, but let's explain it differently. If you no longer love them, that means you "hate" them. Why? Because you "love" them "less", that puts it into the category of "hates" according to what the Bible says. So if you love anyone less than you use to, then there is a challenge for you.

I'm sure someone is saying, but you don't know or understand what this person or that person had done to me. They ruined me, my career, they put me into debt, they abused me physically and/or emotionally, they didn't love me, he didn't help me around the house, she always griped and moaned, etc. etc. etc. There are so many things that can be said here that will come to the same conclusion.

So how do you know if you are on the right path and loving people correctly? As always, let's see what God's Word says about this.

Matthew 5:23-24;
23 "Therefore, if you are offering your gift at the altar and there remember that your brother or sister has something against you,
24 leave your gift there in front of the altar. First go and be reconciled to them; then come and offer your gift. (New International Version)

1 John 2:15; *Do not love the world or anything in the world. If anyone loves the world, the love of the Father is not in him.* (New International Version)

If you are not speaking with someone because you are mad, upset, bitter at them for doing something you didn't like or perceived to be harmful to you, then you do not love correctly. It's the absence of love. We as Christians need to love everyone. That includes those we think hurt or continue to hurt us. In the eyes of God, every one of us can and are commanded to love everyone. How can this be? Because we are different now. When we trusted Jesus Christ, we became a new creature. We love because we want to love others, not because we have to love someone. We love them because they need that love in their lives, regardless of whether or not they see it that way or not.

Galatians 6:15; *Certainly, it doesn't matter whether a person is circumcised or not. Rather, what matters is being a new creation.* (GOD'S WORD® Translation)

2 Corinthians 5:17; *Therefore, if anyone is in Christ, he is a new creation; the old has gone, the new has come!* (New International Version)

The first level of love is loving our family, which includes parents, brothers and sisters, spouse and your children. This isn't the reward level. That is coming up later.

Matthew 5:46-47;
46 If you love those who love you, what reward will you get? Are not even the tax collectors doing that?
47 And if you greet only your own people, what are you doing more than others? Do not even pagans do that? (New International Version)

If we are to live a fulfilling life, we need to follow what the LORD says concerning loving Him and others. Next is the second level of love we need to achieve.

Love

Level 2

I realize I may never get the chance to see, or to shake hands with, my readers. However, when they finish reading this book, I hope they start to apply the suggestions and see the opportunities that are contained within it. Then they can fully understand the greater life that is out there, waiting for us to discover.

This book is about the wiles of the evil ones. They are on the offensive, in or around your life. They are trying to make you or put you in a position that you will do something that will bring absolute heartache and destruction into your life. The evil ones want you to continue to be deceived. By him keeping you deceived, you will not see what he is doing to you, yours, and others around you.

This level 2 is when you love people outside your immediate family. This includes cousins, aunts and uncles, maybe grandparents, distance cousins, and co-workers. Then there are your friends and acquaintances too. Include with them those people who go to your church.

This isn't the reward level yet. Now for some, this can be challenging depending on how they are looking at it. Learning to see and love other people as the LORD sees them will change your life completely. This love is not how the world loves, but how our God loves us all.

Love

Level 3

This is the reward level. The third level is where you love someone on the street, in a grocery store or at the bank, who you don't know. If you have your own business, your competitors are part of this group also. You love those who don't love you. Those people include those that might hate and despise you for any reason and you might not know why either. They might seek your destruction. They might attack you openly with words without regard as to if they do hurt you. More than likely, they will rejoice if it does hurt you.

When you can expand your love to include these people, then you are entering the reward territory that Jesus is talking about in the verse below.

Luke 6:31-36;
31 Do to others as you would have them do to you.
32 "If you love those who love you, what credit is that to you? Even sinners love those who love them.
33 And if you do good to those who are good to you, what credit is that to you? Even sinners do that.
34 And if you lend to those from whom you expect repayment, what credit is that to you? Even sinners lend to sinners, expecting to be repaid in full.
35 But love your enemies, do good to them, and lend to them without expecting to get anything back. Then your reward will be great, and you will be children of the Most High, because he is kind to the ungrateful and wicked.
36 Be merciful, just as your Father is merciful. (New International Version)

Why is this reward territory? You are giving and helping someone where there is no financial or personal interests in it for yourself. You pay for someone's meal. You tell the waitress or waiter to tell them that it's taken care of and that the LORD truly loves them. They will never know who you are. When you find someone in need you might send them money anonymously in the mail. They might never know who sent it or why.

Matthew 6:18; *so that it will not be obvious to men that you are fasting, but only to your Father, who is unseen; and your Father,* *who sees what is done in secret, will reward you.* (New International Version)

Here are some one-liners about love that the world teaches. I don't believe there is a scriptural basis for them. Here is just one of them. "Spend your time on those that love you unconditionally. Don't waste it on those that only love you when the condition is right for them."

We are commanded many times to love one another. I don't know where there is a limit to that command either… if there is one.

Luke 6:27-30;
27 "But to you who are listening I say: Love your enemies, do good to those who hate you,
28 bless those who curse you, pray for those who mistreat you.
29 If someone slaps you on one cheek, turn to them the other also. If someone takes your coat, do not withhold your shirt from them.
30 Give to everyone who asks you, and if anyone takes what belongs to you, do not demand it back.
31 Do to others as you would have them do to you. (New International Version)

Could verse 31 above be the golden rule that people talk about now a days?

Luke 6:31-36;
31 Do to others as you would have them do to you.
32 "If you love those who love you, what credit is that to you? Even sinners love those who love them.
33 And if you do good to those who are good to you, what credit is that to you? Even sinners do that.
34 And if you lend to those from whom you expect repayment, what credit is that to you? Even sinners lend to sinners, expecting to be repaid in full.
35 But love your enemies, do good to them, and lend to them without expecting to get anything back. Then your reward will be

great, and you will be children of the Most High, because he is kind to the ungrateful and wicked.
36 Be merciful, just as your Father is merciful. (New International Version)

Whenever I read that passage, I see how much more I need to grow, to love other people not just in words, but mostly in action. If I'm going to ask my Heavenly Father to forgive me because I did this or didn't do that, it's pretty clear that I need to do the same to others first.

In my opinion, this is where you love and really don't expect to get anything in return. When you love, you love because the person you are loving needs it when they don't understand or know they need it. You love not for the heavenly reward. It really doesn't enter into the picture. You see the bigger picture. You are looking more and more through your spiritual eyes and seeing eternity. You see where people might end up, in the lake of fire burning with fire and brimstone. You see, people need your love.

Jesus revealed many things to us because He has the highest form of love for us. If we want to be like Him, then we must do the things He did.

Matthew 26:50; *Jesus replied, "Friend, do what you came for." Then the men stepped forward, seized Jesus and arrested him.* (New International Version)

In every version, I was able to check, Jesus used the word "friend" when He said that to Judas. Can you imagine that? Here, Jesus is being arrested and will eventually die on the cross for our sins. And what did He do? Called him, "Friend". Can you call someone a friend when they don't meet your expectations? Do you refrain from getting mad or upset at them when they don't follow or do all of your instructions? How about when they don't meet your expectations?

Romans 12:17-21;

17 Do not repay anyone evil for evil. Be careful to do what is right in the eyes of everyone.
18 If it is possible, as far as it depends on you, live at peace with everyone.
19 Do not take revenge, my dear friends, but leave room for God's wrath, for it is written: "It is mine to avenge; I will repay," says the Lord.
20 On the contrary: "If your enemy is hungry, feed him; if he is thirsty, give him something to drink. In doing this, you will heap burning coals on his head."
21 Do not be overcome by evil, but overcome evil with good. (New International Version)

Now that is an interesting verse, isn't it? Overcome evil with good. Remember what I wrote above when I said that evil is the absence of love? God says that all good things come from the LORD God. So when we repay evil deeds with good ones, we are doing that out of love. By doing that, we are expressing love to that individual. When we turn a light bulb on in a dark room, it becomes illuminated with light. When we turn on the furnace when the house is too cold, warm air replaces the cold air. When we love someone who are doing evil things, we are giving that person something they so desperately need.

Romans 14:10-13;
10 You, then, why do you judge your brother or sister ? Or why do you treat them with contempt? For we will all stand before God's judgment seat.
11 It is written: "'As surely as I live,' says the Lord, 'every knee will bow before me; every tongue will acknowledge God.'"
12 So then, each of us will give an account of ourselves to God.
13 Therefore let us stop passing judgment on one another. Instead, make up your mind not to put any stumbling block or obstacle in the way of a brother or sister. (New International Version)

James 4:11-12;
11 Brothers and sisters, do not slander one another. Anyone who speaks against a brother or sister or judges them speaks against the law and judges it. When you judge the law, you are not keeping it, but sitting in judgment on it.

12 There is only one Lawgiver and Judge, the one who is able to save and destroy. But you—who are you to judge your neighbor? (New International Version)

1 John 4:17-19;
17 This is how love is made complete among us so that we will have confidence on the day of judgment: In this world we are like Jesus.
18 There is no fear in love. But perfect love drives out fear, because fear has to do with punishment. The one who fears is not made perfect in love.
19 We love because he first loved us. (New International Version)

Did you catch that last verse? We love because He, The LORD loved us first. So doesn't it make sense that we need to FIRST show genuine love and affection towards others, just like the LORD God did to us? By others, I mean ALL, EVERYONE, ANYONE, etc.

1 Peter 2:12; *Live decent lives among unbelievers. Then, although they ridicule you as if you were doing wrong while they are watching you do good things, they will praise God on the day he comes to help you.* (GOD'S WORD® Translation)

Ephesians 4:31-32;
31 Get rid of all bitterness, rage and anger, brawling and slander, along with every form of malice.
32 Be kind and compassionate to one another, forgiving each other, just as in Christ God forgave you. (New International Version)

If you really want the LORD to use you, then dedicate yourself to learning 1st Corinthians 13. Know it inside and out. And live it. Why? If you were to look closely at the life of Jesus, that is what He always did.

Let's go beyond excuses for why we do or did this or don't do that. We are better than that. We are a new creature in Jesus. So let's not hold onto the old.

James 4:13-17;
13 Now listen, you who say, "Today or tomorrow we will go to this or that city, spend a year there, carry on business and make money."
14 Why, you do not even know what will happen tomorrow. What is your life? You are a mist that appears for a little while and then vanishes.
15 Instead, you ought to say, "If it is the Lord's will, we will live and do this or that."
16 As it is, you boast in your arrogant schemes. All such boasting is evil.
17 If anyone, then, knows the good they ought to do and doesn't do it, it is sin for them. (New International Version)

Now Jesus gave us some more commands to follow right along this line.

John 13:34; *A new command I give you: Love one another. As I have loved you, so you must love one another.* (New International Version)

John 13:35; *By this all men will know that you are my disciples, if you love one another."* (New International Version)

John 15:12; *My command is this: Love each other as I have loved you.* (New International Version)

John 15:17; *This is my command: Love each other.* (New International Version)

This concept is mentioned many times in the Bible. Hmm.... It seems to be very significant. Maybe we should change our lives to accommodate this seemingly very important teaching! Why? Because just like that lady (a precious saint of the LORD) I mentioned at the beginning of this chapter, maybe we need to do it so other people who don't have any hope, who don't feel loved will be able to see and feel it from His redeemed people. As a result, people will be drawn to Jesus so He can minister to them just like He did and continues to do to and for us!

Psalm 37:8-9;
8 Refrain from anger and turn from wrath; do not fret—it leads only to evil.
9 For those who are evil will be destroyed, but those who hope in the LORD will inherit the land. (New International Version)

Proverbs 10:12; *Hatred stirs up quarrels, but love makes up for all offenses.* (New Living Translation)

Proverbs 16:28; *A devious person spreads quarrels. A gossip separates the closest of friends.* (GOD'S WORD® Translation)

Proverbs 19:11; *A man's wisdom gives him patience; it is to his glory to overlook an offense.* (New International Version)

Proverbs 24:29; *Do not say, "I'll do to him as he has done to me; I'll pay that man back for what he did."* (New International Version)

Zechariah 7:9; *"This is what the LORD Almighty says: 'Administer true justice; show mercy and compassion to one another.* (New International Version)

Matthew 5:21-22;
21 "You have heard that it was said to the people long ago, 'You shall not murder, and anyone who murders will be subject to judgment.'
22 But I tell you that anyone who is angry with a brother or sister will be subject to judgment. Again, anyone who says to a brother or sister, 'Raca,' is answerable to the court. And anyone who says, 'You fool!' will be in danger of the fire of hell. (New Living Translation)

Matthew 6:14-15;
14 For if you forgive other people when they sin against you, your heavenly Father will also forgive you.

15 But if you do not forgive others their sins, your Father will not forgive your sins. (New International Version)

Matthew 15:18-19;
18 But the things that come out of a person's mouth come from the heart, and these defile them.
19 For out of the heart come evil thoughts—murder, adultery, sexual immorality, theft, false testimony, slander.'" (New International Version)

Matthew 18:21-22;
21 Then Peter came to Jesus and asked, "Lord, how many times shall I forgive my brother or sister who sins against me? Up to seven times?"
22 Jesus answered, "I tell you, not seven times, but seventy-seven times. (New International Version)

That amount of seventy times seven is interesting. Once you understand that love doesn't keep track of wrongs, then you will come to the understanding that a person will never get to the seventy seven times. Why? Because love doesn't keep track of wrongs! A person who loves wants to restore the relationship to its fullest possible extent. Thereby, you always start all over again at zero!

Mark 7:20-23;
20 He went on: "What comes out of a person is what defiles them.
21 For it is from within, out of a person's heart, that evil thoughts come—sexual immorality, theft, murder,
22 adultery, greed, malice, deceit, lewdness, envy, slander, arrogance and folly.
23 All these evils come from inside and defile a person." (New International Version)

Luke 17:3-4;
3 So watch yourselves! "If a believer sins, correct him. If he changes the way he thinks and acts, forgive him.

4 Even if he wrongs you seven times in one day and comes back to you seven times and says that he is sorry, forgive him." (GOD'S WORD® Translation)

Acts 20:35; *In everything I did, I showed you that by this kind of hard work we must help the weak, remembering the words the Lord Jesus himself said: 'It is more blessed to give than to receive.'"* (New International Version)

Romans 2:1-4;
1 No matter who you are, if you judge anyone, you have no excuse. When you judge another person, you condemn yourself, since you, the judge, do the same things.
2 We know that God's judgment is right when he condemns people for doing these things.
3 When you judge people for doing these things but then do them yourself, do you think you will escape God's judgment?
4 Do you have contempt for God, who is very kind to you, puts up with you, and deals patiently with you? Don't you realize that it is God's kindness that is trying to lead you to him and change the way you think and act? (GOD'S WORD® Translation)

Romans 12:10; *Love each other with genuine affection, and take delight in honoring each other.* (New Living Translation)

Romans 13:9-10;
9 The commandments, "You shall not commit adultery," "You shall not murder," "You shall not steal," "You shall not covet," and whatever other command there may be, are summed up in this one command: "Love your neighbor as yourself."
10 Love does no harm to a neighbor. Therefore love is the fulfillment of the law. (New International Version)

Romans 15:1-3;
1 We who are strong ought to bear with the failings of the weak and not to please ourselves.
2 Each of us should please our neighbors for their good, to build them up.
3 For even Christ did not please himself but, as it is written: "The insults of those who insult you have fallen on me." (New International Version)

Galatians 5:22; *But the fruit of the Spirit is love, joy, peace, patience, kindness, goodness, faithfulness,* (New International Version)

Philippians 2:3-4;
2 then make my joy complete by being like-minded, having the same love, being one in spirit and of one mind.
3 Do nothing out of selfish ambition or vain conceit. Rather, in humility value others above yourselves, (GOD'S WORD® Translation)

2 Peter 3:9; *The Lord isn't slow to do what he promised, as some people think. Rather, he is patient for your sake. He doesn't want to destroy anyone but wants all people to have an opportunity to turn to him and change the way they think and act.* (GOD'S WORD® Translation)

Colossians 3:5-10;
5 Put to death, therefore, whatever belongs to your earthly nature: sexual immorality, impurity, lust, evil desires and greed, which is idolatry.
6 Because of these, the wrath of God is coming.
7 You used to walk in these ways, in the life you once lived.
8 But now you must also rid yourselves of all such things as these: anger, rage, malice, slander, and filthy language from your lips.
9 Do not lie to each other, since you have taken off your old self with its practices
10 and have put on the new self, which is being renewed in knowledge in the image of its Creator. (New International Version)

Colossians 3:12-14;
12 Therefore, as God's chosen people, holy and dearly loved, clothe yourselves with compassion, kindness, humility, gentleness and patience.
13 Bear with each other and forgive one another if any of you has a grievance against someone. Forgive as the Lord forgave you.
14 And over all these virtues put on love, which binds them all together in perfect unity. (New International Version)

1 Peter 1:22; *Now that you have purified yourselves by obeying the truth so that you have sincere love for your brothers, love one another deeply, from the heart.* (New International Version)

1 John 3:11; *This is the message you heard from the beginning: We should love one another.* (New International Version)

What I found very interesting was when I watched the movie on the "Gospel of John" by Visual Bible International Inc. for maybe the third time. One part jumped out at me towards the very end. I found it absolutely fascinating. It really explained the love, the forgiveness the LORD has towards us.

John 21:9-19;
9 When they went ashore, they saw a fire with a fish lying on the coals, and they saw a loaf of bread.
10 Jesus told them, "Bring some of the fish you've just caught."
11 Simon Peter got into the boat and pulled the net ashore. Though the net was filled with 153 large fish, it was not torn.
12 Jesus told them, "Come, have breakfast." None of the disciples dared to ask him who he was. They knew he was the Lord.
13 Jesus took the bread, gave it to them, and did the same with the fish.
14 This was the third time that Jesus showed himself to the disciples after he had come back to life.
15 After they had eaten breakfast, Jesus asked Simon Peter, "Simon, son of John, do you love me more than the other disciples do?" Peter answered him, "Yes, Lord, you know that I love you." Jesus told him, "Feed my lambs."
16 Jesus asked him again, a second time, "Simon, son of John, do you love me?" Peter answered him, "Yes, Lord, you know that I love you." Jesus told him, "Take care of my sheep."
17 Jesus asked him a third time, "Simon, son of John, do you love me?" Peter felt sad because Jesus had asked him a third time, "Do you love me?" So Peter said to him, "Lord, you know everything. You know that I love you." Jesus told him, "Feed my sheep.

18 I can guarantee this truth: When you were young, you would get ready to go where you wanted. But when you're old, you will stretch out your hands, and someone else will get you ready to take you where you don't want to go."
19 Jesus said this to show by what kind of death Peter would bring glory to God. After saying this, Jesus told Peter, "Follow me!" (GOD'S WORD® Translation)

So the setting is they probably stayed on the beach the entire time. Jesus had bread ready for them. They brought some fish to cook on the fire too.

What is interesting is Jesus asked Peter three times if he loved Him. Notice each question was becoming shorter. Then Peter responded three times. Then Jesus gave him a slightly different command to carry out each time. It was an interesting sequence, to say the least. I'll talk about that in a few moments.

There are those who say it was to remind Peter of when he denied Jesus three different times. But notice when Peter said; "*Yes, Lord, you know that I love you"*, He didn't dispute it. And neither did any of the other disciples. Why? To find that answer, we need to go to the following passage.

John 21:4-7;
4 As the sun was rising, Jesus stood on the shore. The disciples didn't realize that it was Jesus.
5 Jesus asked them, "Friends, haven't you caught any fish?" They answered him, "No, we haven't."
6 He told them, "Throw the net out on the right side of the boat, and you'll catch some." So they threw the net out and were unable to pull it in because so many fish were in it.
7 The disciple whom Jesus loved said to Peter, "It's the Lord." When Simon Peter heard that it was the Lord, he put back on the clothes that he had taken off and jumped into the sea. (GOD'S WORD® Translation)

Who was the first one out of the boat? Who was the one that couldn't wait to get to Him? Who's the one who thought it was so important to be with his Master, his Savior, his LORD, his God that he didn't want to wait till the boat reached the shore? It was Peter. Despite that moment when he lost it and denied the

Jesus three times when He was on trial, he wanted to be with Him more than anything. His first thought was to be with Jesus.

Right before Jesus was arrested, in Peter's misguided love and passion for Him, he drew a sword he had and cut off the servant's ear. Then Jesus healed the servant's ear. Image having that happen to you, when the person you are arresting just restored your ear miraculously.

When the other disciples scattered when they arrested Jesus, Peter hung around to see what will happen.

When Mary visited the tomb and discovered that the body of Jesus was missing, she ran to Peter and the other disciple, whom Jesus loved to tell them.

Let's get back to Jesus talking with Peter on the beach. I would like for you to notice the progression of what He wanted Peter to do. Let's take them one at a time.

1. The first time Jesus said in response to Peter's answer to "Do you love me more than the other disciples?", "Feed my lambs". What could this possibly mean? This first instruction at that time to Peter was to feed (spiritually) all the new converts that would become known to this day as Christians or in some areas of the world as believers. Like lambs are baby sheep, so are newly converted people to Christianity. They need to be nurtured as they grow in the knowledge of Jesus.
2. The second response from Jesus when He asked Peter if he loves him, "take care of my sheep". This is primarily a duty that a shepherd would perform like watching over the flock. It could even be something like what a pastor of a church would do.
3. The third and final answer was to "feed my sheep". Jesus' last instruction at that time to Peter was to take the mature Christians or believers that are growing in knowledge of Him and help them to mature in the knowingness of Him.

Jesus let Peter know in His unique way that he was forgiven and told him what was going to happen to him. Why did that exchange occur? I guess or imagine the Lord Jesus knew Peter's heart and possibly realized that it might hold him back of doing the work Jesus wanted done by Peter if He didn't tell him those things. Maybe it was as simple as all is forgiven so let's move forward and do the work I have for you to do.

The Love Jesus Showed to Us

Let's look at some of the many things that Jesus did for us out of love for each and every one of us. With all the physical and mental pain He endured up to this point, He still was thinking of us more than himself.

Luke 24:26-28;
26 Did not the Messiah have to suffer these things and then enter his glory?"
27 And beginning with Moses and all the Prophets, he explained to them what was said in all the Scriptures concerning himself.
28 As they approached the village to which they were going, Jesus continued on as if he were going farther. (New International Version)

A very big part of love is showing compassion. Here are the verses that deal with having compassion just in the New Testament alone.

Matthew 9:36; *When he saw the crowds, he had compassion on them, because they were harassed and helpless, like sheep without a shepherd.* (New International Version)

Matthew 12:7; *"But if you had known what this means, 'I DESIRE COMPASSION, AND NOT A SACRIFICE,' you would not have condemned the innocent.* (New American Standard Bible)

Mark 5:18-19;
18 And when he had come into the boat, he that had been possessed with the demon prayed him that he might be with him.

19 Yet Jesus suffered him not, but saith to him, Go home to thy friends, and tell them how great things the Lord hath done for thee, and hath had compassion on thee. (Webster Bible Translation)

Mark 6:34; *When Jesus landed and saw a large crowd, he had compassion on them, because they were like sheep without a shepherd. So he began teaching them many things.* (New International Version)

One of the best things one can do for anyone else is to love them no matter what they do or don't do for you.

Matthew 22:36-40;
36 "Teacher, which is the greatest commandment in the Law?"
37 Jesus replied: "'Love the Lord your God with all your heart and with all your soul and with all your mind.'
38 This is the first and greatest commandment.
39 And the second is like it: 'Love your neighbor as yourself.'
40 All the Law and the Prophets hang on these two commandments." (New International Version)

I'm going to challenge your thinking here a bit by asking you a question. This question will hopefully let you see the bigger picture. The solution will allow you to see the full circle of why the answer to our problems here is "love". There are more songs are written about love than any other topic. Note what Jesus said; Love God with your heart, your soul, and your mind.

Now Luke and Mark add another item to the mix about how to love God… with all your strength.

Luke 10:27; *He answered, "'Love the Lord your God with all your heart and with all your soul and with all your strength and with all your mind'; and, 'Love your neighbor as yourself.'"* (New International Version)

Mark 12:30-31;
30 Love the Lord your God with all your heart and with all your soul and with all your mind and with all your strength.'

31 The second is this: 'Love your neighbor as yourself.' There is no commandment greater than these." (New International Version)

First off, that word "neighbor" means basically everyone. If you don't believe this, check out these verses.

Luke 10:36-37;
36 "Which of these three do you think was a neighbor to the man who fell into the hands of robbers?"
37 The expert in the law replied, "The one who had mercy on him." (New American Standard Bible)

The LORD wants us to love everyone, no matter what. Maybe it is a parent that says some things to you that are less than uplifting. Sometimes it can be very hurtful to you for whatever reason. It cuts right down into the depths of your heart. It might hurt so bad that you want that 'eye for an eye' and 'a tooth for a tooth' vengeance. Is that the proper way of handling the situation? Is that the proper way of honoring your parents?

Maybe it's a son or daughter not doing their homework, taking out the garbage or doing the dishes. They are not doing what you want them to do. Do they talk "back" to you disrespectfully? Does that or the other things they do or say make you want to yell or get angry at them or give them the silent treatment? Hmmm… Love sees beyond the emotion. Love looks deeper than what was said. It notices there is something else there that caused or causes that type of reaction. More on this a bit later.

Then there is the spouse not doing or helping you out with the work that needs to be done around the house. Instead of them out cutting the grass, cleaning up around the house, maybe cleaning the basement or helping out with the laundry, etc. what are they doing? Laying on the couch or playing on the computer instead of helping you.

Let's not forget the people you work with at the office. How about that boss who might say some things that might get you upset on the inside. Or how about that co-worker who seemingly rubs you the wrong way, if you know what I mean. Hmmm… In honor preferring one another.

We can use any excuse we can think up to talk ourselves into thinking we are justified in how we react when we think we are wronged. Sometimes we talk ourselves into getting angry or upset… sometimes to the point of retaliation again others.

Now here is the bigger picture for you. So here is the question for you. Why did The LORD give us the Law? This is an interesting question. Why DID He give us the Law? He knew we would break it. He knew we would add to and take away from His law. So why did the LORD give us the Law?

I've heard a few people who had some unique comments about it. One response was He knows we can't keep the law. That brings to mind the next verse.

1 John 5:3; *For this demonstrates our love for God: We keep his commandments, and his commandments are not difficult,* (International Standard Version)

Another one is, so He can show us His grace and make it available to us. Then there is, so He can give His mercy. Yet another is so that the Messiah would come and pay the penalty for our sin. These are interesting answers.

If the LORD knew we would not keep the Law and sin against Him, why bother giving it to us? To hold us accountable when we stand before Him in judgment at the end of time? That is exactly what will happen. Another one answered with because He loved us.

No doubt you might be scratching your head right now wondering huh??? I understand the reaction. Let me explain further.

He loved us so much that He gave us the law. Why? This is something for you to ponder. There is an answer. And it is simpler than you might think. Here are some hints.

As we know, He made everything.

John 1:3; *Through him all things were made; without him nothing was made that has been made.* (New International Version)

The LORD made everything here; He made the moon and the stars and hung them in the sky.

Psalms 8:3; *When I consider your heavens, the work of your fingers, the moon and the stars, which you have set in place,* (New International Version)

He also hung the earth on nothing.

Job 26:7; *He spreads out the northern skies over empty space; he suspends the earth over nothing.* (New International Version)

He gave us the other planets and the air we breathe. Perhaps He tossed a hunk of rock through the universe. Maybe He designed it so it would orbit and show itself streaking across our sky. Maybe He gave it a tail so we can see it very clearly. He created all the plants, the water, the sky and made rain. He created animals of so many varieties; those that walk upon the land, that fly in the air, and swim in the sea. We, as humans, are fearfully and wonderfully made as it states in the psalms.

Psalm 139:14; *I praise you because I am fearfully and wonderfully made; your works are wonderful, I know that full well.* (New International Version)

He knows all our thoughts better than we do.

Psalm 17:3; *Though you probe my heart, though you examine me at night and test me, you will find that I have planned no evil; my mouth has not transgressed.* (New International Version)

Revelation 2:23; *I will strike her children dead. Then all the churches will know that I am he who searches hearts and minds, and I will repay each of you according to your deeds.* (New International Version)

We may think we are hiding our secrets, but the LORD knows them; He knows them all.

Psalm 44:21; *would not God have discovered it, since he knows the secrets of the heart?* (New International Version)

Psalm 139:1-4;
1 You have searched me, LORD, and you know me.
2 You know when I sit and when I rise; you perceive my thoughts from afar.
3 You discern my going out and my lying down; you are familiar with all my ways.
4 Before a word is on my tongue you, LORD, know it completely.
(New International Version)

There are many more verses that state how much the LORD knows about what is happening here. That includes everything we say, do, and think. Despite the fact that He knows everything about everything around here, He still loves us far more than we can ever possibly imagine. Because of that love for us, He gave us the law.

If you carefully look at the environment the Garden of Eden was in, you would understand great many things. Everything was provided for Adam and Eve. All the food they needed was right there, ripe for the picking. So they didn't need to go to any grocery store to purchase any food. It was all around them. They didn't need clothes because they were not ashamed. The clothing industry wasn't needed. The temperature was so perfect they didn't need coats. There was no need for rain gear. Water never fell from the sky back then. It never got to hot or too cold. It was just right. There was no need for a fire to keep warm or air conditioner. There was a river nearby so they could wash off, take a swim in a temperature controlled river. As they swam in it, they could see gold and the many precious metals that were in it. When they lay on the beach along the river, they could enjoy a nice tan. This is what the LORD created for us at the beginning. We long for it. We really don't mind working. We just don't want the challenges with bills, going to the grocery stores, buying clothes, cleaning the house, buying cars, etc. etc. etc.

Furthermore, if you look at what Jesus is preparing for us after the Great White Throne judgment that is described in the Book of Revelation chapter 20 and beyond, you will notice everything will be different. It will be like the Garden of Eden, but much more enhanced. It will be so grand, so magnificent, so breath taking it will boggle the mind.

1 Corinthians 2:9; *However, as it is written: "What no eye has seen, what no ear has heard, and what no human mind has conceived" the things God has prepared for those who love him—* (New International Version)

If Christians are no longer under the Law, why did Jesus give His disciples a new commandant right before they left to go to the Garden of Gethsemane? And what is that commandment? "To love one another." That is a commandment, that's for sure. So why did He give us that law if it was going to be abolished in a short time later?

John 13:34; *"A new command I give you: Love one another. As I have loved you, so you must love one another.* (New International Version)

John 13:35; *By this everyone will know that you are my disciples, if you love one another."* (New International Version)

John 15:12; *My command is this: Love each other as I have loved you.* (New International Version)

John 15:17; *This is my command: Love each other.* (New International Version)

Matthew 5:16-17;
16 In the same way, let your light shine before others, that they may see your good deeds and glorify your Father in heaven.
17 "Do not think that I have come to abolish the Law or the Prophets; I have not come to abolish them but to fulfill them. (New International Version)

So I will leave you with this question. Why did the LORD love us so much that He gave us the law?

I will end this book with the following text from the book of Judaism, edited by Arthur Hertzberg, George Braziller. New York 1963. It is pages 155-156;

The wicked emperor Hadrian, who conquered Jerusalem, boasted, "I have conquered Jerusalem with great power." Rabbi Johanan ben Zakkai said to him, "Do not boast. Had it not been the will of Heaven, you would not have conquered it." Rabbi Johanan then took Hadrian into a cave and showed him the bodies of Amorites who were buried there. One of them measured eighteen cubits (approximately thirty feet) in height. He said, "When we were deserving, such men were defeated by us, but now, because of our sins, you have defeated us"

If America is defeated or destroyed, it will be because of God's people who have sinned and not repented of our pagan sun god worship, participating in their festivals, and for not loving each other as Jesus commanded us.

It is my most sincere hope, dream, and aspiration that all who read this book will be enlightened and seek out the LORD.

Daniel 12:3; *Those who are wise will shine like the brightness of the heavens, and those who lead many to righteousness, like the stars for ever and ever.* (New International Version)

Numbers 6:24-26;
24 "The LORD bless you and keep you;
25 the LORD make his face shine on you and be gracious to you;
26 the LORD turn his face toward you and give you peace."' (New International Version)

Printed in Great Britain
by Amazon.co.uk, Ltd.,
Marston Gate.